Revolutionary Laughter

The World of Women Comics

Edited by Roz Warren

The Crossing Press ▪ Freedom, CA 95019

Attention Funny Women!

If you're a female comic or humorist and wish to be included in the sequel to this book, or in an upcoming Women's Glib collection, please write Roz for submission guidelines at Box 259/Bala Cynwyd, PA 19004. (Enclose a stamped, self-addressed envelope) or E-mail Roz at RozWarren@AOL.com.

Thanks A lot!

To: Laura Post, without whose help and support I would never have completed this book. Deni Kasrel, for working even harder on this book than I did, and for taking the hit when you-know-who came gunning for us. Elaine Goldman, because this book was her idea, and because she doesn't try to second-guess me (much). Laurie Kimbrough, good neighbor and conveniently located terrific typist, for doing right by the transcripts. Pat Miller, for telling Brett I was cool. Amy Sibiga and Brigid Fuller, for continuing to put up with me. Gail Leondar, for being a great publicist (and pal). Rick Smith, for being the best hubby a gal ever had. Tom Smith, age 6, for cheerfully screening millions of hours of performance videos with me (and returning so often to Maxine Lapiduss' "The Jelly Donut Saga" that we both have it memorized). And to Judy Tenuta, for bravely jumping into the host's lap when we were on TV together so that I didn't have to.

Most of the material in *Revolutionary Laughter* is based upon interviews with the comics or information contained in press kits provided by the comics or their representatives. This is not true in all cases, however. While every effort has been made to contact those represented in this book, we did not receive responses from all the performers. For the few performers who did not respond, the information presented in *Revolutionary Laughter* was researched from various public sources.

Copyright © 1995 Roz Warren
Cover design by Amy Sibiga
Interior design by Victoria May
Printed in the U.S.A.
Credits are noted on page 299

Library of Congress Cataloging-in-Publication Data

Revolutionary laughter : the world of women comics / edited by Roz Warren.
       p. cm.
    ISBN 0-89594-742-0 (pbk.)
      1. Women comedians—United States—Biography. 2. Women comedians—United States—Interviews. I. Warren, Rosalind, 1954–
PN2285.R46 1995
792.7'028'082--dc20
   [B]   94-45793
                                                  CIP

Contents

Introduction

Revolutionary Laughter: The World of Women Comics is the eighth book in the Women's Glib Contemporary Women's Humor series. Prior books collected cartoons, essays, stories, light verse, and one-liners. Revolutionary Laughter is a departure both because it focuses on performance and also because it's as much about the humorists themselves as about their work.

Some definitions and disclaimers: Revolutionary Laughter is about living performers actively involved in stand-up comedy or comic performance: thus, women like Gracie Allen, Moms Mabley, and Gilda Radner are excluded. (And folks like Bette Midler and Whoopi Goldberg, who nowadays are more actresses than stand-ups are but briefly noted.) Also, the focus is, with only a few exceptions, on solo performers rather than on performance groups and on spoken humor rather than on song and cabaret.

This isn't a "best of" book. I don't claim that the women included here are the top women working in comedy today or that anybody who isn't in this book isn't funny. Instead, this book is about women at all levels of the profession, from superstars like Brett Butler to performers who are just starting to make a name for themselves. *Revolutionary Laughter* provides an overview of a working career in comedy, not a view of (or from) from the top.

Revolutionary Laughter isn't a critical study. I make no effort to rank, rate, or criticize the women in this book. My purpose is to help spread the word about the work they're doing. I want to increase their audience, help their fans get to know them better, and, with them, explore comedy as an art form and a way of life.

Each of the performers included is profiled. Many are interviewed. Because the interviews took place over a year's time, some things have changed. When interviewed, Brett Butler was just beginning work on "Grace Under Fire"; she didn't yet know it would be a major hit. Margaret Cho speaks of her ideas for a sitcom; now she stars in one. I've brought the profiles up-to-date as much as possible, but I have left the interviews intact as accurate records of a particular point in each comic's career.

Revolutionary Laughter has been a team effort. At the start I brought in writers Laura Post and Deni Kasrel to help me with the interviews; other writers joined the book as it developed. Bringing in different writers opened the book up by bringing in new perspectives and voices. Humorist Patty Marx, who wrote monologues for Mo Gaffney's popular TV show, "Women Aloud," interviewed Mo for the book. Laurie Stone allowed me to reprint a few of her insightful essays from the *Village Voice*. When film critic Kathi Maio mentioned she'd watched (and videotaped) every episode of "Roseanne," I convinced her to write my "Roseanne" section. She went on to write sections about Tracy Ullman and Judy Tenuta as well. Other writers who appear in these pages include Susie Day, Victoria Brownworth, and Ellen Orleans. (Not to mention Trey Graham, author of the piece about Thea Vidale, who has the distinction of being the only man involved in this project.)

Getting this material wasn't always easy. Some comics were too busy working to talk with us. Others just didn't care to. Some managers didn't want to let their stars speak with us without a clear financial incentive. (One comic even threatened to sue me unless I paid her $5,000 per quote.) On a bad day, I'd spend hours on the phone, wrangling with press agents, managers, and other reps. Sometimes it seemed the more famous the comic, the more people she had on her payroll whose sole job was to tell people like me to get lost. I'd begin to feel as though I spent all my time jumping through hoop after hoop after hoop, only to get a door slammed rudely in my face. (Sometimes it was different; sometimes the door was slammed politely.)

But most days weren't like that. Mostly, this book was a joy to work on. I was impressed with the warmth and the wit of these women, as well as by their generosity. Brett Butler took time off from working on "Grace Under Fire" to give me terrific, from-the-heart answers to a huge list of questions. In the space of one week, Kate Clinton, Marga Gomez, and Judy Tenuta all came through with terrific interviews. Bertice Berry not only answered all my questions but she also told me that she loved *Women's Glib*. Talking with comics was always a hoot. They were funny; they were smart; they were articulate. It was terrific. There were rough spots, but in putting together this book, we all laughed a lot.

The interviews are the heart of this book. Women talked at length with us about career ups and downs, stage fright, the sexism of comedy clubs, getting started, audience response, and the motivation and mechanics of comedy. They explored what works and what doesn't, how to come up with and polish material, and how to get guys to laugh at Bobbitt jokes. They talked about the lives they've led and the sacrifices they've made. Joy Behar describes being an early feminist in the male-dominated world of comedy clubs. Suzanne Westenhoefer talks about breaking into straight clubs with queer comedy. Maxine Lapiduss talks about writing for sitcoms like "Roseanne" and "Home Improvement."

Some were "on" for their interviews; the result is pure entertainment. Others were more analytical. Some had axes to grind; some were on top of the world, having a ball.

All the women in this book have one thing in common: intelligence. There are no stupid stand-ups. (No stupid successful ones, anyway.) These women are all very smart. They're also very motivated. Comedy is hard work. (As the old saying goes: Dying is easy, comedy is hard.) You've got to be motivated to travel around the country getting up over and over again in front of crowds of strangers who may not laugh.

Revolutionary Laughter explores this drive, but in the end, like the power of laughter, it remains a mystery. What made Suzanne Westenhoefer defy the entire comedy establishment by performing lesbian comedy in straight clubs? Where did Joan Rivers get the belief in her own vision required to completely redefine women's role in comedy? How was Brett Butler able to transform herself from battered wife to sitcom star?

These women are driven. This isn't normal. Their lives aren't routine or humdrum or everyday. This just isn't life as most of us live it. And as Joy Behar puts it: "Stand-up isn't exactly the least neurotic thing to do. There's something wacky about it."

Comedy is communication. Comics are communicators. They're also, especially women comics, rule breakers. These are all women who want to communicate with us badly enough to do what it takes to get to a stage, find their audience, and make that audience love them. They've all had to overcome a lot to find that audience. But they made it up on stage, and some, like Roseanne, have changed the face of our culture. It's a tough job. But they claim the love and support they get from their audience make it all worthwhile.

It's been said that if you want to tell people the truth you'd better do it with a punch line, or they'll kill you. These women have power because they're all telling us their truths, whether it's through political comedy about major issues, social commentary about men and women, or silly observational humor about cats.

We all need a good laugh. Laughter is a mystery; it's also crucial to our sanity. In this book you'll get to know teachers and healers, angry women and goofy women, sages, poets and clowns. We need them all.

Comedy is half music.
                    —*Joan Rivers*

Comedy is tragedy, plus time.
                    —*Carol Burnett*

Humor is just truth, only faster!
                    —*Gilda Radner*

Comics are angry people
    with something to say.
                    —*Roseanne*

Diane Amos

by Roz Warren

San Francisco comic Diane Amos says her act is about "folks white people would like to look at up close on a bus but never would. I bring these
characters to the stage, so you can see what makes them tick." Amos's character monologues introduce her audience to her past, her heritage, her
friends, and her insights. For instance, she compares three cultures by
"becoming" a white woman, then a Latina, and finally a black woman telling
off a boyfriend. Noting that the kitchen is a favored venue for arguments, she
asks the audience, "How many men here have been hit by mashed potatoes?
Tell the truth!" "Don't argue with your mate in the kitchen," she advises guys,

"because we know where everything is, and you don't!" Other bits include one on what you need to know if you want to take your black friends skiing and a riff about being the straight child of lesbian moms ("Black Mom" and "White Mom").

Before starting to do stand-up five years ago Amos performed improv for over a decade with groups like the National Theater of the Deranged. The years of improv make her very comfortable with her audience. Her free-wheeling style, she says, is inspired by comics like Lucille Ball. "Lucy was so willing to be wacky and go out of her way and not look like anyone else when she was being funny," Amos explains. "You know, shoving bonbons in her face faster than anyone. I've always admired her for being 'unbeautiful' when being funny."

Amos became a single mom by choice in her late twenties (son Kelvin is now eight). She does commercials (for Pine Sol). She's won thousands of dollars on television game shows, including $14,750 on "Wheel of Fortune."

Amos feels empowered by her comedy career. "When you work for yourself," she says, "you're empowered in a way not usual in this society. It's like any woman who owns her own business." To quote the *San Francisco Examiner*: "'Healing Comedy' is what Diane likes to call her act, and it is, but you may die laughing."

Joy Behar

by Deni Kasrel

When Joy Behar was emerging on the stand-up circuit, she stood out for being one of the few females working in what was largely a man's world. Back then, feminism was just budding, and live comedy was primarily a guy gig. Times have changed, and though women have gained a lot of ground in the comedy circuit, Behar still stands out. She makes sure of this with her delivery —she's loud, brash and has real attitude—and with content that smashes false idols and pretty much tells it like it is.

Joy says many people have told her she reminds them of a relative or a good friend. That's probably because both on stage and off she's a real person. There's no pretense or put-on. Of course brutal honesty is often threatening to those with thin skin, and Behar has found this out the hard way. She was fired from a popular New York call-in radio show for daring to stand up to such big media hypes like Rush Limbaugh.

This hasn't stopped her from pointing the finger, and sometimes giving the finger, when she thinks something or someone is wrong or unjust. When George Bush was leading the country, she scoffed at his claim of being the education president. "Oh sure, "she huffed, "lucky for us he's not the nutrition president. We'd all starve."

Before coming to comedy, Behar worked as an English teacher. This proved to be good preparation for her career as a comedian, since her classes were like a challenging audience. She describes her students as hard-core New York kids, who would set fire to their parents. "I tried to make it relevant. I'd say '*Whom* do you wish to kill? Not who'."

She's appeared in a few movies, including Nora Ephron's *This is My Life*, which tells a tale similar to Behar's own. Like the movie's main character, Behar got into stand-up when she was a single, divorced mother with a kid.

Getting up in front of a crowd is difficult and risky, believes Behar. She's got the balls and the gall to do it, in part thanks to having been brought up in Brooklyn, where being tough and streetwise is the norm. Being possessed of those traits, plus having a quick wit and keen mind, makes Behar a joy to behold.

Kasrel: Did you always know that stand-up was the right career for you?

Behar: There were always clues that I should have been doing stand-up, but I was too intimidated. In the sixties, there were no female comedians. There was no club scene. Hardly anything was happening. Then in the early seventies, I read an article about Elayne Boosler in *New York Magazine*. I was a housewife with a baby at that point, being a mom. I was taken by the fact that there was a woman doing stand-up. It was almost like I was jealous.

Kasrel: What about people like Carol Burnett?

Behar: They're funny, but they're actresses, not comedians. I'm talking about standing at a microphone and talking to an audience. I loved Carol Burnett's work and I loved Imogene Coca, but I had no interest in being Carol Burnett. Somehow that didn't grab me.

Kasrel: You wanted to do stand-up.

Behar: But it was too hard. I had a child. I couldn't stay up late. I was living too far away. I was a professor's wife. I was ensconced in that life. Then the years went by and my daughter got older. I got a divorce and I was fired from "Good Morning America." I was in the position of "use it or lose it."

Kasrel: You always had doing stand-up as a goal in the back of your mind, but you didn't see a way to do it?

Behar: Yes. I think if I look back on my entire life—even as a child I could always hold an audience's attention. Any time. I used to be the Bible reader because I could hold the attention of the audience. It's just that I was scared. I had huge stage fright. The fear of humiliation was always with me.

Kasrel: But then you went into a profession that's fraught with that, right?

Behar: Stand-up comedy is very difficult in the beginning. You have personal things you have to overcome. You've got audiences that don't particularly want to watch you. It's a highly skilled job.

Kasrel: And you were a divorced single mother. It must have been very hard.

Behar: I was on unemployment insurance. I was broke. I was getting a little child support, not much. I started to sort of claw my way up. Interestingly enough, after about six months I landed myself a major thing. I was on "The New Show" on NBC, the first show Lorne Michaels produced after "Saturday Night Live." I made short films with Tom Schiller, who'd been the film person on "Saturday Night Live." Unfortunately, "The New Show" folded. I got an agent and I started to do the clubs.

Kasrel: At some point you just decided you were going to go out and try to be a stand-up?

Behar: I'd dabbled before that. When I was at "Good Morning America," every once in a while I'd invite people from my office to come to a place called Mickey's, and I'd do an evening. But the idea of going to the big clubs—the Improv, Catch a Rising Star—was too intimidating. Also, the process is humiliating. You have to take a number. You have to wait. People judge you. It's outrageous.

Kasrel: But you did it. What made you go through that?

Behar: Once you get on stage and you have a good response from the audience and that happens a few times, you see that you have something. And that little something pushes you to the next time. But at first, even when I'd do well, I wouldn't go on stage for another six months. In the beginning of your career, you're petrified that it's not going to work. Just because you did well the last time is no guarantee it's going to happen again. As a matter of fact, a lot of times it doesn't. So who needs it? You don't want to do it. You'll do anything not to get on stage.

Kasrel: But you did. There's something there that says "do it," right?

Behar: There's a compulsion of some kind. Stand-up isn't exactly the least neurotic thing to do. There's something very neurotic about it.

Kasrel: What about having to leave your child at night?

Behar: That's hard. The industry is not supportive of that. This is the feminist issue. The industry doesn't give a shit if you've got a kid. There was one club owner, a woman—I said to her, "Look, I have a job and I've got a kid, and I can't really hang out late. Can't I just go on at ten and then go home?" But she had this Nixonian idea that loyalty meant everything. She said to me one time, "Joy, it's not about your talent. You are very good, but other people hang out more than you do and I have to give them preference."

Her club went under, so she was obviously doing it wrong. It is not about loyalty. It is about talent.

Kasrel: Describe your slant as a comedian.

Behar: My persona is a woman who is in your face and who basically knows who she is.

Kasrel: Let's talk about the idea of being an in-your-face comic. You do it and it works. Other people try to do it and the audience doesn't get it.

Behar: I don't want to blow my horn here, but if you're going to have an attitude, which I have, you have to have the ammunition to back it up. That's what Dennis Miller once told me: "You've got the 'tude, but you've got the ammo."

Kasrel: What do you mean by ammo?

Behar: You need to have material to back up what you are doing up there. You have jokes. You've got an act. You've got a brain. It's the same with actors. Some actors are completely vapid: they're walking through a scene and you know that nothing is going on in their heads. But watch somebody like Anthony Hopkins—you know something is always working in his head. Some comics have a brain working and some don't. The ones who do are much more interesting. Robin Williams—he has a brain working. Even working from prepared material, you see that there's content, and that he's given it thought. And if something happens in the moment, his brain will kick in.

Kasrel: And your own style?

Behar: It's a person who has an attitude about life, who takes a position, and who has a slant. I'm inquisitive. I'm very curious about the audience. I'll ask them questions about themselves.

Kasrel: Can't that be dangerous? Not every comic wants to deal with the audience, right?

Behar: But that's another reason that some comics are more interesting than others: they deal with what's going on. They're not afraid to find out what's happening in the moment. It makes for a much more interesting show. If a person is a genuine comedian, she can have fun with whatever is in the house that night.

Kasrel: By "genuine comedian" I assume you mean a natural ability to be funny, which you have. But sometimes, even as funny as you are, not every night works.

Behar: You still have audiences that are dead or audiences that don't get it. You always have that.

Kasrel: So what do you do?

Behar: You hope that you can get out without committing hara-kiri on the stage. I've heard stories about really, really famous comedians who, for instance, die at the Concord in the Catskills. It doesn't matter how advanced or how famous or how popular you are; each room presents a different problem. And sometimes it's going to be difficult.

Kasrel: Your act is very much about how we live in this world. You use street language. You talk like a real person. You present yourself as somebody who is similar to, or at least accessible to, the people in your audience.

Behar: I think that my particular appeal is that people think that they know me. I hear it all the time: "You remind me of my girlfriend Joanie. She was always a pisser." People come to see me because they're comfortable with me. They know there's going to be a party. It's going to be fun and everybody is going to be safe. Nobody is going to walk out of there feeling bad. But I'm edgy, too.

Kasrel: Being edgy is risky. How do you do it without being insulting?

Behar: It's the same in life, you know? Some people have a way of saying the truth that doesn't make you want to strangle them.

Kasrel: Do you feel that what you're doing is saying the truth?

Behar: I try to get as close to it as I can. Sometimes I get into trouble with it.

Kasrel: What kind of trouble?

Behar: For instance, I was recently interviewed, and in the middle of the interview, the interviewer told me that Bill Clinton's mom, Virginia Kelly, had died that day. I commented that it was good timing for her because it was right in the middle of the Whitewater scandal. I said, "It's funny how people will die just when they're supposed to die." I've always found it fascinating that people will, oh, wait until after Christmas to die. I said, "She figured that she's sick. She's going to die. Her son is in trouble. Maybe this will get the press off his back."

The Daily News picked up this one comment and printed it. A letter was written the following week saying that it was the most insensitive and nasty thing to say and I hope that Joy Behar never encounters such misery. What I said was misinterpreted.

Kasrel: Your comment was taken out of context. It can happen to anybody on almost any topic, I guess.

Behar: I guess it's a radical statement to say, "Well, the woman timed her death beautifully." But it's the truth as I see it. I don't think that's a hostile statement. I happen to be a huge fan of Clinton's.

As a comic, you're always taking a risk that people won't like what you say. It's a very risky business. You're taking a risk that what you say will be mis-interpreted. You're taking a risk that you're going to be humiliated on stage. You're risking that you aren't going to be funny. You're risking that you won't be able to make a living at this. There are a million things that you're risking here. I'm coming back to what I said before, which is that it's neurotic. There's something wacky about it.

Kasrel: You're risking all of this—what's the payoff for you?

Behar: The payoff is that they're laughing, which is an enormous payoff, and that you're expressing yourself in a position of power.

Kasrel: Making people laugh strengthens you or gives you a sense of purpose?

Behar: Yeah, it does. All my life I've had social worker tendencies, which is why I was originally drawn to teaching and to working with disadvantaged kids. Even now, I feel the need to do, and I get very edgy when I can't. When I don't feel that I'm contributing something, I get a little edgy and I feel that life is meaningless.

Kasrel: You have leftist politics and feminist content. You cover issues that are important to you, right?

Behar: It's not just the content. It's also the fact that you're in a room creating laughter, and that's a highly remarkable thing. Life is such a minefield. Every day is so laden with difficulty for many people. To be able to suspend that reality for even half an hour and have people just forget there's an earthquake or there's cancer, that there's misery everywhere—that's something.

Kasrel: What are some of the issues you like to cover?

Behar: I focus on the topics that I find interesting. Some subjects just lend themselves to humor, like Lorena Bobbitt. Lorena Bobbitt was a gold mine. You just know there are jokes there.

Kasrel: Why is Lorena Bobbitt a gold mine?

Behar: For one thing, it immediately made men nervous. Every woman in the world who has been oppressed by a man or read about women who are oppressed yearns for some kind of retaliation. Look at the popularity of *Thelma and Louise*. Even though rationally we say, "That's not the way to do it," and "She should have been able to leave," there's something in a woman that says, She did what she had to do. Especially in a country where justice is meted out rather poorly and there isn't enough protection for women. Women feel that Lorena was empowered in a certain way by what she did. But men have a very different reaction.

Kasrel: Absolutely.

Behar: If you say "Bobbitt" the men in the audience boo and the women cheer. But then I'll go along doing the material about it and the men will be laughing. Cutting off a guy's dick, there's something funny about it. Because they love it so much, I guess, and because it's so revered by men. They adore it. And so now a woman just says, Oh yeah? Fuck you. And there is something funny about it. Even men have to agree that it's funny.

Kasrel: Still, it's a pretty touchy subject. Every comic draws the line somewhere. You say, "I'm not going to make a joke about this. This is not territory that I think is funny." How do you determine where to draw that line?

Behar: It has to be humorous to me. I have to be able to find the humor in it. I'm not saying, "There are subjects that are verboten." I just don't see the humor in them.

Kasrel: It's a personal choice?

Behar: I think so. The key for me is to make fun of the oppressor. I don't appreciate comics who do gay-bashing jokes or who attack the underdog, like Dice does. That's no challenge. Take on the oppressor. Take on the big guy.

Kasrel: That's what you do, right?

Behar: I've taken on Rush Limbaugh; I've taken on Howard Stern. I called Stern a miserable cocksucker in an interview, and he was furious with me.

Kasrel: He can say it but you can't, right?

Behar: Exactly. He can't stand anybody to say anything critical of him, because he's so paper-thin. He appeals to people who are also very thin-skinned and who are frightened about their own lives. They make racist jokes and trash women. It's easy. But I say to all these guys, Let's see you take on somebody bigger than you. That's the comic's job, to tell the king that he's merely mortal.

Kasrel: Why is that?

Behar: Because power corrupts, and so you need somebody to put a few holes into powerful people.

Kasrel: And humor is a way of doing it?

Behar: Humor is an incredible tool. It's gotten me into trouble, but I've also used it to get out of trouble.

Kasrel: What kind of trouble?

Behar: I was always funny in class. I'd get into trouble with other kids sometimes and then use humor to get out of trouble. Humor can be a great defensive weapon.

Kasrel: How did you learn to use your sense of humor to defend yourself?

Behar: I grew up in a very tough Brooklyn neighborhood. All the girls were wearing dungaree jackets, that sort of look, and I'd be wearing Bermuda shorts. I was a tweedy kind of kid in a tough neighborhood. So I was targeted as some kind of weird nerd.

I was also very smart in school. I was an only child and I was treated like a princess in my family. I was taken to the theater, while these kids were hanging out on the stoop. The teachers liked me because I did well in school, but I could also function in the neighborhood because I was funny. I was one of the girls; I wanted to have some fun out there. But kids from out of the neighborhood would come in and start fights with me, because I looked like a goody-goody.

I didn't want to fight, so I developed a verbal way to deal with life, a verbal defense. I'm very much against violence. But I do like verbal feuding. I enjoy a good argument.

Kasrel: Let's talk about the language you use in your act.

Behar: A lot of my language is Anglo-Saxon, but I'm not vulgar, ever. I don't do doody jokes or fart jokes. I'll do a dick joke, though. A dick joke is a beautiful thing.

Kasrel: Can I quote you? A dick joke is a beautiful thing?

Behar: Of course. But that's not scatological. I cannot stand toilet humor. I'm not into fart jokes or describing certain sexual things. That stuff isn't interesting to me; it's infantile.

Kasrel: In a magazine interview you talked about using direct language, words like queer, for example. You've said that you take the original insult and reclaim the word and make it your own. What do you mean by that?

Behar: It empowers you not to be victimized. One of the reasons people become comedians is so they can say these things about themselves first. For instance, growing up I had really, really kinky hair. Everybody used to tease me about it; they called me Brillo head. My fifth grade teacher used to call me Brillo head. I was hurt by this, so finally I started to make jokes about my hair. I'd say, "I've got a Brillo head" first, before anyone could say it to me. This defuses it; it takes away their power to hurt me.

Kasrel: What about the danger of being perceived as self-deprecating?

Behar: I could never understand why "self-deprecating" is such a bad thing, as long as you're on top of the situation. Joan Rivers is sometimes perceived as being self-deprecating, but Joan Rivers is a multimillionaire who is sixty and looks forty…

Kasrel: Phyllis Diller has also been criticized for being self-deprecating.

Behar: Phyllis is one of the strongest people I know. She has an extremely positive attitude towards life. She runs around the country making a living at making fun of herself. I don't think there's anything wrong with that. I don't squirm when I hear her say something about being flat-chested. Who cares? *She* knows it. She's at the microphone telling *you* this. Why be upset by that?

They always pin this on women. Rodney Dangerfield can't get no respect; that's all he talks about. Does anybody say he's self-deprecating?

Kasrel: If it's a man, that's just his schtick, but if it's a woman, she's accused of putting herself down? Are there other types of discrimination? Do you think that men are perceived as being funnier—even before they open their mouths—than women?

Behar: That was certainly true in the past; it may not be true anymore, because now there are so many women comics. In the past, being funny was just not part of a woman's role. It was the boys who were always the cut-ups in school.

Kasrel: They say boys will be boys and girls will be girls. They don't mean the same thing.

Behar: When they say girls will be girls, they mean girls will be bitchy and catty and sit quietly and be good. Well, that's unacceptable to me. First of all, I was never that quiet or good. And I certainly didn't think that the boys should act any wackier than the girls.

Kasrel: You were coming up in comedy at the same time the feminist movement was gaining momentum. Do you think that had an influence on your career?

Behar: The feminist movement had a lot to do with there being more women comedians. Slowly but surely, it started to sink in that we could do what the guys can do. All my comedian friends who are women have a similar story—they were funny in school, but they didn't know what to do with it.

Kasrel: They'd go to a comedy club and the owner wouldn't hire them?

Behar: Comedy was a boys' club. They'd support each other. The girls were insignificant.

Now that I'm one of the seniors and I've been around longer than a lot of the younger guys, they'll come over and tell me that I'm very funny. But when I was coming up, it was rare for a male comedian to compliment a female comedian. They'd stay in the room when another guy was on, then when a girl went on, they'd leave the room.

Kasrel: Really? That's terrible.

Behar: I got plenty of it. Also, women were encouraged not to support each other. I hope that's changing. The men who ran the clubs would say, "You're going to be the only girl, which is better for you because you don't want to be repetitious." Meanwhile, there'd be five boys in a row talking about masturbation, but that obviously was not repetitious to them. They could listen to it until the cows come home. But if a woman gets on and talks about a women's issue and then another woman gets on and talks about a women's issue, that's the end of it. They can only have one. The women were encouraged to see each other as competition.

Kasrel: Has that attitude since changed?

Behar: I have a number of close friends in the business and we're very supportive of each other. We commiserate plenty. We've learned not to be so competitive with each other.

I was older than everybody else when I started, and more of a feminist. I was in my thirties, and these girls were younger. I knew immediately that we should support each other. I remember saying often that the more women there are doing it the better it is for all of us, because the audiences will get used to seeing women on stage. That was a concept that I grasped right away. But a lot of women didn't.

Kasrel: Let's talk about your radio show. What was the format? People would call in and you'd talk about the issues of the day? That can become political.

Behar: Very. It was a different level of expression for me. With stand-up, you have to stay within the act because you know that's going to work and you're there to get laughs. But on the radio you can take the day's newspaper and comment. You can take a position. I have very strong opinions, and I'd state them, and then people would call to argue. It becomes a town meeting. I liked that a lot.

A lot of times it wasn't very funny, but I got more skilled as I went along. I learned to control myself, and to give good answers. Although sometimes it would just be a brawl.

Kasrel: Once you announced that on the next show you were going to read a list of ten reasons why Rush Limbaugh couldn't get laid.

Behar: The program director called me up and said, "I don't think you should do it, because it's a personal attack."

Kasrel: As if Rush doesn't personally attack people.

Behar: Exactly. I said, "He's calling my friends feminazis. *That's* a personal attack." Gloria Steinem happens to be a friend of mine. The producer said he didn't think I should read the list. I said, "Am I going to get fired if I do?" And he said, "Well, I don't think you should do it." What does that mean?

Finally I told him, "I'm not going to read the list, but I'm going to tell my listeners that I was told not to read it." So it became more of a free speech issue and was actually more interesting than if I'd been allowed to read the goddamned thing.

Kasrel: But you did end up reading it eventually, right?

Behar: The next time I did my act at a club, the minute I got on stage my fans started yelling, "The list! The list!" I happened to have it with me. So I read it.

It was just a joke. It was a joke about Limbaugh. They can't take a joke, these people. They can only dish it out.

Kasrel: Do you think the censoring had something to do with your being a woman, or was it because Rush is such a powerful media presence?

Behar: Rush is a big ratings-getter. They're always intimidated by that. Also, talk radio is very right-wing. You've got Limbaugh, you've got Bob Grant in New York, who is slightly to the right of Attila the Hun.

Kasrel: So how did you like even being in that environment, you know, working with a bunch of skunks?

Behar: I didn't like it. But it's the same thing as being with a bunch of male comics when I was coming up. That was difficult too, but when you got on stage, it was the audience who decided if you were good, not the other comics. When you're on the radio, it's the audience who decides, not the people running the office. My ratings went up steadily and I got a lot of fans.

Kasrel: Then what happened?

Behar: They fired me anyway. They said they were changing the format, which was a lie. The person they put in there had the same format. She didn't do anything differently. My theory is that they couldn't control me, and they didn't like that.

Suzy Berger

by Roz Warren

Suzy Berger is a successful stand-up comic. So successful, in fact, that recently she had to take a vacation from her other vocation, that of a drama therapist. To hear her tell it, the two careers have much in common. As a therapist, Berger encourages her patients to express themselves through improv. For example, she's been known to bolster her patients' assertiveness by "casting" them as Captain Picard in "Star Trek." "I try to work with whatever they give me," she says. "For some reason, they all love 'Star Trek'." Onstage, Berger jokes about topics ranging from lesbians to lightning bugs. But she also "improvs" a therapist character, who offers to help solve the audience's problems. "Does anybody have a problem?" she'll ask. Getting no response, she'll comment, "Okay. This is denial." Eventually, somebody always offers up an actual problem, "and then I'll go with it." She says she is amazed by what people will reveal about themselves in that setting, so she's careful to treat her audience with respect. "I'll use the problem to joke around, but I'm very careful never to make fun of the person. I try to be kind. I just want to show people that there's levity in every situation." Berger also throws a few psychology-based jokes into her act, like: "Everyone says that having a multiple personality is so terrible. I don't think having ninety-two personalities is so terrible. I think it's wonderful. Because I know so many people who don't even have one."

A native New Yorker (she retains a New York accent), Berger moved to San Francisco in 1982, where, encouraged by comic Lea Delaria, she began performing "out" lesbian comedy at gay/lesbian clubs. Berger successfully made the crossover to mainstream clubs with a gig at the Punchline in 1984. Since then she's played both gay and mainstream clubs all over the country, and she has appeared on National Public Radio and "The Mo Show." Last year, she shared the bill with comic Sandra Bernhard at a Gay Games benefit show, and coming up is a show in San Francisco with Robin Williams.

Warren: When did you first realize you could make other people laugh?

Berger: In school, with a captive audience.

Warren: Did you get in trouble for being class clown?

Berger: I remember one occasion when my mom was called to school for a parent/teacher conference. My teacher complained, in my presence, that I'd entertain the class and make them laugh. My mother responded, "Suzy wasn't solely to blame. The other students were just as guilty for responding and encouraging her." I was shocked, and so was my teacher. I was also validated. From that day on, I realized how important audiences were.

Warren: Did that encouragement inspire you to become a performer?

Berger: That, and a need to express myself. Performing allows me to achieve a heightened state of consciousness. It's spiritual for me, maybe shamanistic.

Warren: What kind of comedy are you most comfortable doing?

Berger: I prefer comedy that's inviting and enjoyable, not confrontational on a personal level. I'm disappointed when people are reluctant to sit in the front row for fear that they'll be made fun of. Why pay a two-drink minimum for hostility when you can get it for free?

Warren: Who makes *you* laugh? Who has influenced your humor over the years?

Berger: I really enjoy Madeline Kahn, Robert Klein, and Bette Midler. I was profoundly influenced by gay comedy pioneers, like Lea Delaria, Tom Ammiano, and Danny Williams, to name a few. My greatest mentors, though, have been audiences. They've taught me and encouraged me to trust myself and them.

Warren: You've always been an "out" comic. Did you ever consider being closeted?

Berger: I couldn't imagine being a closeted performer. Censorship and comedy are quite opposite. It's really important to give credit here to Ron Lanza and Donald Montwill, the owners of Valencia Rose and then of Josie's in San Francisco. They took the risk of showcasing gay and lesbian comedy before it became chic.

Warren: How do you develop your material?

Berger: I have creative bursts walking down the street or at one in the morning. I keep pen and paper on my nightstand. I also incorporate material from my conversations with others when I get them laughing. I also enjoy performing at a specific event which triggers material for that audience.

Warren: Like the show you did for Jews at a Chinese restaurant on Christmas Eve?

Berger: Exactly. "Kung Pao Kosher Comedy" was an alternative event, just for Jews who feel disenfranchised during the holidays. Some Jewish people resist all the attention Christmas receives. So I did jokes like: "What's the problem with Christmas—shouldn't we be celebrating the birth of a Jew?" Or "My gentile friends don't know what Chanukah is about. They ask, 'Is that when you don't eat for eight days?'"

Warren: How do you integrate being an out lesbian comic into an event like that?

Berger: I got up there and did five minutes that weren't gay, and then I came out to them. And I still had them. Gay material is a lot like Jewish material. If comedy is good, it's universal. It does translate. I did one line about being a lesbian: "You know, my family always *said* no man would be good enough for me," and they just lost it. Because don't they *all* say that to their daughters?

Warren: How does it feel to connect with a crowd of strangers like that and make them laugh?

Berger: It's a wonderful, synergistic experience. It's a unique opportunity to be very familiar with a lot of strangers. A good joke is worth a thousand words. It's a fabulous feeling to communicate and to get laughter as a response. And doing lesbian comedy is empowering—to take my life and perceptions, no matter how different, and know by their immediate laughter that I'm understood and accepted.

Warren: Are there ever times when it just doesn't work and you just can't make that connection with your audience?

Berger: Not very often. I believe that my attitude can transcend any obstacle. If I'm dealing with a particularly homophobic audience, for example, it's my job to address that reality and speak to those fears. I'll ask, "Don't any of you know a lesbian besides me? Didn't anybody have high school gym?"

Warren: What impact do you want to have?

Berger: I'd like to think that I challenge conformity and apathy. I'd like to set an example of someone who is true to herself. As Shakespeare said, "It is a fool's prerogative to utter truths that no one else will speak." I speak my truths in the guise of foolishness.

Bertice Berry

by Roz Warren

An award-winning lecturer, stand-up comic, Ph.D., and host of her own talk-show, Bertice Berry has carved out a unique niche in the world of entertainment as a scholar with a positive message *and* a terrific sense of humor.

Bertice Berry was teaching sociology and statistics at Kent State University where she'd received her doctorate in sociology, when a colleague urged her to give stand-up a try. She'd become one of the university's most popular teachers by using humor as a teaching tool in her lectures about tough issues like racism and sexism.

After winning an amateur night contest at a local comedy club, Berry began traveling the country to perform at other clubs, while continuing to teach and write. Finding entertainment a "powerful tool for reaching people," she decided to go into comedy full-time. Her hip, smart, and upbeat act was an immediate hit on college campuses. Berry was voted Campus Comedian of the Year for both 1991 and 1992. She made about two hundred live appearances annually as a comic, as well as many television appearances.

Berry's act focuses on creating racial and gender harmony, increasing self-esteem, and accepting diversity. Her humor is tough but never mean-spirited. By letting her audience in on the joke, she often jolts them into rethinking some of their assumptions and biases. One example is a story she tells of an on-the-road encounter: "I travel frequently and every day I'm in a different hotel. A couple of times, people have mistaken me for part of the housekeeping staff. The other day a man said to me, 'You can come into my room now and do your job.' So, I went in there and told him some jokes!"

Berry also covers topics like dating and celebrities (including doing a terrific Tina Turner imitation) but the core of her act comes from using comedy as a tool for better understanding. Berry shows her audience that by laughing with each other we can learn to respect each other, as when she tells her audience: "I don't look like Whoopi Goldberg, but people confuse us because we're both black and have dreadlocks. The other day a lady on the bus said to me, 'You look just like Whoopi Goldberg'. I told her 'You're fat and white, but you don't look like Mama Cass!'"

Berry's act amuses, informs, and transforms. While much of it is grounded in instances of racism or sexism that have upset her, Berry keeps her tone upbeat and optimistic. Her teaching experience has enhanced her talent for easy, authoritative give and take with her audience. She takes her role as a teacher seriously. "My material is all positive for blacks and women," she says. "I'm a spokesperson for everything I believe in. I got into comedy to help people look at themselves and know that they're as good as the next person, so they'd feel better about themselves and then start embracing others. The ability to do that, for me, is very important."

Berry sees the transition from stand-up comic to talk-show host as only natural. "I'd been doing a talk-show on the road every day," she comments about her act. "Basically, I'm a road comedian and sociologist."

Berry grew up poor in Wilmington, Delaware, the sixth of seven children, and was the first of her family to attend college. Is becoming the host of a national talk-show the achievement of the American dream? "I achieved that years ago," laughs Berry. "The American dream for me was to be able to pay my bills on time. Anything else is just dessert."

(Note: Bertice Berry's talk-show went off the air between the time when this interview was conducted and the time when this book was printed.)

Warren: As an educator, you used humor as a teaching tool. In hosting "The Bertice Berry Show," you often use humor to communicate with and establish rapport with both guests and audience. What about humor and comedy makes them so effective at getting through to people? How did you start using comedy to communicate?

Berry: I started using comedy as a child. My family used humor throughout our poverty; we learned to laugh at all kinds of situations. For instance, in the sixties my brother heard some radical say there was no God. He thought that he could bring that stuff home, and he came in saying, "Ain't no God. Ain't no God." My sister said, "Okay, well, where *is* God?" He was like, "I'm the God. I'm the God." So she says, "All right God, fix the holes in all these children's shoes!" We laughed at the situation and learned that there was power in humor.

I was probably the least funny of all of my siblings. I was very, very serious. But I started using humor when it was time to teach, because I knew that if something was interesting, funny, or bizarre people would remember it. If they remembered it, it would make them want to learn more about it.

Humor is effective at getting through because it breaks down barriers. Everybody laughs, and when you find the common denominator of laughter, you have a great deal of power.

Warren: Your message as a stand-up comic was a very positive one of empowerment and self-respect. In your act, you acted as a role model, showing your audience how to counter ignorance, stupidity, and prejudice with truth and humor. You showed people how to use wit as a tool, turning around tough situations with humor. Your message also included the importance of having fun with a troubling situation rather than letting it overwhelm you. What led you to develop your act in this direction? How did you learn these lessons yourself?

Berry: Again, that was through poverty. My mother is a recovering alcoholic. When I was growing up, she was a serious alcoholic, and dealing with that situation you had to find some kind of escape. My brothers and sisters and I would get away and manage to laugh at it. Even my mother, in a sober state, would try to laugh and explain that there would be a better time. It's hard to do that, but it was all we had.

What led me to develop my act in this direction? It wasn't a question of which way it would go. It's what I had to do. There was no reason for me to use humor to just make people laugh. I don't think I can afford to do that. I don't have that kind of time, as a woman or as an African-American. I don't have time to just be funny; I have to say something as well.

Warren: I know that you want "The Bertice Berry Show" to convey the same positive message as your act. How does operating within this new format change things? Can you compare the experiences of doing your act and doing your show?

Berry: In the act I have a structure that I'm going with, and the humor flows from that. With the show, there's a structure that the producer and the guests give me, and my humor has to respond to it. I'm reacting to the structure rather than creating it.

Warren: Has hosting a daytime talk-show mean you have had to change your message or the way you deliver your message?

Berry: Absolutely not. I'm sure that there are people who would like me to, but there's no way I can do that. The power of doing the show is that I can say all the things that I'd said with my act, but I'm saying them every day to a much wider audience and to people who wouldn't have necessarily come out to see me perform.

Warren: In hosting your show do you find that you have to censor yourself, rein in your personality or your politics?

Berry: In the beginning, you say, "I haven't done this. I don't know how to do this, and I'll listen to those who claim that they do." But I've found that my gut, my own instincts, are what I should listen to, so I've thrown away the teleprompter and all the cue cards, and I just kind of fly. It's a lot of fun to really delve into each issue, to try to see all sides of it and to meet all of the folks and see what they think.

Warren: Both as a comic and on your show you establish great rapport with your audience. How did you develop this skill? Did it come from teaching?

Berry: Yeah, that skill is definitely one that came from teaching. As a teacher, you've got to look in the eye of each of those students. Sometimes you have a class of two hundred and you know that they're with you at that moment. But if you see that even one of them isn't getting it, you know you need to back up, because for every one that has that look of "I'm not getting it" there are another ten that aren't going to show it. You learn to know when it's working. You learn to feel the groove of it.

Stand-up takes it up another level. You know immediately when you've hit home with an audience. You also know why. Sometimes you don't like the *why*. I don't like it when an audience only laughs at a joke that they perceive as a put-down. When I feel that happening, I immediately stop and say, "This is not what comedy is supposed to be about." I have the opportunity to do that on the talk-show as well.

Warren: How would you describe your approach to your audience?

Berry: On the show, we think of our audience as a village. In olden times, if there was a problem or a difficult situation, you took it to your village. If there was a joyous announcement, you took it to your village. We just don't have that anymore. In most neighborhoods, we no longer even have a sense of community.

With the show, we want to recreate that village atmosphere, where people feel free to interject their perspective and their *why* on that perspective. It's been phenomenal that folks here not only tell us what they think but they share stories about their personal experience and why from their experience they think that their perspective may be accurate. That's very powerful, because you get all of those opinions and outlooks mixed together, and somehow in there you get a shakedown to get into the best of all possible truths.

Warren: Has humor always been an important part of your life? Have you always been funny?

Berry: No, I've not always been funny, but it's always been an important part of my life. I had to learn to be funny.

Warren: What is it about your world view that makes you need to find the humor in things?

Berry: I've thought about this for hours and hours and hours. I have this theory that we're all in a cage. Most people are in the center of that cage, dancing happily, and they're laughing, but it's not a true laugh. They don't know the truth that this is a cage. There are many of us who've ventured far enough out to have found out that this is a cage. We spend a lot of time screaming and yelling to those in the middle that this is a cage. It's an exercise in futility; they don't want to see it.

I finally learned that I was wasting time and energy. I was casting pearls to swine. I needed to talk to folks who were where I was. That meant that I had to come together with people who I'd been taught not to accept; I had to embrace people who saw that it was a cage for other reasons. Maybe because they were homosexual, or Jewish, or poor and white, or oppressed for some other reason. Maybe they were white males who had experienced things from another side.

It was crucial to embrace folks who weren't necessarily in my circle but who saw the cage. Once I did that, my task was to throw a party with these people, a big old party that could not be ignored by the people in the center. Little by little those people would say, "How come I wasn't invited?" And they'd move further and further out to where our party was. You can't afford to leave your party to go to theirs. When you get off your path to try to convince somebody to get on yours, you're off your own path. You've got to stay on your own path, because it's the only way you can be an example.

The best thing you can do is to make tracks for somebody else to follow. Once they realize that there's a party going on out there, they can come out and see for themselves that this is a cage and be empowered in truth and in love.

Warren: Why is it important that it be done with love?

Berry: There's no way I can be effective in getting people to see that there's a need for change if I'm mad about it. How can I have a glimpse at peace and truth and try to share it with somebody in anger?

I went to a peace march once with my cousin. We couldn't find the peace march, and we started to get really mad about it. Then it occurred to me that there was no way I would convince somebody that there was a need for peace if I was mad. So we started marching, just the two of us, singing "We want peace." Immediately two other people came up and said, "We're looking for the march, too." I found out that a lot of people looking for peace are simply lost. We're all lost. And once we find each other, there will be a lot of power in coming together and working for change. But we have to do it in humor and in love.

Warren: Many people have compared you to Oprah, but if you remind me of anyone it's Carol Burnett.

Berry: Roz, what a compliment.

Warren: You have a similar wit, and warmth. I also see a similar sense of strength, as well as zaniness. Am I nuts? Did you watch her show as a kid? Did she influence your humor?

Berry: You hit the nail right on the head. The very first skit I did was in high school with my best friend Tia, and the both of us were elements of Carol Burnett on that park bench saying, "Here pidgie, pidgie." What I want to achieve with my show is that same rapport Carol had with her audience.

They could ask her any question and know that she'd answer it. They were her family.

Warren: Who are your other comic influences, and what about their work inspired you?

Berry: Loads of people have influenced me. I used to sneak down to the basement and play my mother's Moms Mabley records when she wasn't at home. Moms Mabley was bold enough to say incredibly tough things. They were politically dangerous, but she said them anyway, and she said them in such a way that you *had* to laugh. It was scary that this older black woman would have the nerve to say these things, and I loved that.

Warren: There are more and more funny women on television, women like Roseanne, Brett Butler, and Thea Vidale. Why are television audiences so eager to hear from strong, funny women?

Berry: I think because we're honest. We remind a lot of people of their mother, or of a lover they'd like to have. Or of a sister who told you the truth and still loved you. We remind them of a teacher that they had who was tough. Someone that they love and respect—that's what they're seeing.

Warren: Roseanne once said, "Comics are angry people with something to say." Do you agree?

Berry: Everything that I've said as a comic started as something that made me angry, and I realized a need to turn it around and force people to see it. That's the two-edged sword of comedy.

Warren: Much of the humor in your act is based on your angry response to racism, sexism, and homophobia. Why were you willing to take on such tough topics?

Berry: It's what I have to do. You see these things and you've got to respond. I can't *force* people to accept my views. It's tougher and much more empowering to make people see your side or your perspective, and that's what I want to do with humor.

Warren: You're one of the few heterosexual comics to include material about homophobia in your act. This shouldn't be unusual, but it is. What moved you to include this material?

Berry: Oppression is oppression is oppression. If somebody is putting their foot on your head because you're homosexual, the foot does not hurt less than it would if you were black. It's the same kind of oppression, and you've got to speak out about it.

What amazes me is when some African-Americans say, "How dare homosexuals say their plight is one of civil rights? They shouldn't be trying to join us on our bandwagon." That's crazy. If one more person is on this wagon, it's a little stronger. It doesn't matter why they came on the wagon. But a lot of people seem to find power in oppression. I don't. I've found power in recognizing oppression and overthrowing it. The only way to do that is to have the force of others doing that with you. It makes sense. It's logical. It is right and it is righteous.

I could easily say some of my best friends are homosexual, but it's not necessary. This is my family and we are in the same situation and have the same voice.

Warren: You've gone from educator to stand-up comic to talk-show host; with each career change your audience has expanded. Has your relationship with or responsibility to that audience changed?

Berry: There are more people watching me and listening to me now, but a station manager in Cincinnati once told me a very powerful thing: "Talk to one person at a time. If you talk to one person at a time, you're going to reach all of them."

Warren: You've come very far, very fast. Within a brief span of time, you've gone from being a private person in academia to a public figure in the entertainment industry. How has this changed your life? How has this changed *you*?

Berry: My life has changed, but I haven't changed, and I don't intend to change.

The people around you start changing. They start expecting that you've become the image on television and that you can't be approached. People will see me shopping at K-Mart and they'll say, "I can't believe I'm seeing *you* here!" or "You look just like Bertice, but I know Bertice would never be here." That's crazy. I've got three kids; I'm definitely going to be at K-Mart.

I've gone very far, but it's not been fast. From the time I was cleaning toilets when I was twelve, that was a part of working on what I'm doing now. It hasn't been as fast as people feel that it is, and it's been very tough, incredibly tough.

Warren: Tell me something about your background. Is your family close? Are you like your mom, or your sisters?

Berry: I believe that you're a product of everybody you meet and know. Sometimes I don't like that, because there are aspects of myself that I don't care for, and I know where they come from. But I know I'm responsible, ultimately.

My family is very close. I talk to my mom five times a week, sometimes about nothing, sometimes about things that are a little tough. I'm just finding out who my father is and getting in touch with that side of my family.

Warren: Are you a feminist? Is there such a thing as feminist humor?

Berry: There's a feminist perspective in humor, definitely.

People think feminists don't have a sense of humor, but the only way you can call yourself a feminist in America is to laugh, you know? If you ask people the important questions, you usually get feminist answers. If you ask, "Do you believe in equal pay for equal work? Do you believe that women and men should have the same rights?" people say yes. That would make the majority of us feminists.

Betty

by Laurie Stone

Think of girl gangs ... composed of princesses. Think of Bette Midler ... before she became a Disney character, when, as the Divine One, she channeled Mae West, bawdy and bold, her own fool but nobody else's. Think of girl bands, like the hellzapoppin' combo in *Some Like It Hot* and the real-life International Sweethearts of Rhythm, an interracial ensemble that blew tight, swinging tunes during the forties. Think of the Andrews Sisters with rich fantasy lives, unfurling and unchecked. And you have something of Betty.

Betty consists of twin sisters Amy and Bitzi Ziff, who don't inordinately resemble each other, and Alyson Palmer. The trio is a band, knowing and relaxed with each other and with their instruments. They sing three-part harmonies that are thrillingly woven and mellifluous, then take jolting twists. And they're partial to hard-driving rock rhythms with punk, new wave, and Caribbean beats; most of their tunes are composed by the threesome.

Betty is richly comic, part home movie, part artful contrivance. It's a dream pajama party, with every wish of wildness and silliness indulged. Diversity is prominently featured. The Ziffs are diminutive and pale-skinned.

Palmer is statuesque, her complexion café au lait. Bitzi's mane is red, Amy's blond, and Alyson's brown, but they're all frizzed, and electric current seems to flow from the tendrils.

The performers are wired, connected to one another, yet each projects an individual persona. Bitzi, boogying solo and flashing a sleek midriff, is an earthy imp sporting a slender nose ring. Alyson, wielder of the bass guitar and master of electronic gadgetry, is a glamorous wizard. And Amy, who does most of the talking and delivers monologues between musical numbers, translates the associations, mannerisms, and verbal tics that trail the trio like jet streams.

Favored themes are standards of pop—love gone sour and feelings of freakiness—but they're freshened with puns and double entendres. In "Go Ahead and Split, Mr. Amoeba Man," the women quip, "I can't divide my love again." At one point, Amy declares, "I can't decide whether to ride girls or boys." Long take. "Bicycles, that is." In "First Date," about a happening that doesn't, they croon, "I shaved my legs for nothing." After the song, Amy stares out. "You weren't feeling sorry for us in that last number, were you?"

References whiz by, but an intelligent, foxy tone is sustained, and this, above all, lifts the evening from a revue to a work of theater. The name Betty evokes Betty Crocker, conjurer of all that's homey and secure. The women of Betty hold the stage, their skilled hands on the controls; they are delighted with each other's company. They are anti-Betty Crockers, and yet Betty is homey, a sister act, with inside moves and code phrases.

Ambivalence is paraded and examined, as are the pleasures and tensions of being part of a group—even a group of outcasts banded together. The urge toward individuality is countered with a yearning to meld into a united, harmonic voice. Sisterhood is at times an amulet, at others, an albatross; in one bit, parasitic twins are described.

Much performance art skirts definition to mask the fact that it has nothing to say. Betty frolics adeptly with multiple and simultaneous impulses: with the desire for men and women, straights and gays, blacks and whites, team players and renegades. These women refuse to lop off portions of themselves, but there's no piety in their stand and no exclusivity in the pleasure they generate. Betty satirizes insider humor, letting everyone in on the joke.

Matina Bevis

by Roz Warren

"I've always had an intense amount of attitude," says Matina Bevis, "and I'm very quick on my feet." No wonder her career in stand-up is going great guns. Bevis got into comedy performance in a roundabout fashion. Working as a carpenter at Robin Tyler's Southern Women's Music and Comedy Festival, she impulsively entered the festival's talent show. "I did about ten minutes, and I was a scream."

Present at the creation of Matina's stand-up career were both Tyler and Lynn Lavner. Tyler was impressed enough to ask the fledgling comic to perform at her upcoming West Coast Music and Comedy Festival and on one of her Olivia cruises. Bevis is grateful for Tyler's mentoring. "I've been working steadily ever since I first stood up," Bevis says. "You've got to love that."

As a kid, inspired by TV comics like Joan Rivers, Totie Fields, and Phyllis Diller, Bevis wanted to be a stand-up. She even majored in theater in college, but she found that "at five foot ten, there are really no leading-lady roles." But there was plenty of work for "an electro-lesbian," Bevis's term for "a dyke who's mastered every tool known to womankind."

Bevis doesn't have much time for her toolbox these days, since she's usually on the road performing at women's festivals and comedy clubs. "To be serious about stand-up," she says, "you've got to travel nonstop. It's not a part-time job. You've got to be out there all the time, or you get out of shape." She jokes that she makes it home so rarely that she's forgotten her dog's name. "I go home and dust off my dog and it's like, 'Don't tell me. I know your name. Starts with an *M*, right?' " But the joy of performing makes it all worthwhile. "You take the audience's emotions and you work them, literally, into whatever you want. It's a very intense thing. It's the most incredible high in the world."

Maureen Brownsey

by Laura Post and Roz Warren

"I'm going to be a big star!" proclaims Maureen Brownsey at the start of her set. "In California, we call that sort of statement creative visualization. In the other forty-nine states, it's called self-delusion."

Well, maybe not in Brownsey's case. Everyone always knew she was going to be a comic when she grew up. "I was a goofy little kid," she recalls. "I was always saying things that were somehow on a different wavelength, and everybody would laugh." A natural clown, Brownsey also had a knack for spotting silliness. At nine she reduced her older sister to tears by mocking a sentence from a beloved Nancy Drew book. "Nancy's boyfriend Ned has come to visit, and he tries to kiss her," remembers Brownsey, smiling, "and Nancy actually says 'Oh Ned Nickerson, you ninny, the neighbors'."

Brownsey's role as a jokester continued through grade school: "By fifth grade I could imitate anything Lily Tomlin did the night before on 'Laugh-In'." She did, however, briefly go through the obligatory wanting-to-be-a-martyr stage. "All little Catholic school girls want to be nuns," she explains, "but there were those problems with dogma."

These days, Brownsey more than fulfills her early promise. Her act is swiftly paced and upbeat and includes jokes about body piercing, underwear inspectors, Republicans, and job hunting. ("When I was applying for a job I went from having no discernible skills to lying about having no discernible skills.") About personal ads, she quips, "A truly honest ad would say, 'I want to date myself, only with more money'."

Besides being a successful comic, Brownsey is also a filmmaker: "I like art forms that cost a lot of money with outrageously small chances for success." Her first film, *True Blue*, starring comic Karen Williams, has done well; a future project will involve Williams and comics Marga Gomez and Suzy Berger. Brownsey holds a graduate degree in film from San Francisco State University, where she's also worked as an instructor. "It was great!" enthuses Brownsey. "It's important to torture young minds."

Brett Butler

by Roz Warren

Brett Butler, star of the hit ABC sitcom "Grace Under Fire," describes herself, and Grace, as a "straight-shooting southern woman who's both proletarian and literate." Grace is an oil refinery worker and single mom with three kids, who's escaped an abusive marriage. Butler herself married at age twenty and endured an abusive relationship for three years before getting out. The comic doesn't have kids, but "with four younger sisters and eleven younger cousins I grew up with a baby on my hip."

Butler (who was named after Lady Brett Ashley in *The Sun Also Rises*) was born in Montgomery, Alabama, and grew up in Marietta, Georgia. Her father walked out on the family when she was four. Her mom remarried when Brett was six.

Butler started doing stand-up at local comedy clubs while working as a waitress after her divorce. She also performed her act at battered women's shelters. She did five hundred shows in her first year, performing what she calls "good-old-girl insult comedy." Her approach was wickedly honest and autobiographical, as when she mocked her ex: "Once a friend of my ex-husband came up to me and said, 'Your ex-husband jokes are mean'. I said, 'That may be true, but which among his friends has been cruel enough to explain them to him?' "

Just four and a half years after she started doing stand-up, Butler had earned her first "Tonight Show" spot. She did more television work, with appearances on HBO, Showtime, "Hollywood Squares," and a stint as a writer for Dolly Parton's variety show, before landing the role of Grace.

Her fans love Butler because she's a survivor. Because she's funny as hell. And because she doesn't take shit from anyone. Or as *TV Guide* put it: "Brett Butler has had her heart broken, her face punched in, her dreams laughed at, but she's never given up."

Warren: When did you first realize you could make people laugh?

Butler: When I laughed myself. Not at myself, just when I laughed. The women in our family are particularly funny—nothing was ever profane, but it always seemed like some salty, iconoclastic banter was going on when we all got together. I have four younger sisters, and making them laugh was the finest part of my youth, other than when they were funny, too. Actually, I might have done real stand-up comedy at a younger age than any comedian working today. I was eight years old, and I told a mixture of George Carlin jokes and things my kid sisters said around the house, for example, "When my mother bought training pants for the baby, one of my sisters asked, 'But where are the wheels?!' "

Warren: How would you describe your humor?

Butler: I think what I do is an extremely personal take on my own inconsistencies as a person combined with not suffering fools gladly. I often react [on stage] in small ways to heinous behavior in others and then in big ways to the stupid things we all do, realizing that, for me, these exaggerations create a belief system all my own, without regard to whether anyone can relate. My feelings are what they relate to, not necessarily the experience.

Warren: What kind of comedy are you comfortable with? Uncomfortable with?

Butler: I am comfortable with humor that often makes others *un*comfortable. I am uncomfortable with simplistic observational comedy, things that are generic and devoid of any opinion. However, comedy that upsets me—and as a total defender of the First Amendment I hate to say this—is hate comedy. What is worse than the comedian who does it are the audiences that buy into it as a group. Lately this seems to have been stolen from the exclusive province of white males, and now it is being used by black comedians, women, and homosexuals. Personally, I never thought it gave an enemy power to behave like them, except on a battlefield. I recently saw a talented lesbian comedian close her show with an impression of a man performing cunnilingus: it was as shallow, erroneous, and one-sided as anything Dice Clay ever did. The sad part is that some think this is progress.

Warren: How did you decide to become a performer?

Butler: After my stint as a child comic, I didn't do it again for sixteen years. I never set foot, as we say down South, on stage for that whole time, and probably didn't think of it consciously. I believe that performing lived inside me and was gestating, or in chrysalis, or whatever metaphor of growth you choose. When I did get on stage again, after a grim first marriage, I felt that I had things to say and knew that time and more experience would get me to say them. It has been eleven years, and now I know that the reverie I have at night, right before I go to sleep, is a tour guide of future progress: wherever I see myself in that moment will happen if I just keep getting under the light and writing. I suppose performing decided on me, as much as anything.

Warren: What makes you laugh?

Butler: Generally, autobiographical comedy—"comedy vérité" makes me laugh, whether it is the outrageous pain of Richard Pryor or Sam Kinison or the characterizations of Lily Tomlin and Jonathan Winters. It doesn't have to be "true" for the comedy to be autobiographical. When Winters does some weird character, it is from a combination of something he noticed once and his private take on it. I enjoy dark comedy, comedy about things thought of as sacred or even sad, but not comedy that fulfills itself on the pain of others.

Warren: Who have been your influences and mentors as a comic?

Butler: I watched television continuously as a child and lived for the moments when the comedians performed. I honestly liked them all. They were the heroes of my youth, my skydivers, athletes, the whole ball of wax. My influences have been Richard Pryor, Jonathan Winters, Robert Klein, and when he first started, Robin Williams. I don't think I have ever laughed as hard as when I heard Pryor's "Was It Something I Said?" for the first time. I still think he's the best comedian who ever lived. As I go further into the craft, I like what Lenny Bruce did and strive to reach his level—politically and personally—on stage. Of course, at the end he got so sick with addiction and persecutory self-absorption, he helped no one, not even himself.

As far as personal mentors, Robert Klein saw me when I was first starting out down South and encouraged me to go to New York. He gave me some phone numbers and really followed my career. And I owe special homage to my mother, who encouraged me even when I was eight and wanted to do schtick at school. She acted like every third-grader in the world wanted to be a stand-up at a school pageant, and she helped me organize the material. She didn't stop there, either. When I began the work, she was almost the only parent of any of my peers who thought the work was honorable and worthwhile, and she has never stopped believing in me.

Warren: What is feminist humor? Is there such a thing? How is feminist humor different from other humor?

Butler: Now I will give my jaded answers! Before I reply, I want to paraphrase some old, dead white male—it might have been Oliver Wendell Holmes—who said that injustice will never be destroyed until those not affected by it are as outraged as those who are. Feminist humor is humor that empowers those who perform it and who listen to it. It does not walk loudly, necessarily, but the strength is unmistakable. I wish it were more aligned with the humor of other subjugated groups—multiracial, ethnic, international comedy would mix like salad with feminist humor.

The shrill cries of any of us who decry the differences among people and do not see what is the same do not belong in comedy. Too often I will finish a show and a woman will come up to me and say, "That was great. I love how you pick on men. You should do more of it." Often, after the same performance, a man will come up and say, "I like the way you get dumb women. I could get along with a broad like you." To me, both of them miss the point: I try to excoriate the ignorance, prejudice, and shallowness of certain mindsets. When I give them a character, the gender is secondary to the point of my joke.

Feminist humor comes in all colors and sizes, and men are just as capable of doing it as we are. I have been on more shows featuring "all-female comedians" only to mourn the lack of my feminist men colleagues who should be there, too. Affirmative action is an ugly thing to see in art.

Oh, hell. I am an artist. What am I talking about?! To make any of this academic rots what I do on stage. I will leave this to the studiously inclined and say simply this: feminism, just like all mind-expanding beliefs, is easily recognized when it happens on a comedy stage. It adheres to old ideas like a pesky bit of knowledge that there's no room for in some places. It lifts, but it does not separate!

Warren: How do you develop your material?

Butler: I carry paper with me everywhere, and when I don't have it, I write on my hand or arm or whatever is handy. At night, I have learned to write in the dark in a pad that lies by my bed. I tape shows—audio only—and try to listen to the tape as soon after a show as I can. I pay attention to what makes me mad—often there is something very funny in it. I try to take the anger and the ridiculousness of whatever it is to the most exaggerated level and just play with it.

As far as writing goes, most of it is done with just the hull of an idea. It fleshes itself out on the stage and often goes someplace entirely new once I do it there. I keep every joke I ever wrote. Age gives a new perspective that pays off in the reworking. Much of my "new" stuff is old stuff reworked and refined and done now in a basically unrecognizable way.

The most important thing I do is get on stage as much as possible, and I have done that for the entire time I've been a comedian. The only way to get better is to do this. My first two years in comedy, I did five hundred shows a year. I would go up to bands in Houston and ask to go on between their breaks. Lord, the nerve of me. But it worked, and my fear gradually eased.

Warren: How does it feel to make people laugh from a stage? To bomb?

Butler: The words I use to describe the first part of this question are always either religious or sexual. Bear with me. It feels holy to make people laugh. When comedy works, it is a circle that goes from the performer to the crowd and back again. Although the comedian is the one elevated on the stage and illuminated by light, the audience participates just as directly in the process. Like the moment in sex in which both partners "become as one," the room is filled with the uniting of spirits for a common cause. There is hardly any place I would rather be than in the midst of such a circle. Conversely, when I tell a joke and one person laughs very hard and alone, that feels great, too. I feel the human connection very specifically, and that is rewarding in a private and funny—to me—way.

On the subject of bombing, like the marriage I left in which I was battered for three years, I honestly feel that I had to go through that to become who I am now. Today, after thousands of performances, a quiet room is more of a mystery than it is upsetting. That might not be as egotistical as it sounds. I am there wondering what to do next, but not doubting myself as a person or performer. I rarely become defensive, but I just try to go further in tried and true material, or I go ahead and do all the new stuff I can do. With such moments, you can't lose. The room can only go up from there! Funny thing about bombing: often on the nights you think you did, the people will tell you later that they loved what you did. Some crowds are just shy, I reckon!

Warren: What impact do you want to have? What are your dreams?

Butler: The impact I want to have is this: I want people to know that what they see on stage when I am performing is the product of a life well examined and that I like myself in spite of the foibles and frailties I display. This is a freedom I have earned. If people can see it when I work, then that is having an impact. They may not like me, but they will respect what I do.

In this age of cosmetic perfection and political dissembling, comedians give permission for the flaws to exist—the little ones, anyway—while they (we) work to weed out the big ones. I read somewhere that truth is becoming profane and illusion sacred. Comedy, when it works, flips this around, and if I can do this a tenth of the time I am on stage, I will consider myself a success.

My dream is to continue this process. Right now in my career some extraordinary things are happening to me, and they are a combination of my working hard to be ready and getting that break you hear about in show biz. If it all ended tomorrow, my dreams still would have come true: I took big chances, followed through with discipline, and made room for disappointment along the way. I have seen myself grow from an unsober, fearful person to one who takes care of herself and works hard with much joy. If I keep doing that, then my dreams are already happening.

Fran Capo

by Roz Warren

Fran "Supermouth" Capo is better than anybody else at what she does: talking. Fran is listed in the *Guinness Book of World Records* as the "World's Fastest-Talking Female" and has been clocked at 603.32 words per minute. She first won the record after racing through the Ninety-first Psalm at warp speed (585 words per minute) on "Larry King Live." Fran's son Spence is a record breaker too: at age two he was credited by the Professional Comedians' Association as being the world's youngest professional comic. (His act includes mini-impressions of Joan Rivers, Elvis, Andrew Dice Clay, and Richard Nixon.)

Fran's act includes telling fairy tales at hyperspeed ("The Three Little Pigs" takes her twenty seconds) and zipping through passages from the Bible. A crowd-pleaser on her frequent television appearances is phoning a local take-out restaurant and ordering everything on the menu at lightning speed. Her unique verbal skills have also led to radio and movie spots, including a turn as a motormouth secretary in *Lonely In America*. She's also popular as a public speaker on topics like humor in everyday life.

As a kid growing up in New York City, talking fast was a survival skill. "I learned to talk fast because the pace here is fast," she explains. "It began in sixth grade. If you didn't answer right away, the teacher called on someone else. I'd memorize ten different answers to say in the same amount of time, so he could pick the right one." Fast-talking continues to be a useful skill. When she fights with her boyfriend, Fran jokes, it's over so fast "he doesn't realize it happened!" She's also "fast-talked" her way out of speeding tickets: after listening to her, Fran says, the cops usually just walk away smiling. Another plus: "I save a lot of money on long-distance phone bills."

Margaret Cho

by Susie Day

Margaret Cho made TV history when she became the first Asian American to land her own network series: ABC's "All-American Girl." Cho, who has long poked fun at the way Asians are portrayed on network TV, parodies such a show in her act, including a snappy theme song: "She's not wearing a wedding veil/'cause she's the kind of bride that comes in the mail!" There are more extraterrestrials on TV than Asians, notes Cho, who argues that the popular "Kung Fu" should have been retitled "That Guy's Not Chinese!"

Cho's sitcom, like her life, is about being both Korean and American; her comedy is informed by the experience of "not fitting in" with either culture. Korean women, notes Cho, are taught to be "beautiful, silent flowers." Cho's street-smart, wisecracking Valley Girl persona fights this stereotype while embracing her identity as an Asian American. (Ironically, when she went on "Star Search," the producers asked Cho if she could be "more Chinese.")

With her life and with her humor, Cho challenges the geisha stereotype. "Men look at me and think I'm going to walk on their backs or something," she laughs. "I tell them, 'The only time I'll walk on your back is if there's something on the other side of you I want'."

(Note: This interview took place shortly before "All-American Girl" went on the air.)

Day: Do you change your material depending on your audience?

Cho: Not really. I perform mostly at colleges now, and sometimes they'll ask me not to do any material on abortion. Which I don't, anyway, because I think that everybody in their right mind is pro-choice. Sometimes I'm asked not to use foul language, and I comply with that, because that's not really what I do.

Day: How did you get into comedy?

Cho: I was involved with theater for many years. I started when I was about thirteen, doing different shows. I eventually went to the High School of Performing Arts, much like the one that's immortalized in the film *Fame*. I got a lot of exposure to the arts in my upbringing. My parents owned a bookstore in San Francisco. My mother sang and played classical guitar and my father and I both played piano. It was an artistic family, and I kind of continued in the family tradition.

My father's a comedy writer. It's kind of embarrassing—he writes "Toastmasters" books in Korea. He lives in Seoul now. So I was always sort of surrounded by mirth and music when I was growing up. I started doing comedy when I was in college. Before that, doing community theater and children's theater, I was always very castable. I got work all the time. I always got leads in plays, a little star. But I found out, when I got into the real world, that it wasn't like that at all. There were no parts for Asians and no good parts for women. I couldn't get work.

It was really hard for me to get going or make money or do anything, so I decided I was going to do comedy. At the time I was working with an improv group that had a lot of stand-up comedians in it, and they helped me because they thought I had potential. I started doing stand-up five years ago. Eventually I decided to quit school and go on the road and perform.

Day: Did your parents support that choice?

Cho: They were very upset. Even though they supported me in my artistic endeavors, they really looked down on the fact that I wasn't finishing school, and they didn't want me in nightclubs every night. I think they would have preferred if I were a writer or something more respectable, because a comedian is ... my mother used to say sarcasm is the *lowest* of the arts. And it's so true! [*laughs*]

They wanted me to pursue something a little bit more upscale, uptown. But I loved the raw feeling of comedy. Comedy is entertainment in its purest form, because it's just you and a microphone and an audience. There's no music, there's no play to support you. You're not an actor, really. It's just you, laying out your life for people. I really love it. I feel very fortunate to have achieved the success that I have, because it's something that I enjoy doing so much. Performing is a reward in itself. So I'm very happy with the way things are right now.

Day: Do you want to stay in stand-up or would you like to get back into theater?

Cho: I'd like to get back into theater. I'd like to get into film and television. Some people in Los Angeles are interested in developing a sitcom around me and what I do onstage. But it's very difficult, because it's something that's never happened on television. They've never had a show based around an Asian person.

Somehow Hollywood seems to think that if you have an Asian or a Latino in the cast, or even an African-American, you need to explain why they're there, like "This is my adopted sister." It's very strange. They can't just be there, which is the way it is in real life. I'm battling that right now. I want to be represented in a way that I'm comfortable being represented, you know? I want success on my own terms, which may take longer. But I think it's better in the long run.

Day: Is the appeal of stand-up the fact that you have so much more control over your material? You can create what you don't have on television or in the theater.

Cho: Exactly. It's all mine. I can say and do what I want to. It's a wonderful form of self-expression. I'm talking about my life, so it's very personal, very self-indulgent, which is why I like it.

Day: Have you received support from other Asian performers? Do they see you as breaking new ground?

Cho: I've received tremendous support from other Asian performers. Other comedians have also been very supportive. And I feel I've inspired other people to pursue comedy who probably wouldn't have.

Asian culture can be so oppressive about the choices that you make in life. It's very rare to find a family that supports going into the arts. They have such a struggle when they come here, and they spend all this time working and slaving so that their children can have a better life, and not throw it away on some artistic endeavor. They want their kids to be doctors, lawyers, which they feel are "real jobs." So it's very difficult. A lot of people let their parents take charge of their lives in that way. But I think I've encouraged people to break away from that.

Day: And is your family coming around?

Cho: Oh, they're completely supportive. Now they're very happy. They see me on television and they realize, Well, she's not at a nightclub; she's right there. I've actually had a show broadcast in Korea, which made them really, really proud and happy. I think it's given them new hope. They're excited because they have a daughter they can say has done something that nobody else's daughter has. That's another big Korean thing. It's like: "My kid's at Stanford." "Well, *my* kid's at Princeton." "Well, *my* kid was on TV with Bob Hope." You know? "Top that!"

Day: How would you describe your appeal? Who is your audience?

Cho: A lot of my humor has to do with feeling like you don't really belong. I come from a very traditional Korean background, but with a lot of American influence, so I grew up in a very confused atmosphere. Most Asian Americans do, I think, because they're raised in a very strict, traditional Asian household, yet they have to deal with their friends on the outside who are very Americanized. So you grow up with these two cultures, not really feeling that you belong. I think that comes through in my act.

It's the universal feeling of not really feeling that you belong anywhere. I appeal to people who are sort of disenfranchised. There's a lot of talk about Generation X, which is my generation, feeling as if we don't really fit in anywhere. And, if anything, maybe that's my audience.

I also have a big Asian following, because they like to see what I'm doing. I'm a "positive" image.

Day: So you play to Asian audiences as well as mostly white audiences?

Cho: I also spent a lot of time on the black comedy circuit. When I was working in San Francisco, there were a lot of black comedy clubs in Oakland that are amazing to me because they've existed for many years and have produced their own comedy, their own talent. Comedians that you probably would never see, although lately there have been more African-American comedians, on shows like "Def Jam." I spent a lot of time performing at those clubs. I just performed everywhere I could. Leather bars. I was very popular in leather bars. [*Laughs*]

Day: Ideally, what do you want to do with your comedy?

Cho: To see how far I can take it. Ideally, I'd really like to make a difference in the world. A long-time dream is to start my own film company, where I would produce my own films and TV shows about things that concern my generation and our issues: racism, sexism, homophobia, AIDS. I'd like to tackle issues that are important to me and that Hollywood tends to shy away from. I want to be Barbra Streisand, basically. [*Laughs*]

Day: What's it like being on major TV shows like "Arsenio"?

Cho: It's great. I used to get really scared when I did television, but I don't anymore, because this is my job. If I got scared every time I went on, I don't think I could do it. I had a great time on his show. I really enjoy being on television. It just expands your audience exponentially. It makes it so huge. It's very exciting.

Day: What is it like performing if you don't get nervous? Do you get a high?

Cho: Yeah, it's exciting. I enjoy pleasing people. I'm very codependent; I want to make sure everybody's okay. So I do get a rush from it. It's an amazing feeling to talk and have people physically react to the things that you're saying, to laugh and applaud. It's not like anything else. I don't know what it would be like to be a singer, but I do know what it is to be loved by a lot of people, and that's just great.

I'll probably continue performing live for the rest of my life, because I've become so addicted to that rush—or whatever it is—that I don't think I could do without it.

I know that if I haven't performed for, say, a week, which is very rare, I feel I'm not in my head that day. I work 350 days a year. I very rarely take a day off, and I love my work.

The only thing that gets difficult is traveling. I'm very paranoid. I shove all the furniture up against the door, Connie Francis-style. And it gets more intense as I grow more successful. But I still love performing. I don't think I could ever stop doing that.

Day: Who have been your influences?

Cho: There are so many people that I really admire and respect for their work through the years. M.F.K. Fisher, I love her. I think she's brilliant. I love Sandra Bernhard, and of course, Lily Tomlin—who doesn't? Madonna. Art inspires me. I'm a big pop art fan. I love Andy Warhol. I also love people who were reckless with their lives, like Edie Sedgwick. Living out the fantasy of life as art, the decadence. I know it sounds so pretentious but I love glamorous people. I love drag queens. I love Camille Paglia. Those are the kind of people who really inspire me, people who live to extremes.

Day: What advice would you give to women who want to get into comedy?

Cho: Go for it! And don't get discouraged. The first year I did comedy, I bombed every night. For a year. And I still never lost sight of my goals. Just persevere, because they'll all pay. Just say that in your head; that's like my mantra: "They'll all pay." If something happens to you and it really upsets you, just calm yourself down and just think, Well, it's okay because they'll all pay.

Day: Karma?

Cho: Yeah.

Day: Unfortunately, you're usually not around to see karma happen.

Cho: But you know it will. That's the satisfaction.

Kate Clinton

by Roz Warren

Kate Clinton is America's most beloved lesbian feminist comic—a field in which, until recently, there hasn't been overwhelming competition. A native of Syracuse, New York, Kate was a high school English teacher before turning to stand-up in 1981, the year Ronald Reagan became president. Or in her words, "I began performing political comedy the same year Ronald Reagan began performing his." (Recently, Clinton has begun referring to herself as "Hilarity Clinton—Bill's sister.")

At first, Clinton performed in women's bars, church basements, and at women's music festivals for mostly lesbian audiences: "I didn't want my life goal to be simply making straight people laugh." Her comic persona combines cynicism, common sense, and queer politics. She always begins her show with the words, "Thanks for coming out."

It took a while for the rest of the world to catch up with Kate, but her off-Broadway show, *Out Is In*, is currently a big hit, and reviewers are scrambling for adjectives to describe Clinton's audience-friendly performing style. She's being called gracious, warm, savvy, engaging, friendly, unintimidating, maternal (!) and astute. One critic even called Kate "the lesbian you'd want to bring home to meet your parents."

Clinton's comedy combines expert puns, solid one-liners ("Is Janet Reno a lesbian? I don't know—but her hair is!"), family history (she calls herself a "recovering Catholic"), and brilliant free-associational riffs on topics both personal and political. One example is her discovery of a "bathroom moment motif" underlying opposition to contemporary civil rights movements. In *Out Is In*, Clinton tracks segregationist concerns about shared drinking fountains through the ERA's shared-bathroom debate up to today's gays-in-the-military flak about shared showers.

Clinton also pokes fun at her own community. In her current show, she returns often to a chant she heard at the March on Washington: "We're dykes! Don't touch us! We'll hurt you!" One critic has suggested that Clinton's act constitutes "an adult education class on lesbian feminist politics."

Being an out lesbian has always provided Clinton with plenty of good material, but in recent years her focus has moved from bawdy lesbian in-jokes ("She wouldn't say the word *lesbian* if her mouth were full of one.") to include barbed political commentary as well. She refers to politicians as "the ethically challenged" and proposes, as a country fair attraction, a Sam Nunn slapping booth. Addressing the gays-in-the-military issue, she labels the "don't ask, don't tell" policy "a screen door to the closet."

Clinton, who coined the term "fumerist" (feminist humorist or humorist who fumes) sees comedy as a force for social change: "People are more open to a lot of things when they're laughing." About women and humor, she says, "Women are funny, and we have been laughing together for survival for years."

Warren: For years you played to mostly lesbian and feminist audiences; now you're appearing off-Broadway. Do you need to work harder to get your current audience on your wavelength?

Clinton: I've been performing for twelve years, so often when I play a mostly lesbian or feminist audience they've been coming to see me every year for that many years. I walk out and they start clapping. I can say hello and they'll applaud, they've been so well trained. With my New York audience I don't always get that same riotous acceptance right away—but I do by the end of the show.

Warren: There's always been a strong sense of community in your audience. It must be tougher now that you're no longer "preaching to the choir." There's more pressure on you to succeed, and you're facing more challenging audiences. Is performing still fun?

Clinton: I just finished with seventy shows, and there was only one that wasn't fun. The work it takes to get to the stage is the hard part. When I walk on stage—that's the fun part. If you don't have fun there, forget it.

Warren: Are lesbians actually becoming more mainstream, or is "lesbian chic" just media hype?

Clinton: It's a little bit of both, I think. But we'll take it!

Warren: Is the current lesbian visibility something that's going to last?

Clinton: There's a surge forward and then the wave recedes, but we've made progress. I believe in the power of words. For instance, look at the number of people who are now able to say the word *penis* because of the Bobbitt thing. I've never heard that word so much in my life, which demystifies it. I think that's wonderful.

Warren: Once people can say words like *penis* or *lesbian* we can actually begin to communicate about these things.

Clinton: The word lesbian didn't use to be out there much. It never banged me in the head when I was growing up. But now there's a chance that it will light on someone and she will think, Oh, this is what I am, or, This is a definition of life that some people lead. That's pretty extraordinary. But because of the visibility, there's the inevitable backlash. In a lot of ways, I think that this current focus on the penis is part of that. Because if lesbians are chic, men are really threatened.

Warren: You've always said that your goal is not to make straight people laugh, that you were performing for the lesbian community. But now that you're off-Broadway you're clearly making straight people laugh ...

Clinton: It's still not my goal. If they come, it's fine. But I still like to amuse lesbians.

Warren: What's your take on "political correctness" and comedy? Some people feel there's something wrong with this whole notion of fairness and inclusivity. A lot of comics are very defensive about being criticized for not being PC.

Clinton: Labeling something politically correct is such a hideous conversation stopper. All it means is that people are unwilling to deal with the issues of racism and sexism and homophobia. For a while, I was doing a line about racism. I'd say, "Well, I can see we've really done our outreach and *she's* here." It made the audience really uncomfortable. I *wanted* them to be uncomfortable. *I* was uncomfortable.

Warren: You often address serious issues like racism and homophobia with your humor. Do you find there's a bias against humor, that people feel that if your delivery isn't solemn then your message can't be serious?

Clinton: Absolutely. Even from my childhood. I could be baring my soul to someone, but if I made a light remark it would negate everything I'd just said. People would say, "I don't know when you're being serious and when you're being humorous."

Warren: Why do you think people treat *humorous* and *serious* as two mutually exclusive categories?

Clinton: Too much Calvinism? [*laughs*] I'm not sure. I think there's a really hideous kind of puritan ethic that makes people feel that if it doesn't hurt and it's not painful it really doesn't mean anything. You know—no pain, no gain.

I also think it's fear. There's something about humor that involves really letting go and being out of control, which people really fear. They fear it now more than ever. Which is why there's a longing for one answer once and for all. It's an incredible rigidity based on fear.

Warren: And yet if you do get people to laugh you can get them to listen to you.

Clinton: I know there are people who come to my show who are only there because they think it's good for them. I got a wonderful review in *The New York Times*, and for two weeks after that review came out I had a sense that people were coming to the theater thinking, I know this will be good for us. Or maybe they'd come to the show because they have a child who's gay and they're thinking, I know Bob would appreciate it. But that's okay, because I know they heard things they would never ever hear if they hadn't been laughing or around people who were laughing.

There's a window of vulnerability that opens up when people are laughing. They let down their guard and new ideas can come in.

Roz: Has the fact that you're addressing this new audience changed your act or the way you present your material?

Clinton: I think the context has changed. I don't think the content has changed.

Warren: Your attitude and values haven't changed over the years but your material has changed to a certain extent. It started out very much about being a lesbian and coming out and lesbian culture, and now it's more outward-looking. You're commenting on the culture at large and making jokes about politics. You've making jokes about Janet Reno's hair …

Clinton: I love that joke! It's still very clear that I'm a lesbian when I do my material, but my world has expanded, and I can comment on it.

Warren: You're doing a lot of television work. Do you enjoy it?

Clinton: I'm liking it more. I still can't watch myself.

Warren: You're kidding! Why not? Is it that you don't like the format or you don't like the way that you come off? What is it you're uncomfortable with?

Clinton: I have no idea what it is, but seeing myself on television isn't a thrill. I know some people who'll just watch their reel over and over again. It would be good if I did because I'd know what not to do. But I can't.

Warren: I recently saw you on a PBS all-woman comedy special, "The World According to Us." It was a great show—so funny and so political. It reminded me of "Saturday Night Live" in its heyday, when everybody in the cast was funny. Except that everyone in this cast was also a woman and a feminist. Was that show fun to do? Had you ever worked with a group of women like that?

Clinton: No, and I loved it. It was a blast. It was a pure joy working with women like Alison Martin and Bertice Berry. Bertice does a Tina Turner imitation that kills. I laughed so hard I couldn't even breathe.

Warren: You acted in some sketches in that show, which is new for you. They were terrific. Will you be doing more sketch comedy, more acting? Maybe your own sitcom?

Clinton: No. No, it's too frightening. Although since I've been in New York I've read for a couple of movies. What I'd like to do is a Rush Limbaugh type of show. I want to talk for half an hour. I could do that.

Warren: You've always started your act by saying, "Thanks for coming out"?

Clinton: At first it was just a pun. Then I realized that for a lot of people it was a big act of courage to come to a show of a known lesbian. So I've always meant it.

And when I say it to a really straight audience, I say: "Just checking."

Warren: For years you've joked that being a lesbian comic wasn't necessarily a wise career move. Yet right now lesbian comics are really hot.

Clinton: I know. Now to have a gimmick you need to be a lesbian comic with a boyfriend.

Warren: What makes lesbians such good comics?

Clinton: A lot of things. First of all, what's outside the norm is funny. So women are funny because the norm is clearly male. Lesbians are even further outside the norm than other women, so we're *really* funny. Being so far out gives you that skewed kind of sense of irony that's really critical for humor.

Warren: There are so many gay and lesbian comics these days. Do you welcome this, or do you feel that all these newcomers are moving in on your turf? What's your feeling about it?

Clinton: I feel relieved. I think it's great. It used to be kind of lonely to be a lesbian comedian. There wasn't anyone whose material you could look at or get together with and talk about the business.

Warren: Comedy is said to be a fiercely competitive field. Is that any different among lesbian and feminist comedians? Is there a sense of community or support that outweighs that career-mindedness?

Clinton: There's a certain level of competitiveness. It is cutthroat. It is a killer. But that's okay. I think it really can make people sharp. At least I hope so. I want the best gay and lesbian comedy on television. I don't want, "Take my boyfriend, please." I want it to be really interesting and twisted and fun.

Warren: Perhaps you don't feel threatened by the new gay comics because it was your turf for so long and you're so good at it that you don't really feel anyone is challenging you.

Clinton: Oh, but I've really been pushed this year. To be better on television. To be better in performance and to tighten up things. While it's wonderful to do a ninety-minute show, you also have to hone your six minutes for when you need it. It's been very challenging for me. I've really had to be more disciplined.

Warren: Suzanne Westenhoefer told me that after she did her first show in Provincetown, even though she'd never met you, you phoned her to give her encouragement and advice.

Clinton: I really enjoy Suzanne. She's just so kick-ass, you know? I've learned a lot from her attitude.

Warren: How does her attitude differ from yours?

Clinton: First of all, she did her act in straight clubs. That's a *big* difference. I think that's fabulous.

Warren: I don't understand how Suzanne is able to get away with doing material making fun of how bad straight guys are in bed. To straight audiences! And the guys in the audience are laughing. How does she pull that off?

Clinton: I think it's the laughing. The threat is there, but it's defused by being able to laugh about it. I really believe that if you have the right angle, and sometimes the right anger, it will work.

Warren: Which other comics do you admire? What about Joan Rivers?

Clinton: I think she's fabulous. That she's still alive and surviving what they put her through is wonderful.

Warren: Her career was such an uphill climb. They made it so tough for her. You were a real pioneer, too, and the only one doing what you were doing for a long time. But you always seemed to be enjoying it. I don't get the sense that she enjoyed it at all.

Clinton: But I never performed in places where I *wouldn't* enjoy it. I didn't beat myself against the wall in a comedy club. Instead, I said, "Okay, I'm going to do the Unitarian church this year. Then next year, I'll do a small theater, and then I'll do a big theatre."

Warren: Coming back to Suzanne. Your phoning her like that was such a generous thing to do. Do other women comics support each other that way?

Clinton: Oh, I think so. Rosie O'Donnell has been very helpful to other comedians. Roseanne is also very supportive of the woman comics she's worked with. The boys have always had that old boys' network, and now women are supporting each other, too. I remember Suzanne telling me that when she was first appearing at one of the comedy clubs in New York, the guys were giving her a hard time. Like: "Lesbian humor? Where can you go with that?" And Joy Behar would go over and tell them to cut it out.

Warren: Do you find there's a difference between the way men and women respond to your show?

Clinton: What's been interesting to me is having the Upper East Side, minked, liberal couples come to the show because "I know Bob would like it if we did." I see these couples in front of me and very frequently the woman never hears what I say except through her husband's ears. But there was one couple that I loved, because she heard me directly and laughed her head off and he watched her and enjoyed her having a few laughs. I thought, Oh my God. *They've* got it together.

Warren: Perhaps because there are so many straights coming to see your show the reviewers—the straight ones, anyway—seem to use the same adjectives over and over to describe you. "She's warm! She's maternal! She's friendly!" One even called you "the lesbian you'd want to bring home to meet your parents."

Clinton: Better lock up your mother!

Warren: [*Laughs*] But clearly, they're dealing with this notion that straight theatergoers might assume that because you're a lesbian you're scary or threatening. They're trying to reassure them.

Clinton: I knew somebody who was talking to this big reviewer in New York who was saying, "Oh, but isn't she just a man-hating lesbian?" And my friend was saying, "No—go see."

Warren: She's more than just a man-hating lesbian. [*Laughs*]

Clinton: Actually, straight women do much more scathing material about men. They live with them. They really care about it. When I talk about guys, I'm stretching.

Warren: How has comedy changed in recent years?

Clinton: It bothers me that so much of our common language is now based on television and that I have to talk about television.

Warren: You've got to know what "Beavis and Butthead" is.

Clinton: It's really frightening. It's ugly.

Warren: In fact, your show is very literate and very smart. Can your audience keep up with you?

Clinton: I have a friend who tells me, "I know before I go to your show that I have to read some magazines to know what the hell you're talking about."

Warren: Personally, I think that's a plus. When you started out, there were no other uncloseted lesbian comics. It was pretty much assumed that you had to stay closeted to become successful. Did you ever consider staying in the closet?

Clinton: Oh God, no. Never.

Warren: Do you ever look at all of the lesbian comics performing now and think, Gee, if I were starting out now it would be so much easier?

Clinton: Everything comes in its time. I had a lot to learn about comedy. I had a lot to learn about myself. Now, I'm exactly where I need to be right now with the confidence I need to do it. I've had a life. I have a home. I know when the plants are coming up, you know? That's been wonderful. Now things have speeded up, and this year has been enormous. I'm in warp speed.

Warren: You sure are. Are you enjoying that?

Clinton: Yes, but I'm also looking forward to having some time to reflect.

Warren: You've achieved success without compromising yourself and without closeting yourself. There are plenty of lesbian comics who have achieved success at the cost of being in the closet. What's your take on that?

Clinton: Some of those people are my really close friends so I have to respect their choices. But I know for myself it's been wonderful. I have to do it this way.

Cathy Crimmins

by Roz Warren

Cathy Crimmins shares her birthday with humorist Dorothy Parker, so maybe it's no coincidence that Crimmins is an accomplished humor writer and social satirist, whose essays (with snappy titles like "A Period Is Just The Beginning Of A Life-long Sentence") appear in magazines from *Redbook* to the *Village Voice*. Crimmins started out in stand-up, but took a detour into writing humor books that mocked yuppies (*Entrechic*), guys (The Secret World of Men), kitties (*The Quotable Cat*), and other facets of modern life. All were popular, but Crimmins outdid herself with *Curse of the Mommy*, a wickedly accurate portrait of a mommy's life, including chapters like "Honing Your

Labor Pain Vocabulary" and "The Road To Hell is Paved With Good Nintendo." The success of *Curse* spawned a new stand-up persona for Crimmins: the "Anti-Mom."

Who is the anti-mom? "She's someone who might have heeded her biological clock," explains Crimmins, "but will need another eighteen years to figure out if it was a false alarm." The anti-mom is that delinquent mommy who forgets to carry Kleenex, cannot name all the Muppets, and throws her *own* tantrums in supermarkets. She's the mom who vows never ever to spit on her kid to clean her. To help her out, Crimmins has even developed an anti-mom manifesto, including items like "I will continue to wear dry-clean-only garments," "I will never learn to use a rectal thermometer," and "I will never actually eat Cheerios."

Crimmins' anti-mom act works because she's revealing a basic truth about motherhood: even the most devoted Donna Reed wannabe eventually realizes that being a mother "combines absolute joy with absolute, brain-numbing tedium." Or as Crimmins has summed it up: "Every mom has an evil twin who might get kicked out of Mr. Rogers' neighborhood."

Warren: How did you become the "Anti-Mom"?

Crimmins: I never liked babies or children. So the question was, Can a woman who doesn't like children actually have a child? I've wanted a child; I just never thought I would have one. Somehow, I always thought nature would stop me. My own mother, when I told her I was pregnant, said, "You're kidding!"

Warren: But doesn't every mom have some anti-mom in her? You were on a radio call-in show recently, and women were phoning in from all over to "come out" as anti-moms. One woman even phoned in from the hospital where she was in labor.

Crimmins: Everyone was telling me how glad they were that I'm saying out loud what so many women think about motherhood. It's the final taboo. People don't want to admit that having children is 97 percent drudgery and 3 percent pleasure.

Some of the men I know are very uncomfortable when I complain about children or motherhood. It's very threatening to men. They think any woman who complains about mothering is unfeminine, that there's something unnatural about it and something wrong with her. I think women understand that taboo innately.

Warren: Women making jokes and being funny about any topic can make some men uncomfortable. Have you found that to be true?

Crimmins: Humor is very aggressive and a lot of men are nervous around aggressive females. I hate to say it, but you almost have to take on a male persona to be funny.

Warren: What's the difference between thinking like a male and thinking like a female?

Crimmins: The female side of me is always a little worried about what people are going to think. Part of me still wants to be a nice girl and not hurt anyone's feelings. That's the reason I'm uncomfortable making fun of real people. I like to create archetypes to play off of.

Warren: In contrast to someone like Joan Rivers, who dares to make fun of specific people.

Crimmins: That kind of humor exposes the hypocrisy in all of us, which is why it's so popular. We all make nasty comments behind people's backs. For a woman to have the guts to say those things directly is admirable.

Of course, that's the humorist in me speaking. The nice girl part of me is thinking, Oh God, I could never do that!

Warren: Instead, you make fun of yourself. The anti-mom shtick is very much based on your own experience. It's not self-deprecating, but you do make fun of the situations you find yourself in.

Crimmins: I think of myself as being perpetually stuck in a Hitchcock movie where I feel as if I'm in the wrong life. It seems like a dream to me that I now have a husband and a child and a career. That I'm already thirty-eight years old seems astounding. I try to approach humor from that slightly alienated stance. I'm always saying to myself, Who am I? How did I get here?

Warren: Many humorists seem to have grown up with that kind of slightly off-center perspective.

Crimmins: I'm just beginning to realize how alienated I was as a child. My public stance is that I had an incredibly happy, well-adjusted childhood, which I did in that I was adjusted within my home. But my family was very odd, and my father was very odd, especially.

I just went to my high school reunion and realized that I was one of the strangest people in my high school. No one else had the same kind of ideas or values. I was wearing 1940s evening gowns to pep rallies. My three closest friends were gay, black, and Jewish. I was reading Bertolt Brecht. My high school was in a completely rural area, and I was listening to "Bobby Short Sings Cole Porter." I mean, no wonder.

Also, I've always been a really tall woman. So I stand out and I intimidate guys. That's always set me apart.

Warren: Do you intimidate them because you're tall or because you're quick-witted?

Crimmins: It's a really, really scary combination. And on top of that, I never learned the rules about how to behave as a female. I didn't learn how to flirt. I didn't learn how to look at people's engagement rings. Basic skills like that.

Warren: You said your family was odd and your dad was very odd. What was so odd about your dad?

Crimmins: He had a bizarre sense of humor. If somebody died, for instance, he'd say, "Well, he won't do *that* again!" He couldn't take anything seriously. I inherited that from him. He was a nutty guy. He was always getting ideas, some of which would reverberate in my life. For instance, when I was in fourth grade, he convinced me that it would be really funny if I stuffed my stocking cap with newspaper and went to school with it standing straight up on my head. So I did it. I stood around on the schoolyard like that, and the boys started trying to hit the hat off of my head, and I got sent to the principal's office.

Warren: It sounds as if he was a big influence.

Crimmins: I'm so similar to him that my mother calls me "Dave in drag."

Warren: For a while you stopped doing stand-up in order to concentrate on doing radio work and writing humor books. Now you're going back to performing. Why?

Crimmins: I liked stand-up, but I didn't like the audiences very much. I was working in comedy clubs around Philadelphia. The audiences were basically drunken twenty-year-olds from Cherry Hill, New Jersey, who wanted blow-job jokes.

I knew I was really losing it when I was so desperate for their approval that I started including a douche-bag joke. It got the biggest laugh of anything I did, but it was my least clever routine.

Warren: So what made you quit? You just got fed up?

Crimmins: Yeah, and I got pregnant. That made doing stand-up very difficult. On the other hand, the best radio work I did was when I was pregnant. I loved the idea of not having to tell anyone that I was pregnant. The day before I had my daughter, the host of the show said, "So, Cathy, what are you doing this weekend?" I said, "I'm having a baby." That's how we announced it on the air.

Warren: Why are you getting back into stand-up?

Crimmins: I miss it. It's also hard to get recognized as a humor writer without a following as a performer. It's like song writers singing their own songs. If you look at the great comedy writers, they always end up performing their stuff. People like Steve Martin, Woody Allen, and Elaine May all started out as writers and eventually went into performing.

Warren: Are these your comic influences or role models? When you were young, were you aware of comics?

Crimmins: Oh yeah. I loved stand-up as a kid, and comedy songs and comedy performers. I was the biggest Smothers Brothers fan on the face of the earth. I was a Bob and Ray fan because my father had told me so much about them. My father and I also listened to Gene Shepard.

Warren: When we were young, there weren't that many women doing comedy.

Crimmins: Phyllis Diller. She was the first female comic I ever saw. My husband calls himself "the Fang of Philadelphia."

Warren: In a way she was the first anti-mom. She mocked the role of the perfect wife and mother and joked about how inadequate she was to that task. Your anti-mom act is a similar thumbing of your nose at what people expect women to be and do. What do you feel is the difference between what she did and what you're doing now?

Crimmins: What I do is more aggressive, as befits my generation. Although I think it's my daughter's generation that will make the real changes, because they won't even be thinking about some of these issues. I was born in '55, and that leads to a lot of ambivalence about gender roles. My daughter will grow up without a lot of the gender stereotypes, so that won't be part of her humor.

Many women my age still define motherhood as being what our mothers were. In certain ways, my daughter is much more nurtured by my husband than by me, and she has a different relationship with me than I had with my mother.

Warren: Your comic persona grew out of your book *Curse of the Mommy*. What made you decide to focus your act in this way?

Crimmins: I've always been something of a chameleon in that with each humor book I've assumed a different narrative voice. I'm very proud of that skill, but it doesn't help you as a performer, because what the public needs there is consistency. They want to know who you are. Each stand-up has to have some kind of hook—like Judy Tenuta being the Petite Goddess.

Warren: You've written six humor books. Do you find that it's tough to get people to take your work seriously because you're a humorist?

Crimmins: A friend of mine overheard an editor at one of the New York publishing houses talking about my work. She said, "Cathy Crimmins is really intelligent for a humorist." They don't realize how smart you have to be to make fun of things!

Warren: Growing up, were you confident that you were the center of attention or did you have to fight for the attention?

Crimmins: I was the firstborn daughter. There were only two daughters, and we were taught that we were superior to everyone else in the world. My parents always told me I could do anything. I have almost too much self-confidence.

We had a very strong family culture. We believed that "the Crimmins way" was the way to do everything. My father used to pretend we had this religion called the Crimminsonian religion. He was the Pope. My sister and I were the nuns.

I also had a great relationship with my mother, who encouraged me to be happy. I had an idyllic female upbringing in the sense that I never thought about my appearance. I never even thought of the connection between putting food into my mouth and my body at all. I was taught—and this has been a real problem for me as a budding novelist—never to notice what other people looked like.

Warren: That confidence is probably why even when you make fun of your own shortcomings you come off as strong and in control rather than self-deprecating.

Crimmins: But there are moments in every woman's life in which she feels as though she's in over her head. I think motherhood was it for me.

I'm fascinated by Carol Gilligan's work on adolescence. She found that girls are going full force and achieving and all of this great stuff is happening and then suddenly they hit adolescence and everything stops because they want approval. They want to fit in. They want boyfriends.

I didn't hit that at thirteen or fourteen, and I don't know why. But I did hit it when I had a baby.

Warren: You didn't feel entirely confident that you knew what you were doing in the same way you had before.

Crimmins: Exactly. Could I achieve what I had always wanted to achieve and not screw up another human being in the process?

Some women reach it when they get married and their personalities are squashed. I had a bad first marriage, which kind of squashed my personality for a little while, but my personality doesn't seem to be squashable for long.

Warren: You don't talk about that marriage in your act at all. In contrast to Brett Butler, for instance, who does wonderful material mocking her first husband. Your material comes from your own life, but there are some things you don't talk about.

Crimmins: I'm sort of a puritan in a certain way, too. I've noticed that about myself. I don't talk about my own sex life in my act, for example.

Warren: But you did talk about it recently on a nationwide television talk-show.

Crimmins: Oh, about the multiple orgasms?

Warren: Can you tell us that story?

Crimmins: I was asked to go on a talk-show. The topic was "real women respond to sex surveys." I guess I was so thrilled to be labeled a real woman at this time of my life that I decided to go on.

There were several producers on this show, and each producer was pushing his or her guest by prompting the host with cue cards that were based on pre-interviews they'd done with us. During my interview, I'd asked if there was going to be a segment on multiple orgasms. My producer said, "Gee, no, we hadn't thought about that. Do you have them?" I said yeah, I did, and I could feel myself blushing to the roots of my hair as I was talking. I was thinking, Well, yeah, but I'm not going to talk about *that* on television.

So there we were in a segment about faking orgasms and a few other orgasmic topics, and I saw this cue card being thrust toward the host. In great big letters the cue card said, "ASK CATHY ABOUT MULTIPLE ORGASMS."

It was one of the worst moments of my life. All I could imagine was everyone I knew sitting in front of the television set, my mother, my elderly aunt—everyone.

Fortunately, they went to a station break, and I was saved.

Warren: If you're a writer with a book to promote, you're expected to go on television and put yourself on display like that. It almost seems as though there's not much difference between that and getting up on stage as a stand-up.

Crimmins: When you're a stand-up you have more control. *You* decide what your material is.

Warren: What would your life be like if you didn't write humor about it?

Crimmins: It's hard for me to imagine. One thing that's bothered me as I've gotten older is that everything in my life becomes a routine. For example, I'm perfecting a routine right now about taking my daughter's turtle to the vet. I've told this story to six different gatherings of people. It gets better each time, because each time I punch it up a little. I know that eventually I'll use it somewhere.

Warren: Do you keep telling the story because you're good at telling the story? Or is there something else that drives you?

Crimmins: I want attention. I really think that's at the base of all writing and all performing. I'm not happy unless I'm the center of attention. I want to command a room. I don't necessarily like that about myself.

Warren: Are you happy when you *do* command the room?

Crimmins: I used to be, because I used to be less self-conscious about it. But the older I get, the more I realize that my kind of neurotic need to be out there and be confessional and controlling everything with anecdotes is just as much of a mask as being shy and withdrawn. Because people don't really know who I am when I'm telling them those anecdotes. The stories I tell aren't really me, they're already once removed from me.

It's not as if I can help being this way. I don't always like it, but I'm not going to ever force myself to change because it seems to be how I best operate in the world.

Warren: It's also true that mocking people's expectations about the joys of motherhood and allowing other women to express the fact that it can be pretty boring is liberating.

Crimmins: A lot of women have told me, "I felt all of this stuff while I was going through it and never felt like I could utter a peep about it."

Warren: So what you're doing is useful.

Crimmins: Even if it weren't, I'd have to do it anyway.

Mary Jo Crowley

by Roz Warren

Corporate comedian Mary Jo Crowley is in the business of delivering "clean, custom comedy" at meetings and conventions. Business is booming, thanks to Crowley's ability to generate snappy workplace-related one-liners, like: "I like to think of my boss as a father figure. That really irritates her." Working audiences love the chance to laugh at their bosses, their jobs, and themselves, Crowley says. And she enjoys helping them do it.

Crowley wrote her first joke at age seven. (*Why* did the turtle cross the road? To get to the Shell Station.) In high school she was already selling one-liners to professional comics. She continues to sell jokes to the pros (favorite clients are Bob Hope and Phyllis Diller), as well as writing scripts for television shows like "The Golden Girls." Radio stations are also steady customers for Crowley's wit: "They go through a lot of one-liners very quickly." Crowley has worked as an instructor for California's infamous "comedy traffic classes," an experience she describes as "doing stand-up comedy for eight hours to a captive, annoyed audience." She's also developed a workshop about using humor in the workplace: "Take this workshop … Please!"

Crowley performs "clean" comedy, which means that her material is witty but deliberately inoffensive. The raciest she'll get is: "I understand there's a new edition of *Playboy* designed for married men. Every month the centerfold is the same picture." "I'm just not comfortable using four-letter words," she says. "I don't do that in my life, anyway."

Crowley has always been more comfortable in the board rooms and sales meetings of the business world than she is in comedy clubs. Because she holds a degree in journalism and spent years working in public relations before concentrating on her comedy, she has a lot in common with her business clients. "Typically, a business audience is not drunk," she adds, and she considers that a plus.

To customize her comedy for a business audience, Crowley spends hours talking to people about the issues and conflicts that are hot items in the industry. She then weaves together a routine that highlights these concerns, often using the names of people employed in the business. "Common threads in what I do are how people treat each other and what they expect of each other. Take office politics, for instance. There's always someone in the office to whom that's important. The group dynamics of the workplace are pretty similar everywhere. The basis of my humor is everyday situations, the things people say and the things they want to say and don't dare."

Crowley's act works because she combines generic workplace material with jokes targeted for each audience. She asks an audience of bankers, "Why do banks chain down the pens but leave the vault wide open?" She's suggested to a General Dynamics group that they start making their aircraft out of the same material used to make the little black box that preserves inflight recordings through aviation disasters."I don't know anybody else who does title company jokes," she says of a gig at an escrow association conference.

Even though Crowley's brand of clean, corporate comedy isn't radical or on-the-edge, she feels that just thriving in the still male-dominated field of comedy makes her a ground-breaker. "Women comics are pioneers," she observes, "and of course, pioneers are the ones who get arrows in their behinds."

Sara Cytron

by Laura Post

Brooklyn comic Sara Cytron often jokes about becoming the first lesbian president—"President Butch" (with her partner Harriet, naturally, assuming the role of "First Lover"). As soon as she assumes office, Cytron says, she'll appoint Anita Hill to the Supreme Court. "The day of Hill's confirmation," Cytron jokes, "the entire Senate will have to drink Cokes with pubic hairs in them and then turn and face Hill, and instead of singing the national anthem, they'll sing "I'm A Believer."

Cytron's comic imagination mixes the personal with the political, always with a slightly outrageous twist. She delivers her insights into being female, gay, and Jewish in a thick Brooklyn accent at high volume. Cytron is brainy, aggressive, and exuberant. One critic has described her as "a good-natured, big-mouthed, barreling butch from Brooklyn."

The child of "overprotective Jewish parents who raised me to get married and have children," Cytron did get married at twenty-two—to a gay man. "I was sidetracked," Cytron explains. "He didn't know he was gay and I was in denial." Cytron and her former husband came out at the same time. Her act includes a hilarious bit about her family's response when Cytron's ex later married another man.

Cytron's outlook may be lesbian but her appeal is universal, both because so many of her insights are applicable across the board and also because her attitude is consistently warm and upbeat. She covers a lot of ground, from memories of being a young butch shopping with her mother ("Macy's had no department for me") to recently participating in what she jokingly calls "the National Schlep on Washington." Her shows, *A Dyke Grows in Brooklyn* and *Take My Domestic Partner—Please!* mix snappy one-liners with longer stories and pop songs from the sixties rewritten for lesbians ("Runaround Sue," for example, becomes "Lesbian Jew"). Some of her best material is about her family ("the Jewish Waltons") and her lover, Harriet.

Cytron has come up with many memorable lines. On lesbian rights: "The last time most people in this country cared about my rights was when I was a fetus." On politically correct terminology: "I didn't steal this. It was differently acquired." On good vacation spots: "Cardinal O'Connor says all the gay activists are going to hell. So sometimes, when Harriet and I are sitting around wondering where to go on vacation, we think, Well, hell would be nice."

She easily draws the audience into her act. "My parents recently retired," she announces. "Guess where?" She counts, "One, two, three," and the audience yells, "Florida!" Cytron beams. "We were shocked. Shocked! An elderly Jewish couple!? We thought, Tibet, the Yukon … Florida! Go figure!"

Cytron excels at extended riffs on basic issues like women's bathrooms, tampons, therapy, and sex. "I once had a girlfriend," she observes, "who was so guilt-ridden about being a lesbian that the only way she could have an orgasm was if we pretended to be shipwrecked, adrift at sea, far from civilization, never to return. So in order to make this whole thing realistic, I had to buy an inflatable raft, a foot pump, and a bailing bucket …. Then I had another girlfriend who liked sex best under time pressure—when she had to rush. So we used to pretend that she was an air traffic controller who had ten seconds to come before two jumbo jets would collide in midair. That was exciting—the best nine and a half seconds of my life!"

In another appealing bit, Cytron tells the story of a thirty-eight-year-old friend with a new twenty-three-year-old girlfriend, who earnestly tells her, "I want to be the best lover you've ever had," to which the friend replies, "Go ahead, babe, I'm rootin' for you!"

Cytron's life partner, Harriet Malinowitz, a college professor, writes most of Cytron's material. After years of working together, the two are on the same comic wavelength. "We both agree that the act should be a combination of silly, fun material and more meaningful political commentary," says Cytron. *Sojourner* called the team "another Jane Wagner/Lily Tomlin magical combination—but the out version."

When she isn't doing comedy, Cytron has a steady job with a federal agency, whose name she's not allowed to disclose. They know that she's a lesbian, Cytron explains, but they don't want anyone else to know that they know. "In fact the security office had to watch a videotape of my act in order to approve my 'outside employment'," she notes. "They said they enjoyed it."

Post: Were you funny as a kid?

Cytron: I had learned to be a comic by the age of five. I was using voices, faces, and timing to make my family and friends laugh. I *craved* attention and approval—from everyone—at all times —and found that being funny was a great strategy for getting them. With this burning need, I was a major conduct problem in school. Some teachers found creative ways of dealing with my interruptions. We struck certain deals: if I'd be quiet and well behaved for the rest of the time, they'd give me five minutes to perform. For example, my ninth grade English teacher would let me have a few minutes to read a Shakespearean monologue in any accent I chose. My favorite was "Out, damned spot" by Lady Macbeth in a Brooklyn accent.

Post: What about your family? Were they funny?

Cytron: My family is fairly typical of many Jewish families in that storytelling and jokes are the way people communicate. There wasn't a lot of honest and open communication about negative emotion. But laughter was the medium, and everything was a joke. Everything was kibitzing and telling a story and ironic comment. There's no question that with my family and neighbors humor was the way to interact with people. I definitely absorbed that.

Post: Did you have comic role models growing up?

Cytron: Even at a very young age I adored stand-up comics. I absolutely loved watching the old-time borscht-belt comics that appeared on "Ed Sullivan." I was a six-year-old who would stop everything to watch Alan King.

People have told me that in performing I have a very traditional Jewish Catskill rhythm and intonation and style, even though what I'm talking about is lesbian and gay humor. And I still find those comics uproariously funny, although sometimes offensive. Someone like Joan Rivers—she's really, really funny, and yet so much of her shtick has been very deprecating of women and really very misogynist. Yet she's a comic who just makes me laugh.

Carol Burnett was my idol. I taped her show every week. Friends came over to watch the show, but they weren't allowed to talk because I didn't want to miss one second. I used to play the show all week until the next one.

Post: Is comedy still an important part of your day-to-day life?

Cytron: For many years I was always trying to be funny offstage. I needed to be funny all the time as a way of defining myself. I construed any gathering of two or more people as an audience. I was always trying to make people laugh, doing imitations of my family, often very inappropriately. You know—somebody would be talking about their life and all of a sudden I'd do my grandmother.

I had intimacy problems. If given a choice between performing in an amphitheater holding five thousand people or engaging in meaningful conversation with one person, I would unquestionably choose the amphitheatre.

I consider myself greatly recovered now, largely thanks to my life partner Harriet (as well as psychotherapy and homeopathy). Early on in our relationship Harriet made it very clear that I could be very controlling, obnoxious, and dominating, snuffing out all chances for real conversation when people were around me. (She's always been very gentle in her criticism.) Over time, I began to relate in a much realer way with people offstage and didn't feel the same desperate need all the time.

Now that I'm a professional comic, there are many and far more appropriate moments in my life to have everybody be quiet and listen to me.

Post: Do you find that a lot of comics have that controlling pay-attention-to-me temperament?

Cytron: Not all of them, but some are prone to that. Why do people became rabbis, ministers, teachers—a regular gig with an audience listening to you all the time? Partly it's motivated by needing attention, but the best people in these roles have something that they really want to say, something that they want to give, not get.

Some people who get on stage want the audience to take care of them, as opposed to saying, "I'm already taken care of. I'm coming here as a whole person and I love the applause but I really want to share something with you. I really want to tell you something. I want us to think about something together."

Post: How did you get started in stand-up?

Cytron: I took a stand-up comedy class, taught by a mainstream comic. I told him, "I want to do lesbian stand-up comedy." And he said, "Look, I'm not a lesbian. I don't know anything about lesbians, but I can just hear your stuff and help you structure it and give you some technique." And he did help me.

Also, I had a lover of many years who died of cancer, and she was the person who first helped me structure my first few minutes of stand-up comedy. She was the one who encouraged me to take comedy seriously.

Post: Does Harriet work with you on your act?

Cytron: The act is Harriet's and mine together. In fact, without Harriet, there'd be no act. Harriet does most of my writing, and she also directs my performance. I collaborate with her, but she writes the majority of it. She's gotten great at directing me, at telling me when I need to emphasize something, or pause, or punch it up.

Post: Is she a performer herself?

Cytron: No! My life partner is a brilliant comedy writer who's great at writing stand-up but never wants to get on stage. Am I lucky or what?

Ellen Degeneres

by Roz Warren

Laid-back, upbeat stand-up comic Ellen Degeneres has been called a "spiritual daughter of Bob Newhart," "a distaff George Carlin," and "a female Jerry Seinfeld." Like those comic masters, her routines emphasize wry wit, intelligent observation, and quirky twists of reality. The bemused and amusing DeGeneres stars in the ABC sitcom "Ellen," where she plays a character she's described as "myself, if I weren't a stand-up." In other words, a laid-back, urban single woman who hangs out with her offbeat pals. She also maintains an active national touring schedule: devoted Degeneres fans are so familiar with her work that they often yell out requests for favorite routines ("Do 'the elevator!' " "My parents sold me to the Iroquois Indians!") in the same way diehard fans scream for cherished songs from touring rock stars.

Degeneres was born in Texas and raised in New Orleans. (Her brother Vance is the cocreator of Mr. Bill.) She began her stand-up career in 1981, working college coffee houses and eventually became emcee at Clyde's Comedy Corner, New Orleans' only comedy club. Her first big break came when she was named Showtime's 1982 Funniest Person in America by a panel of judges including Soupy Sales, Harvey Korman, and Pee Wee Herman.

In 1986, Degeneres earned the distinction of being the only female comic to be invited by Johnny Carson to sit on the couch in her first "Tonight Show" appearance. Prior to "Ellen," her television appearances included office oddball Margo Van Meter on Fox's "Open House" and nurse Nancy McIntire on the ABC series "Laurie Hill," countless cable television specials and talk-show spots, and some very funny juice commercials.

Lea Delaria

by Laura Post

If you haven't heard of Lea Delaria, you haven't been paying attention. In 1993 alone she appeared twice on "Arsenio" and on countless other shows, emceed the 1993 March on Washington, hosted Comedy Central's "Out There," the first ever gay/lesbian comedy special, and was profiled in *People*. She also made the cover of *The New York Times Magazine* and *Rolling Stone*'s list of "What's Hot."

Delaria's "Arsenio" spot made her the first openly lesbian comic to break into contemporary prime-time television. No longer a lesbian secret, Delaria is being revealed to the world, and we can expect to see more and more of her—more recordings featuring her luscious jazz-scat tunes, more television appearances on talk shows and dramatic shows, and of course, more of her never-subtle, largely improvised stand-up.

Delaria began her comedy career in 1982 in San Francisco, at a gay/lesbian club called Valencia Rose. She was an immediate success, and she continued to be a hit at gay and lesbian venues across the country. She helped found San Francisco's "Gay Comedy Nights" and New York's "People Who Are Funny That Way," won many performance awards, and cut a popular album, *Bulldyke in a China Shop.*

Onstage, she's like nothing you've ever seen before: big, bold, bawdy, and outrageous. (If Jackie Gleason and Robin Williams had spawned a love child, it would resemble Delaria.) Busting right out of the closet and into your face, she'll start her show by exuberantly yelling, "I'm a Big Dyke!" And it gets wilder from there. (She's described herself as "the bad girl of lesbian comedy … Kate Clinton's evil twin.") A high voltage performer, Delaria tears around the stage, riffing on topics from pop culture to lesbian sex, then wades into the audience for some intimate, one-on-one comedy. She's been known to wind up on the laps of female audience members. Even in a large hall, Lea's performance stays intimate.

Nothing is sacred to Delaria, yet somehow, all is respected. Her brashness is softened by her obvious vulnerability. She mocks herself as well as mocking straight culture—she's joked that everything she's ever done onstage has been a futile attempt to get Sigourney Weaver to notice her. Another glimpse of Lea's sweeter side is her singing, which serves to balance out the wilder aspects of her show. In between riotous routines about butt plugs and hellish gynecology appointments, Delaria will pause to sing bebop, scat, and blues in a sweet, sultry voice. ("I've wanted to be Ella Fitzgerald for as long as I can possibly remember," she says.)

Delaria grew up in Belleville, Illinois, "the only city in the world surrounded by an information-proof shield." Because she grew up thinking she was Belleville's "only queer," Delaria has always been committed to being completely out onstage: "I am out there as an open lesbian so that young people won't have to think they're the only ones."

Post: Your career has really taken off within the last year.

Delaria: I'm having the time of my life! But I was happy before. I was making plenty of money. I enjoyed myself. I was getting laid. So now if they ask me to do something I don't want to do, I say no, because I can always do what I did before and be perfectly happy. I've got the best of both worlds. I'm able to do what I want and I don't have to sell out to do it. I can keep my integrity.

Post: But wasn't that always true? You were happy doing what you were doing, so you always felt the prerogative to say no if anyone offered you something you didn't want to do.

Delaria: People did offer me what I have now and I said no because they wanted me to hide in the closet. I'm not going to do that. Look at me. Like I can walk out onstage looking like this and talk about my boyfriends?

Post: My grandmother would buy that. She'd say, "That's a big girl, but she's very sweet."

Delaria: "She's a mannish girl."

Post: Yeah, "Her boyfriend probably has a hard time with her."

Delaria: But in this day and age I'm going to go onstage and eventually someone's going to say, "Look at that big bulldyke. Why doesn't she talk about it?"

Post: Your current level of success started with your appearance on "Arsenio." How did that come about?

Delaria: I did a one-week run at the Highways, in Santa Monica, and there was a very positive article about me in the *L.A. Times*, which generated what is known as a "Hollywood feeding frenzy." Everybody came to see the show; they were buzzing about me all over Hollywood. My phone—it was insane. I'd hang up, it would ring. The "Arsenio Hall" people called and asked for a tape. They booked me off the tape. Right away. That show was a make-or-break situation. If I had bombed, there would be nothing.

Post: Because everyone was watching to see what you'd do with that kind of leeway?

Delaria: And what happened was television magic. It was a kill situation. It was the kind of TV you don't see that often. It was obvious that Arsenio and I liked each other. So we played together on the couch. In the four minutes that I was doing the monologue I was stopped for applause God knows how many times—and that's what did it.

Then I did the second appearance, which wasn't television magic, but it was good solid TV. So it was obvious that I was consistent. Since then, it's just been insane.

Post: You've been very busy.

Delaria: I did the Edinburgh International Theatre Festival, where I won the Critics Award for best comedy. There was a feature in *Time Magazine* about it. I did the Montreal Festival. I've been on British television several times, and I'm negotiating with Channel 4 of England about a series. It's just amazing. I hosted the first gay and lesbian comedy special, on Comedy Central, and there's talk of that becoming a series. I'm guest starring on "Matlock." I'm up for the female lead in the film *Mayor of Castro Street*. And we're negotiating with record companies.

Post: They heard your voice on *Bulldyke in a China Shop* and decided they wanted you to sing—not even to do comedy.

Delaria: What's going on right now is that each aspect of what I do is being recognized. It's wonderful. The "Matlock" thing is serious acting—it's not comedy. The Comedy Central thing is stand-up. And the record deal is music. And I've been talking to people about writing. I'm talking with All Girl Productions about writing a movie for Bette Midler.

Everything I do is being recognized and it's just really amazing. Now if only I could get Sigourney Weaver to notice me ...

Post: Well, you're going to be finding yourself at parties, and Sigourney's likely to be there ...

Delaria: George Michael came up to me at a party and started telling me how funny I was. I was sitting there thinking, This is George Michael. He knows who I am. He knows my name. He thinks I'm funny. You know what I mean? There's a point where you start to pinch yourself. You're thinking, Six months ago, I was in San Francisco doing a run at Josie's Juice Joint.

Post: How are you coping with all this? It seems pretty overwhelming.

Delaria: I try to have thirty or forty orgasms a day. It keeps the stress level way down.

Post: How is your family dealing with it? Your mother was quoted in *People* saying, "I don't believe in homosexuality."

Delaria: What does that mean? "I don't believe in homosexuality." It's not like the Easter Bunny.

Post: If they wanted to keep the fact that their daughter was a dyke a secret, it's no longer a secret.

Delaria: It's okay. They're fine with it. My mom and my sister are coming to my show Friday night. I said, "Listen, if you feel out of place, just hold hands. You'll fit right in." And we all laughed. They've come a very long way from when I first came out to them ten years ago. They're actually very remarkable people.

Post: You were the first contemporary gay performer to make it onto prime-time network television. How have your peers reacted to that?

Delaria: Ron and Paul [Romanovsky and Phillips] came up to me at the march and said, "We were so glad that it was you that was the first one, because no one else would knock that door open wider than you did." Another gay comic might have just pushed it open a little, but when I walked out on "Arsenio" and said, "I'm a big dyke," I kicked that door wide open. I thought that was a real sweet thing for them to say.

Post: I think it's true, too.

Delaria: Maybe. You know, you get nervous. The problem with our community is that we're ready to make anyone an icon at any second. It's not my job to speak for the gay and lesbian community. I speak for Lea Delaria. But what happens is that people think you speak for them. Then when they don't agree with you they get angry.

Post: I want to back up a little and ask you a few questions about your comedy and where it comes from. When did you first realize that you could make other people laugh?

Delaria: I had the perfect training to be a stand-up: Catholic school. Nowadays, kids sue teachers for slapping them, but when I went to Catholic school, if you came home and said, "Mom, the nun hit me," BAM! *she'd* hit you. "You probably deserved it." Then she'd hit you again, you know?

I figured out when I was very young that if I could make the nun laugh, she wouldn't hit me. When the ruler is coming at you, boy, you come up with something funny as quick as you can. I think that's what trained me to stay in the moment and be funny in the moment.

Post: Is anyone else in your family funny?

Delaria: Yeah, the whole family's crazy. We're all cornballs. We're all very funny, sarcastic, silly people.

Post: So your comedy started in school and was supported at home. Did you ever think when you were little that you were going to grow up to be what you are now?

Delaria: I never wanted to be anything else. I always wanted to be an "entertainer"—a person who can do everything. I idealized Bette Midler and Judy

Garland. I idealized Lucille Ball. And men like Jackie Gleason. They could do anything—sing, dance, act, do comedy, do tragedy. All of it.

Post: Did you have any comic mentors to help get you started on your own path as an entertainer?

Delaria: I've always been kind of independent and a loner. My comedy was different than any other queer comedy that was out there, and especially different than any other lesbian comedy that was out there, because my comedy came from a point of rage. So there were really no mentors for me. Now I have—I don't know if you'd call them mentors—but people who are important to me. Like Scott Thompson of Kids in the Hall.

Post: How's he influencing you?

Delaria: We talk about the integrity of being who we are in a world where people are telling us not to be. Ian McEllen is another one. Melissa Etheridge. These are people who influence where I am.

Post: How wonderful to have such talented people to connect with.

Delaria: I just did the Palladium in London with the Pet Shop Boys. We were onstage together and Ian said, "Lea, come here." He knows that I idolize Judy Garland. He sat down on the stage and pulled me over and said, "Sit right here. This is the exact spot that Judy Garland sat when she sang 'Somewhere Over The Rainbow'." I said, "Really?" And he said, "Oh, well, it was here … or over there." It was a really funny moment. So I made him sing "Clang Clang Clang Went The Trolley" with me and he didn't know the words! I told him he couldn't be a faggot until he learned the words.

Post: How would you describe your humor?

Delaria: I would say crazy, manic, but lovable.

Post: It actually seems less manic to me than it used to be.

Delaria: I'm older. My energy's a lot more focused now. It's one of the things that's made me a better performer in recent years. I'm more in tune with my audience, and I'm more in tune with myself. It's less important to me to be showy onstage and more important to be in tune.

Post: You've always been good at being in the moment. You could always take anything that's thrown at you and come up with a funny response.

Delaria: That's why the jazz that I do and the comedy work so well together, because that's what I'm doing with the jazz. That improvisational style.

Post: Has Kate Clinton been an influence for you?

Delaria: She and I have been friends for years. We did a show together for PBS this year. I won an Emmy for a piece I wrote called "The Honeymooners." It was Gertrude Stein and Alice Toklas played like Ralph and Alice Kramden. With Pablo Picasso as Ed Norton. It was a very funny piece. PBS liked the show ("The World According to Us") so much that they're filming four specials. It's an all-women sketch comedy series.

Post: It sounds like you're adapting really well to television, which is a different medium than the live stage.

Delaria: Right. For one thing, that word *fuck* comes into play. And we know when I'm onstage that's my second major word. Before I went on "Arsenio" I was sitting in my dressing room saying, "Fuck, fuck, fuck, fuck, fuck, fuck, fuck." Trying to get it out of my system.

You know, you can say the word *penis* on television, but you can't say the word *vagina*. That is so annoying to me.

Post: Well, that's because people with penises make up the rules.

Delaria: Exactly. You know the word *penis* has been getting a lot of play in the media. Mrs. Bobbitt—I loved that her name was "Bob it."

Post: Who would you say is your audience right now?

Delaria: I have a huge gay following, which I've always had. Gays and lesbians. And hip, young, straight people. And then a lot of older intellectual straight kind of professor types. That's my audience.

Post: Who would you like to be your audience?

Delaria: I'm enjoying the audience I have. Who'd I like to be my audience? Homophobes whose minds I can change. I'm going to college campuses, and I'm talking to people who would normally not listen to me. Changing some people's minds and views—that's the reason I went into this in the first place. I wanted to make a difference. And because I wanted to get laid. Let's face it.

Post: How would you define feminist humor? Is there such a thing?

Delaria: *Vanity Fair* called me up because they were doing an article on jokes that women comics use about men. I told them, "To be honest, I don't male-bash." I'm a lesbian and I don't do it. So I said to them, "I'm a lesbian—what do I know about men? Enough to be a lesbian." To me, that's feminist humor.

It's easier to describe feminist humor in terms of what it's not rather than what it is. It's humor that is not racist, sexist, homophobic, misogynist.

There's a sense of political correctness about it, but in the same way that feminism has changed, political correctness has changed. For instance, after I joked that with Hillary Clinton "finally we have a first lady you could fuck," a girl came up to me on the street and said, "If you'd been a man, I would have punched you in the nose." She was angry at me for being a sexist.

Here's my point. She said, "If you'd been a man ..." But I'm not a man. Not only am I not a man, I'm a lesbian. And the rules in this society are different for me. Not because I make them different for me but because *they* have made them different for me. And until the rules are equal for me I can say things like that. And I'll tell you why. From a purely feminist standpoint, women are not allowed to be sexual, and lesbians especially are not allowed to talk about their sexuality.

So I feel that politically, as a feminist, it's my duty to do that.

Post: And you do it so well.

Delaria: Thanks. I think it really does open up stuff for people. I'm onstage for three reasons. What I'm trying to do with my comedy is the old Lenny Bruce thing. Words are meaningless symbols. Let's take the power out of words and put the power back into meaning, where it should be. Right? Two, to provide gays and lesbians with the kind of role models we didn't have. So some gay kid in Someplace, Minnesota, can look at his TV and say "Wow! She's gay and she's happy. She's on TV. I'm not such a bad person." The third thing is that I challenge the stereotype of what a woman is supposed to be. When I'm onstage, I'm running around. I'm screaming. I'm sweating. I'm coughing and I'm swearing. I'm busting through the walls of what socially acceptable woman's behavior is. That's what I'm trying to do. That's feminist humor.

Post: How do you develop your material?

Delaria: I talk about the things that are important to me. I write every day. I hate it. The actual physical sitting down and writing. I much prefer being improvisational onstage in front of people. And I think I'm funnier that way too. I have no idea why.

Post: What about future plans?

Delaria: I'm riding the wave. Right now there are so many people interested in developing a television series for me that it's hard for me to imagine that's not going to happen. I know there'll be some more albums. And I feel confident about things like HBO specials and stuff like that.

A lot of people say my career is happening because of lesbian chic. Frankly, I'm sick of lesbian chic. I'm a lesbian and I'm sick of it; I can't even imagine how straight people feel. But lesbian chic or not, I think that if you can back up the hype with talent, you're going to be okay. And I feel okay.

I don't know. I mean if this is happening because I'm the Flavor of the Month—lick me! That's what I say. I'm having a ball.

Dos Fallopia

by Susie Day

The Seattle-based duo of Lisa Koch and Peggy Platt, known as Dos Fallopia, take audiences on a fast-paced, feminist romp of a show that combines song, shtick and silliness. Their debut tape, My Breasts Are Out Of Control, introduces listeners to a range of characters, from women's music festival vets Compost Morningdew and Dolphinfree Tunawoman to an all-girl grunge band called Surly Bitches. "I'm Spike, she's Red," snarls the lead singer. "The rest of the band's dead." Other highlights include a "recently discovered recording" of Ethel Merman and Katherine Hepburn entitled "Kate and Ethel: Surf's Up!"

When not performing with Dos Fallopia, Koch—an actor, singer, song-writer and comedian—is a member of the feminist foursome Venus Envy, most famous for their song parody "I'll Be A Homo For Christmas," from the album of the same name. "My specialty is singing like a chipmunk," comments Koch, "and I'm happy to say that this talent has been exposed and exploited on 'I'll Be A Homo'." Koch also performs as a solo act and has an album called Colorblind Blues which includes "Beaver Cleaver Fever," a hilarious ode to June.

Peggy Platt has worked steadily as a stand-up for over a decade, at comedy clubs and on television. She can also be seen as country superstar Euomi Spudd (with Lisa as daughter Wynotta) in the long-running hit show, The Spudds' Absolute Last Final Farewell Tour, cowritten by Koch and Platt.

Day: Ideally, what do you want to do with your comedy? Do you want to change minds? Get people to look at themselves?

Platt: And pay our bills.

Koch: We do it because we love doing it. We're both working artists, and if you can do something that you love and that actually makes money at the same time, that's good. What I like is that the group is an amalgam of a lot of different styles. It's some theater, some sketch comedy, and some music. I'm a musician; Peggy's roots are in stand-up. I've worked in bands; she's worked in improv. She's straight; I'm queer. It's an interesting little mix of worlds, and when we come together, it seems to click.

Day: Do you see yourself as changing the minds of your audience?

Koch: I think so. Our tape, My Breasts Are Out of Control, is being played on college stations, and not just on women's programs. If it's funny, people will listen. Friends tell me that their four-year-old knows all the words to "Fran and Annie's Twelve-Step Day Care." Or that their kid loves the lesbian song and sings it constantly. That's kind of cool. You've got little people who are growing up singing your song because it's a good song to sing. Maybe they don't know what lesbian means, but they're spreading the word.

Day: Your humor turns in part on bringing many different worlds or outlooks together.

Koch: And what works in one world doesn't necessarily work in another. I wore my tie-dyed shirt in Boston yesterday and got lots of looks. I'm a big woman, anyway. So people look at me and say, "My, she's large." But you put a tie-dyed shirt on that, and it's "My, she's large, and she's not *from* here."

People actually wear tie-dye in Seattle, a lot. But Boston, you know, there's a lot of preps here, boy.

Day: How do you develop your act?

Koch: One of us comes up with an idea, then we jam on it. Usually it'll just be bantering thoughts, and we'll come up with something. It'll be like, *Boing!* Then we'll put it together.

Day: How much of your show is by-the-book and how much is improv?

Platt: [*Laughing*] Lisa would like it to be more scripted ...

Koch: Every night is improv night for Peggy. [*Laughter*] I like to have a basis to work from, so some of it does have to be scripted. Then you improvise around that. We've come up with whole new portions of the act ...

Platt: The one that's been rewritten more than anything else is "Politically Correct Aerobics." It was one of the first bits we ever wrote. I had done an aerobics bit and Lisa said, "Let's add something onto it—let's do it for politically correct people." That bit was a thorn in my side—Lisa had a lot more faith in it than I did: "We can make it work! Come on, let's do it again." I will concede that it now works, but that's one that's just evolving constantly.

Koch: I tend to be more anal than Peggy. She tends to be more free-floating. Somehow it works.

Day: You have men singing on your tape. Do you sometimes have men in your act?

Platt: [*Huge laughter*]

Koch: We added guys on the lesbian song ...

Platt: ... because if there are men in the audience, we always make them sing that song.

Koch: [*In deep, "male" voice, to the tune of "Kumbaya"*] "We wish we could be lesbians ..." That's half the fun of that song, making the guys sing along. When we do that song for just lesbians, it's not nearly as funny.

Platt: Yeah, it's not fun at all.

Koch: To have a whole group of men singing, "We wish we could be lesbians" is quite empowering, let me tell ya.

Platt: About making people sing weird stuff, we have a song called "It's My Business," and we made the mayor of Seattle and city council people and prominent Washington State politicians sing "It's my business/it's never been yours./It's my closet/I'll open the doors." And the mayor and his wife—it gives me goosebumps to think about the mayor swaying and singing, "If I want to run naked through Woodland Park Zoo/It's my business/Besides, who asked you?" I mean that's the *best*.

Day: Do you think it would be possible to do the same kind of thing in a big, disempowering place like New York City?

Koch: We've played at fund-raisers for the Human Rights Campaign and for NARAL and NOW and the Democratic party. It's interesting to do our thing for a mixed audience and get them to join in and sing. Otherwise, it's almost like preaching to the converted. It's nice to have people get caught up in the whole thing and sing along and realize it's okay.

Platt: We travel in a lot of communities. We're not separatists in any way, shape, or form.

Koch: A lot of material that's generated from me comes from my life experience, from the fact that I'm queer and the struggle with being queer. Peggy isn't going to have the same experiences. It's like, What is our community? Together, as Dos Fallopia, we have a lot of different communities.

Platt: I don't want to be trite about rainbow community, but if we have any message, it's: What's wrong with an act being straight *and* gay? What's wrong with an act being music and comedy and serious *and* thought-provoking?

Day: How did you come up with Louise Needlemeyer, your character who gives the definitions?

Platt: It's a little bit of our mothers. Okay, it's a lot of our mothers. When I first started doing that voice, Lisa said, "That sounds just like my mother." And I said, "Well, I was imitating my mother." My mother became a feminist and learned a lot along the way and made great strides toward the end of her life. She was always supportive. Lisa talks about her mother saying, "You know, the gays." She's supportive, but she doesn't have the hip lingo.

Louise represents that part of the culture that doesn't know what's going on. People who don't really hate somebody who's different—they just don't have a clue. People who voted against equal rights for gays and lesbians in Oregon or Colorado not because they hate homosexuals but out of ignorance. Maybe someone they respected told them it was bad, so they said, "Okay, I'd better not vote for that." It's not hatred; it's ignorance. It's about education. Before enlightenment is ignorance.

Day: What are your backgrounds? What did your folks do?

Koch: Mine are both elementary school teachers. Retired.

Platt: My parents are both teachers, too. Only my dad never got to teach. There was a glut, and he went back to sales. But he got his degree in teaching. My mother was a preschool teacher, and her mom was a preschool teacher.

Day: When you were kids, did you see yourselves as fitting in?

Koch: I've always felt like I fit in. I was active in athletics and theater and debate and was a good student. Plus, I was funny. So you're sort of everybody's friend, even though you may not be a good friend. Yeah, I was a relatively popular kid in school and had a good time in school. I don't know if that's strange or not.

Platt: I was more the persecuted fat kid. I did those things too, but I also had a mopey part of me that said, "I'm fat. I'm horrible. Everyone hates me." On the other hand, people were voting for me and treating me like I was popular. I think I've always felt like I didn't fit in, definitely. But it's really important for me to be popular. I must try to make everyone like me. I'm less secure than Lisa is.

Koch: I think every artist is insecure.

Day: Is there any time you're onstage that you don't see yourselves as "women comics"?

Platt: That's something that frustrates me, actually. With stand-up, I'd be onstage doing comedy and not thinking about that stuff, then I'd find myself thinking, Gee, I'm the only woman on the bill, so I need to interject this little thought. It's unfortunate that our message has to be so woman-oriented, that we're in a place in society where we both feel that it's important to give a woman's message and a woman's point of view.

Koch: But we're women. I won't speak for Peggy, but pretty much everything I do, music and comedy, has that underlying I'm-a-woman-this-is-what-I-have-to-say.

Platt: But there's a tension underlying that which is frustrating. Like why should we have to get up onstage and keep doing that? I have a bit about menstruation, where I talk about how men don't accept it. They're not educated. Stuff like that. It's really funny and I love the bit, but sometimes when I'm doing it there's also this little edge of sadness. Like: "It's really sad that men don't know anything about women's bodies. Gee, it's unfortunate that we have to keep giving this feminist message. And boy, it's upsetting that we have to sing a song where we say that I'm straight and Lisa's a dyke and it's okay, everyone: hold hands." It's sad that we have to remind everyone that that's okay. There's a little teeny bit of sadness there. [*In mock sensitive voice*]

89

"But isn't *all* humor from sadness? That was *not* a quote; don't ever quote me saying that. [*Again, sensitive voice*] "Our comedy is *pain*-based. I'm really in *pain*, okay?" I hate that. Can't comedy be because you think it's *funny*?

Day: Who do you think is really funny?

Platt: Who are my heroes? [*to Lisa*] Do you have any comedy heroes?

Koch: Carol Burnett.

Platt: Carol Burnett, yeah. She's very good. Lily Tomlin.

Koch: Lily Tomlin. Kate Clinton. Suzanne Westenhoefer. Marga Gomez. Rocky and Bullwinkle.

Platt: Imogene Coca on "Your Show of Shows." God, she was amazing.

Koch: Peter Sellers. Course, he's a boy.

Platt: It's okay to like boys.

Day: What's your ultimate dream of success?

Koch: My ultimate dream of success is to make a living doing what we're doing. Maybe to get a little more television exposure. Get Dos Fallopia on Comedy Central.

Platt: Especially since Almost Live is on there from Seattle, and they're schlock. You can quote me on that. They're pigs, and they hate women.

My dream of success—I used to say the same thing as Lisa, that I just wanted to keep working. But I'm starting to get selfish. I want mainstream acceptance for whatever I say. As long as I'm funny and I'm being a professional and I'm making audiences laugh …

Koch: But we're already doing that.

Platt: More, though. I want more. I want to be on Leno and I want to be on Arsenio and I want people on "Good Morning America" to talk about us.

Koch: Rush Limbaugh's already talked about us. I got a call from a friend in Seattle who said she found out that Dos Fallopia was going to be performing at the March on Washington. She said, "You know how I found out about it? I heard about you guys on 'Rush Limbaugh!' " He apparently grabbed a copy of the *Washington Blade* and was leafing through it, and he picked up on us because we have a weird name. He made a joke about how this was the same group who was the Tubes in the eighties. How clever, Rush. We've achieved fame now.

Day: What advice do you have for women who want to get involved in comedy?

Platt: I'd tell them, Be persistent—it's gonna be weird.

Day: What kind of weird?

Platt: If you're onstage doing stand-up there are male pigs. I don't hate men and I don't think all men are evil, but in comedy clubs, where there's alcohol and things are presented in a hermetically sealed, white, straight male environment, there's bound to be some discrimination against women. Be persistent and keep in there.

Louise DuArt

by Laurie Stone

First, the face is long and sultry. Next, the cheeks are sucked in and an air of strained gentility is conjured. Then the tongue juts out, and a finger is thrust down the throat. Louise DuArt is doing Cher, Barbara Walters, and Joan Rivers with dead-on precision. Cher, her tongue working her lips, slips a long hair out of her mouth and stares at it, enchanted by her display of vulgarity. Barbara, abandoning her usual ramrod posture, hitches her chin and narrows her eyes, going in for the question with razor blades. "Tell me," she says to Katherine Hepburn, uncorking her own prurience to snare this priggish prey, "when you were doing those love scenes with Spencer Tracy, did he ever slip you a little tongue?"

Like other inspired impressionists—Martin Short, Catherine O'Hare, Billy Crystal—DuArt isn't a mimic but a caricaturist, drawing psychological portraits and satirizing manners. She's done all the female and some of the male voices for the life-sized puppets on TV's "D.C. Follies." She's done several Showtime specials and hosted a game-show caprice for Lifetime, in which contestants determine whether outrageous dish about the famous is fact or rumor. But mostly DuArt plays clubs, rotating between small venues like the Backlot in L.A. and glitz-barns in Las Vegas and Atlantic City.

There is something ineffable about her ability to change voice, face—a gorgeous oddness, something in the bones and lineaments that comes along once in a blue moon. DuArt channels Barbra Streisand, Roseanne, Jane Fonda, Liza Minelli, Whoopi Goldberg, and Tammy Bakker. She does men, some in full drag, including George Burns, Woody Allen, Willie Nelson, Henry Fonda, and Popeye. And she sings in character as accurately as she speaks. When her imagination rips, when she free-associates and sends her incarnations ricocheting off one another, there's anarchic madness in her work.

DuArt's malice is exuberant, not bitter or pinched, because she doesn't target the weak and dispossessed, and she doesn't look down at her subjects. They are her alter egos. Onstage, she spews a stream of Joan Rivers venom: "I don't want to say the Queen Mother is top-heavy, but her brassiere has curb feelers." DuArt looks up. "You don't know how *good* it feels to do Joan."

Each of DuArt's impersonations expresses a drive. Streisand is narcissism, Cher exhibitionism, Hepburn self-importance. DuArt inhabits males with the same skill and abandon with which she crosses over into women. In a tour de force sequence, she plays both George and Gracie, changing voice, mannerisms, and moods in the flick of an eyelash. Sometimes, she fractures gender altogether. Onstage, she becomes a wizened, inching George Burns while still wearing high heels and flashing long red fingernails.

Incorporating, appropriating, is the charge that fuels DuArt, and she parades this in two of her wildest turns. For a Showtime special, she introduces Rita Mapp, an idiot savant modeled on Dustin Hoffman's character in *Rain Man*. Rita is a crack impressionist, and as a talk-show panel screams out cues, she snaps from bit to bit, balking at Elvis. "I don't do dead people, definitely not dead people." Between impersonations, Rita repeats herself and breaks a vase in frustration. She's only someone when she's someone else.

A taped piece DuArt screens in her live act is equally self-revealing, a gloss on the impressionist's disposition to seize, possess. She plays Shelley Winters during a police interrogation. We see only Shelley, tires of fat bulging between the ropes that bind her, confusion contorting her face. An offscreen man demands, "What did you do with Zsa Zsa Gabor's former husbands?"

"I … I ate 'em." Her voice quavers.

"All *eight* of them?"

"I ate seven."

"What did you do with the eighth?"

"Froze him."

DuArt says it frightens her to acknowledge the gist of her Shelley Winters routine: that the impressionist is a cannibal, that there is something predatory about the activity, that it involves invasiveness, a plundering of boundaries that women, especially, have been inhibited from attempting, lest they be deemed witches or masculine females. But these thoughts also thrill her. "I'm ready to try a sexual male. I'm going to do Dustin Hoffman in my next special. I love dressing up and becoming that other gender. I love exposing Woody's self-righteousness and the shark in Barbara Walters. You can see her get the tears, and then her mind clicks and she's thinking, Now the camera goes in for the kill."

In front of an audience, DuArt gets to be the puppet master as well as all the puppets. She gets to be shameless, bitchy, erotic, flamboyant, intrusive, and egotistical. "I love it," she says in a voice that's her own and filled with passion.

Mo Gaffney

by Roz Warren, interview by Patty Marx

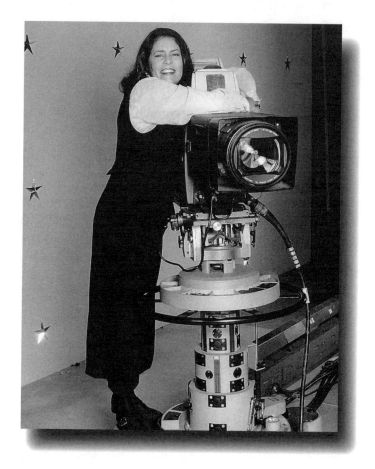

Mo Gaffney began her comedy career in San Diego, as a founding member of Hot Flashes, a four-woman feminist comedy group. She also appeared in the comedy groups Fool Moon Theater and Lipservice. She gained national acclaim when, with Kathy Najimy, she wrote and starred in the feminist comedy classic *The Kathy and Mo Show: Parallel Lives*, a collection of skits and character sketches. The show enjoyed a sold-out off-Broadway run, won a 1989 Obie, was made into an award-winning HBO special, and is still performed by theater groups across the country. Since then, Gaffney has appeared in feature films, on British television, and as the host of "The Mo

Show" for Fox Television. She won an award at the Edinburgh Festival for her work on *The Oppressed Minorities Big Fun Show*.

Gaffney also hosted Comedy Central's popular talk show "Women Aloud!," a mix of comedy, intelligent chat, and politics. She and Najimy are currently writing the film *Bus Plunge* for Hollywood Pictures.

Marx: You know this is ironic, Mo, because you're the interviewer.

Gaffney: I am not.

Marx: You've interviewed more than I've interviewed.

Gaffney: Let's see how much you've learned.

Marx: Quick, give me a tip!

Gaffney: Ask questions.

Marx: Okay. But first, let's just remember to make me look good all of the time.

Gaffney: Patty, that's a brilliant question.

Marx: I feel like I'm calling you up because somebody told me to, and I'm going to ask you out on a blind date.

Gaffney: I'm busy.

Marx: You know that this is for a book about women comedians. So, do you think that there's anything to say about women and comedy that hasn't already been said?

Gaffney: Probably not.

Marx: Okay, that's the end of the interview.

Gaffney: Do you know what? They'd never say, "Is there anything about men and comedy that hasn't been said?"

Marx: No, they wouldn't. They would just talk about comedy.

Gaffney: Right.

Marx: Maybe we should do that.

[*Pause*]

Gaffney: I think that women definitely have a different perspective. There are things that women think are funny more than men think they're funny. We've had to listen to what men think is funny forever. So now that women are being funny, there's just more funny stuff.

Marx: Do you think that men don't want women to be funny?

Gaffney: No, I don't think that's true.

Marx: I don't think that's true, either. Have I left anything out?

Gaffney: I think that pretty much covers it.

Marx: I talked to someone who was an interviewer for *The New York Times* and he said that's the most important question to ask.

Gaffney: What?

Marx: "Have I left anything out?"

Gaffney: You probably have to ask that at the end.

Marx: There's always a catch.

[*Pause*]

Gaffney: Let me put this into perspective for you. I'm sitting on my back porch drinking a Juicy Juice out of a little cardboard container with a straw coming out of it. That's what I'm doing. I'm looking at an orange tree.

Marx: I thought of another question. How important do you think it is to be funny?

Gaffney: It's very important to be funny, but if you can't be funny, it's important to appreciate funny things. I like people more if they laugh at me.

Marx: Absolutely. It's a sign of their intelligence, don't you think?

Gaffney: Today I was at this meeting with my friend Lisa, and she asked, "What did you think of David so-and-so, the business guy?" And I said, "I really liked him." Then I realized that the only reason I'd said that was because he laughed at the things I said that were funny. He's probably an ax murderer. He could kill baby kitties and I wouldn't care, because he thinks I'm funny.

Marx: Do you ever get sick of comedy?

Gaffney: Not if it's good.

Marx: I know this isn't my interview, but I do have the tape recorder, so let me say that so much comedy is bland, because it's all derivative.

Gaffney: They think they've found a formula. Nobody has to be funny in a different way. As long as it looks like a banana and tastes like a banana, there's no reason to make it a better banana.

Marx: People just want the accoutrement of comedy, not comedy. They want the right inflections, they want the right topics.

Gaffney: There's "Seinfeld." Now that's funny to me. That's different and funny. But of course, people are going to do that twenty-eight ways until it's not funny.

Marx: It's hard to be original, but it works when you're original. Well, not always. You could be bad original, I guess.

Gaffney: Even if it's good original, sometimes people ask, "What's funny about that? There's no rubber chicken." Or whatever the thing is now. When you have to explain something that's funny to someone, then it's not funny anymore.

Marx: Do you think that anybody that didn't have an unhappy childhood or an unhappy adulthood can be funny? Do you think misery helps?

Gaffney: I think it does help. But then again you can just be a boring person who's had an unhappy childhood. Most people that I think are really funny, from what I can tell, had some sort of a weird past.

Marx: Mo, what do you want to do next?

Gaffney: Eat dinner, I guess.

Marx: Not after this interview. In life. Do you want to do a talk show?

Gaffney: No.

Marx: Do you want to do a sitcom?

Gaffney: Maybe. Oh, mother of shit, I just cut myself really, really badly!

Marx: Oh my God! And you're not even hysterical!

Gaffney: I'm running water on it and it's bleeding, bleeding. I just like sliced it.

Marx: Where?

Gaffney: My thumb.

Marx: God. Use it to be funnier, Mo.

Gaffney: Huh? My thumb? I hope it stops bleeding.

Marx: Let's talk about bad taste. Are there any topics or issues that you can't be funny about or that you don't think should be made fun of?

Gaffney: That I don't think that I can be funny about? Yes. But I know that someone somewhere can probably be funny about it without being offensive.

Marx: For instance?

Gaffney: Oh, child abuse. I don't think abortion is very funny. Although I've seen someone be funny around that topic. I'm passing out. I don't believe this happened.

Marx: Do you want to take a break so you can bleed to death?

Gaffney: No, I think it's going to be okay.

Marx: Put a tourniquet on it.

Gaffney: I'm pressing it hard.

Marx: How did you do this, was it the Juicy Juice?

Gaffney: No, with a knife. I was cutting a piece of bread from a crusty baguette, and I cut my thumb. It runs in my family.

Marx: Thumbs?

Gaffney: Cutting. Cutting parts of the body.

Marx: You're accident-prone?

Gaffney: Well, I am kind of a klutz. I cut off a piece of my thumb once and had to have my skin grafted. I was very young.

Marx: I know someone whose brother said to her when she was three, "Put your thumb in this bicycle," and she did and her thumb came off. And they sewed her big toe onto her thumb.

Gaffney: So her thumb's a big toe? My thumb had this graft on it that never quite took, you know.

Marx: All right, as funny as this is I have to get back to comedy. We were talking about bad taste.

Gaffney: What I think is really bad taste is unoriginality. Like Andrew Dice Clay.

Marx: What he does passes for humor but it's really only an assault.

Gaffney: I think you have to be a little bit smart to be funny, you know, unless you're accidentally funny.

Marx: Physical comedy, you mean?

Gaffney: Physical comedy, or being so stupid you don't know that you're ridiculous. But normally, you have to be smart to be funny. There's not a modicum of intelligence in what Andrew Dice Clay does. That's what I don't admire at all. There are so many things that can be funny. And when a comic goes back to stuff that is so passé and without merit, I think, You're not funny, you're a hack.

Marx: Do you think …

Gaffney: I just used the word *hack*. Felt pretty good.

Marx: Hack. That's a good word, and it's what you just did to your thumb.

Gaffney: Yeah. It's a funny cut. I don't know what happened. It's like I sliced like a layer off that's still attached.

Marx: I know what you mean, and now you're trying to attach it. Well, just keep holding it on for about three days.

Gaffney: I have to go somewhere.

Marx: To a hospital? But wait—these might be very valuable words: "Mo Gaffney: The Last Interview."

Gaffney: You can say, "When she cut her thumb, of course I didn't know how bad it was …"

Marx: I'll have to say that or I'll look very bad. "She was bleeding to death and still you asked her about Andrew Dice Clay?" they will say.

Gaffney: How sad that would be if my last words were "Andrew Dice Clay."

Marx: Just keep holding your thumb.

Gaffney: I'm doing that.

Marx: Now let me think … why do you think you're funny?

Gaffney: Why do I think I'm funny? Because people laugh at what I say.

Marx: I know your mother says you weren't always funny.

Gaffney: Actually I was always funny, or pretty much always. Maybe in elementary school I wasn't such a hoot, but I could play dodge ball really well, and team ball.

Marx: You could play *Godspell*?

Gaffney: Dodge ball.

Marx: Oh, dodge ball.

Gaffney: In junior high and in high school, it was really important to be pretty or to have big boobs. And I didn't. But if you're funny that's also good. Not as good as pretty. Not when you're in high school.

Marx: No, nothing is.

Gaffney: I wasn't pretty with big boobs. But in the end, I'm much happier to be funny and smart. Now you can buy boobs.

I'm not going to buy any but …

Marx: There are people who don't think it matters to be funny.

Gaffney: Life is so random. You have to be funny, or at least see how things are funny.

Marx: It seems like the choice is to see life as funny or see life literally. If you're literal, the most you can hope for is being bored. And the worst you can hope for is suicide.

Gaffney: I'd have to agree with you.

Marx: Okay, that's what I've been trying all along to get you to do—agree. Finally.

Gaffney: It worked. My thumb stopped bleeding, but it still looks like a blood blister. There's blood under there that wants to come out.

Marx: Don't let it come out yet.

Gaffney: I'm going to just let it sit for a minute.

Marx: I mean, think about it. There's a lot of blood in your body, and it's been staying there for a long time.

Gaffney: Yeah, I don't think that hole is big enough for all of it to come out of.

Marx: Now let me think about being funny.

Gaffney: I'm a little weak from loss of blood.

Marx: You sound anemic. What would you like to do next?

Gaffney: I would like to not bleed to death, number one. But I don't want you to worry—it looks better.

Marx: It sounds better, too.

Gaffney: It was bad. I was very calm, though.

Marx: You were.

Gaffney: When I get off the phone I'm going to scream.

Marx: Do you want me to call 911?

Gaffney: No.

Marx: You're sure?

Gaffney: Call 411 and ask them for a good plastic surgeon. What was I saying? When you write this, you'll have to make me sound more interesting than I am.

Marx: I will. You know what I'm going to do? I'm going to intersperse some Kant.

Gaffney: Some what?

Marx: The philosopher Kant. I'll ask my questions and then just put Kant's answers in.

Gaffney: Good. Get in some Camus, too, because I like that you don't say the *s*.

Marx: The French are funny. The French are very funny because they have *accents graves* and *accents aigus*.

Gaffney: There are a lot of consonants they really don't even say. They spell them in a word and you never hear from them again.

Marx: I sometimes think that when French babies realize that they're going to have to learn a foreign language they're really pissed.

Gaffney: I'd imagine that Russian babies are more pissed off, because they'll have an even harder language to learn.

Marx: Now, let's see. Have we said everything there is to say about humor? Would you like to write unfunny stuff or do you want to stick to humor?

Gaffney: I couldn't write pure drama because that's not how I think. I could write something that's basically a drama, but there would have to be humor in it.

Marx: You know what I want to write? Something that makes the audience laugh and cry so hard they have a stroke.

Gaffney: What I'd like to do is have people actually become ill. You know, in light of my cut. Where people who have stitches, for example—after having something removed —they laugh so hard they split their stitches, literally, and their guts are on the floor. "I laughed my guts up." That would make me happy.

Marx: I laughed so hard I …

Gaffney: … split my stitches. Of course, they don't have stitches anymore, now they have staples.

Marx: You know what else they have? They have a Band-Aid-like material that you spray. Did you know that?

Gaffney: I would think that other things would stick to it. Like stickum.

Marx: That would be handy, in a way, because you could put notes on your leg.

Gaffney: Remind yourself when they have to change your dressing.

Marx: I think it's about time for me to say, "Have I left out anything?"

Gaffney: Probably not. I wasn't very funny.

Marx: No, you were funny.

Gaffney: But you were funny.

Marx: And you were in pain. Comedy is pain.

Terry Galloway

by Roz Warren

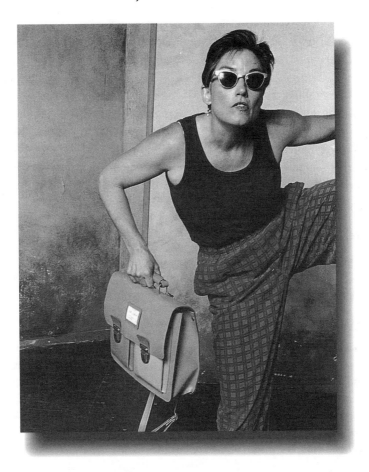

"I'm deaf, I'm weird, and I'm a woman!" cries comic Terry Galloway during her one-woman show, *Out All Night and Lost My Shoes*. And that, in a nutshell, is what Galloway's powerfully funny work is all about. Born in Cold War Berlin and raised in Texas, Galloway became deaf as a child, the result of experimental antibiotics given her mother during pregnancy. Both of her one-woman shows (the other is *Lardo Weeping*) address the pain and isolation of the disabled, giving voice to society's freaks and victims.

With a wild mix of poetry, storytelling, and stand-up, Galloway's work celebrates the power and the rage of the outcast. She tells personal anecdotes, observes weird ironies, and contemplates the meaning behind the animal dioramas in the New York Museum of Natural History. Her take on life is sharply ironic. "People love their freaks," she proclaims during *Out All Night*. "I'm talking from experience here."

Galloway hasn't had an easy life, and she shares her experiences freely with her audience. She describes her stay in a mental hospital (she found she was good at entertaining schizophrenics with puppetry), talks about attending a camp for crippled children, and delivers a lecture on the etiquette of suicide ("Cheesegrater across the wrist: wrong. Carving knife across the vein: right"). Her influences, says Galloway, are William Shakespeare, Oscar Wilde, Louisa May Alcott, Robert Kennedy, and Daffy Duck.

In addition to performing *Out All Night* and *Lardo Weeping* throughout the United States, Galloway has been appointed visiting artist at the California Institute of the Arts and has been awarded a grant by the Florida Division of Cultural Affairs. She's currently working on two pieces, "Peg's Hamlet" and "A Happy Life … If You Can Stand It."

Warren: Do you consider yourself a stand-up comic?

Galloway: A lot of things I've written and performed are funny, but I'm not a stand-up comic. Nor am I really a comedian. My one-woman shows aren't as much comedy as tragedy in burlesque.

Warren: When did you first realize you could make people laugh?

Galloway: I was a child freak, burdened with a hearing aid, thick glasses, baby fat—the works. When I was twelve, my mom and dad both worked, so I'd end up at the junior high school half an hour early each morning, and I'd tell bad jokes to the other early drop-offs to keep them amused until the doors opened. The more jokes I told, the less likely they were to torment or kill me. And the big girls thought I was really cute—in a crippled-baby-seal-clowning-so-as-not-to-get-clubbed way.

Warren: How do you use humor in your life and in performance?

Galloway: My humor is used self-defensively. It's a way of letting others know I'm tough enough to take it, without my actually having to take it. It deals with the books I read, the life I live, the people and circumstances that envelop me, and death, death, death. It's very bleak and blue humor.

Warren: What made you decide to become a performer?

Galloway: I was always a performer. I'd be a performer even if I worked my life away mopping floors. Some of the best performances I've ever seen were given by my two sisters, my mom, and my dad at the dinner table after we'd all had a couple of glasses of wine.

Warren: What's your ideal audience?

Galloway: A big, mixed audience—straight and gay, grannies and queens, in every hue imaginable. People with a sense of irony and a sense of generosity. People who put lots of garlic in everything and always have extra room at the table.

Warren: How do you develop your material?

Galloway: I read. I think about things. I go out to dinner with friends or family, have a glass of wine, and we all start talking and making jokes. And being as deaf as I am, I make everybody repeat their funny lines two or three times—ostensibly so I can hear them, but really so I can store it away for future use.

Warren: Do you ever work with others on material?

Galloway: In developing my cabaret humor I get together with six or seven writers from my group (the Mickee Faust Club) and we drink coffee or beer and eat nachos and toss ideas around. When our minds are warmed up, we start amusing each other. When our imaginations have been engaged, we go off and write, refine the original, crude ideas, meet again, and so on, until idle chat has become a polished skit.

Warren: What impact do you want to have?

Galloway: I used to have grand schemes for shaking the world out of the doldrums and into a fit of laughter—the kind of Zen Buddhist *Ha!* that enlightens. Now I dream of people together, enjoying food and company, puzzling over the oddity of living, laughing at it all. Onstage or off. It no longer matters. I dream of being part of the expansive and humorous nature of things.

Warren: How does it feel when you bomb?

Galloway: Bombing is that dreamlike feeling of being naked in a room when your body is flabby and fish-belly white, and everyone looking at you is an old and hated enemy. A part of your soul is vaporized with shame. You want instant death for yourself and everyone else in the room. You turn into Puck and think, "What fools these mortals be." If only they had half your brain, they'd be laughing their guts out.

Scorn for the audience is a defensive habit, of course. But it does work. And sometimes the scorn is deserved.

Warren: What does it feel like when everything works and the audience is laughing?

Galloway: When all goes well and your jokes are justly adored by the multitudes, all you feel is bliss. You feel happy and maybe just a tad smug. Of course the world loves you. Didn't your mother promise?

Lisa Geduldig

by Ellen Orleans

Lisa Geduldig's mother is a seismologist.

But that shouldn't be too surprising. As Lisa has discovered since moving to the Bay Area, every East Coast parent with kids in San Francisco is a seismologist. Lisa swears that not only does her mother have a Richter scale next to her Cuisinart, but she also has the amazing ability to get through to her daughter when phone lines are down. During the October 1992 earthquake, even while tremors rocked her apartment, Lisa's mother called. Her first words? "Are you going to move?"

Like many comics, Geduldig began her comedy career in high school, where she was a class wise-ass. But it wasn't until 1989, after getting big laughs from a speech she gave at a friend's wedding, that she began performing. Since then, she's been a hit with audiences from London to Provincetown to San Francisco.

Along with her Jewish and lesbian identity, family interaction (or lack thereof) is a big part of Lisa's comedy routine. At one point, she reads a letter from her parents in which they express support for her after her recent breakup and offer to set her up with the nice Jewish girl next door.

The problem with the letter? Well, Lisa herself wrote it. You see, after sending her parents letters filled with thoughts, feelings, and questions, she was tired of getting evasive, emotionless responses. "Now," she says, deadpan, "when I write to my parents, I also include a copy of the letter I'd *like* to receive from them and ask them to sign it and then send it back in the enclosed self-addressed, stamped envelope."

One of Geduldig's talents is to draw from many backgrounds, then add her own twist. She jokes, for instance, about Chinese restaurants filled with Jews breaking the fast on Yom Kippur. "This is odd," she notes, "because Jews aren't supposed to eat pork." From what she observes, however, "wrapping pork in a wonton apparently makes it okay." And it was in a Chinese restaurant, she jokes, that she decided to come out to her parents, which she did by rigging both their fortune cookies to read, "Your son-in-law will be a turkey baster."

Geduldig says she includes a lot of jokes about coming out in her act because "everyone has gone through similar ordeals of having to tell their parents something they don't want to hear."

She makes good use not only of her lesbian identity and Jewish roots but she even turns her height—five feet, one inch—into a draw. Performing at the famous San Francisco gay-comic training ground Josie's Cabaret and Juice Joint, she joined with two other short women to present *Reaching for Laughs: Comedy for the Vertically Challenged*.

While Geduldig often zeros in on her family, she also takes aim at political leaders. Back in the days of Desert Storm she read a front-page article about a zoo elephant that had crushed its trainer. Nothing funny about that, she observed, but she did wonder if the article's subhead, "Testosterone Cycle May Have Spurred Surprise Attack," was accidentally switched from the lead story about Bush launching the Gulf War.

She also notes that Al Gore looks like Superman. "The two of them," she says, "have never been seen together. I rest my case."

Sherry Glaser

by Roz Warren

Sherry Glaser's one-woman off-Broadway show, *Family Secrets,* has inspired critics to compare her with both Lily Tomlin and Anna Deveare Smith. In a series of monologues mixing humor with sometimes painful honesty, Glaser portrays a husband and wife, their two daughters, and the husband's mother, all based on the Bronx-born comic's own family. There's Mort, the deadpan patriarch, a middle-aged accountant and self-described "simple guy from the Bronx," who would do anything to make his family happy. Wisecracking wife Beverly, "the perfect Jewish mother," is a manic-depressive who "tried to make perfect kids, but they wouldn't cooperate." Recovering from a nervous breakdown (she believed she was the Virgin Mary), she's now entered law school and aspires to become a judge. Daughter Fern's story centers around the home birth of her own daughter, which is shared with the audience in harrowing, hilarious detail. (The only way, says Fern as her labor advances, for her lover to realize what she's going through would be if she bit him on the balls, "and I'm talking about every three minutes." She concludes: "I realize why women die in childbirth—it's preferable.") Younger sister Sandra is a sixteen-year-old rebel who has just lost her virginity. Absent is their brother, who has gone from Columbia School of Engineering to a kibbutz in Israel, where he's a shepherd. Finally, there's Grandma Rose, an eighty-year-old who finds love (and good sex) in a nursing home when she marries fellow octogenarian Milton. "If we didn't have families," Rose concludes, "we'd all be strangers."

Cowritten by Glaser and husband Greg Howells, the show is a series of monologues, "but there's never any real idea of what 'normal' is." "Everyone in the family is striving to be normal," says Glaser. For example, the segment where Mort challenges his daughter over a lesbian relationship: when she asks him if it isn't normal to love someone, he says, "Not a woman." The daughter counters, "You love Mom."

Glaser discovered improvisational acting while at San Diego State University. She dropped out of school and began taking improv acting classes and doing street theater. In 1981 she teamed up with several other women comics, including Mo Gaffney, to form the popular feminist theater group Hot Flashes. "We were politically correct," comments Glaser, "*and* we were making a nice living." She left that group in 1985 to form the Egomaniacks, where she developed characters that inspired her first show, *Coping*.

Whoopi Goldberg

by Samantha Rigg

When Whoopi Goldberg hit the world of comedy there was magic. Not since the great Moms Mabley had an outspoken African-American woman expressed herself onstage with such daring and wit. Goldberg has become famous (some would say infamous) for speaking her mind, and for refusing to compromise her personality or her politics. Whether her audience is made up of comedy club fans, the millions of television viewers worldwide who tuned in when she hosted the Oscars, or even the president of the United States, Goldberg calls it exactly as she sees it—and seems to have a hell of a time while she does it.

Goldberg's comedy invites her audience not only to indulge in laughter but also to appreciate the complexity of her characters and the situations in which they find themselves. Goldberg herself isn't simply a comic or even a comic actress. In 1990 she won an Oscar for her performance in *Ghost* (the first African-American woman to win the award since Hattie McDaniel in

1939). (She's also received the NAACP's 1991 Entertainer of the Year award and Harvard University's 1993 Woman of the Year award.)

Born Karyn Johnson in 1949 in a New York City housing project, Goldberg spent much of her childhood and adolescence watching old movies and television comedy. (She's said to have fantasized about being Carole Lombard.) She began acting at the age of eight at the Helena Rubenstein Children's Theater. Goldberg dropped out of high school, actively participated in 1960s counterculture, got married, had a daughter, and moved to Berkeley.

In Berkeley, she debuted *The Spook Show*, an hour-long, one-woman show showcasing four characters she'd honed over the years. *The Spook Show* went on the road in the United States and Europe, and eventually opened on Broadway as *Whoopi Goldberg*. After seeing the show, Steven Spielberg cast Goldberg in *The Color Purple* in 1984. Since then, Goldberg has acted on movie and television screens and sometimes, via voice-overs, as the voice behind the screen. Her films include *Jumpin' Jack Flash, Burglar, Fatal Beauty, Clara's Heart, The Telephone, Homer and Eddie, Ghost, The Long Walk Home, Soapdish, Sarafina!, Sister Act* and *Sister Act II, The Player*, and *Made in America*. She's a voice on the cartoon series "Captain Planet and the Planeteers," and she appears on "Star Trek: The Next Generation." In addition to all this, she's a founding member of HBO's "Comic Relief," which raises money to assist the homeless.

The strength that Goldberg has brought to women and to comedy is immeasurable. She's defied being typecast in stereotypical roles (her first on-screen kiss, in *The Color Purple*, was with another woman). Through the wide range of characters she's played, from the nameless black six-year-old of *The Spook Show* to Oda Mae Brown of *Ghost*, Goldberg possesses a unique comic persona that entertains, teaches, and continually expands the role of women in the field of comedy.

Marga Gomez

by Roz Warren, interview by Laura Post

Born in Harlem to a Cuban comedian and a Puerto Rican exotic dancer, Marga Gomez thinks of herself as an exotic comedian. Her first gigs were in her parents' comedy sketches on the stages of Manhattan's legendary Latino theaters. Marga never spoke more than a line or two, and she had to share scenes with the family chihuahua, but it gave her a taste for show biz.

The hippie life drew Marga from the Big Apple to San Francisco, where she worked with theater groups like Les Nicklettes and the San Francisco Mime Troupe. After touring for several years as an actress, writer, and scenery lugger with Lilith, a feminist theater company, Marga struck out on her own as a stand-up comic.

Marga's solo act combined offbeat character sketches and quirky social commentary with a genuine warmth and caring that endeared her to her audiences. Early material included skits about the hidden lesbians in "The Beverly Hillbillies," one-liners about gender differences ("Women might start a rumor but not a war"), comments about the joys of traveling on public transportation ("Thank you for taking time out from your substance abuse to objectify me"), and the men's movement ("I thought that was called the government").

After a decade of success in stand-up and many awards and television spots (including appearances on Rosie O'Donnell's *Stand-Up Spotlight* and *Comic Relief VI*), Marga developed two critically acclaimed, full-length performance pieces. *Memory Tricks* explores the comic's relationship with her mother, from her mother's flamboyant days as a self-absorbed showgirl to her later struggle with Alzheimer's. *Marga Gomez is Pretty, Witty and Gay*, a monologue Gomez describes as "a comic nervous breakdown," is set on the eve of the comic's appearance as "an adult female homosexual" on a television talk show. Gomez takes the opportunity to explore sexual politics and rewrite the Bible ("You will burn and burn and burn!" she rants in character as a Southern homophobe, "and Jesus loves you"). Another highlight is a dramatic reading from Anaïs Nin's previously undiscovered erotic diary detailing a trip to Disneyland (including a passionate dalliance with Minnie Mouse at the Swiss Family Robinson house).

Gomez is currently developing a performance monologue about her father and working on the screenplay of *Memory Tricks* for *American Playhouse*.

Post: Your career has really taken off in the last year. How has that changed your life?

Gomez: I'm traveling more. I'm getting a lot of emotional and financial support that's allowed me to continue the work I started with *Memory Tricks*. I'm touring both solo shows, writing a third show, and also performing stand-up. I have a lot more opportunities as far as live performance goes. The next thing I really have to crack is film and television.

Post: Your act alludes to your experience of trying out for film roles and the kind of stereotyping you ran into.

Gomez: Yeah, it's pretty depressing. There are a lot of maid roles. That seems to be the only thing they send out Latina actresses for. But I'm under contract right now to write the screenplay of *Memory Tricks* for *American Playhouse*.

I'm going to have to write my own movies because nobody's writing them for someone like me.

Post: I'm surprised that Hollywood people don't recognize your acting talent from a piece like *Memory Tricks*.

Gomez: It's not that they don't recognize my talent. I think they do, because they call me for things. There just aren't a lot of good scripts out there. When I see the movies that do come out, I'm always disappointed. They're always so predictable. I think it's the poverty of characters and imagination in Hollywood, not so much that they don't think I'm good.

Post: After starting out in stand-up, what made you begin to write longer material?

Gomez: I was at an impasse doing stand-up. A lot of it had to do with the homophobia in the comedy scene. I had trouble going onstage and identifying myself as a lesbian comic. I wanted to be out, but I didn't want that to be shtick.

I'm inclined toward storytelling. Even in my stand-up, I created scenes and characters. A friend, Josh Kornbluth, who was having some success with that sort of performance—just telling the story of his life—encouraged me to try it.

I came up with the first version of *Memory Tricks* because someone who had mistakenly heard I was a performance artist called and asked me to perform. I said I would. They gave me a date and I said I'd develop a piece about my mother.

Post: Did *Memory Tricks* change as you continued to perform it?

Gomez: When I first did the piece in 1990, I threw in any cute story I could think of from my childhood. By the time I performed it in New York three years later, the piece had been honed to focus on the story of my mother and me. Everything that didn't serve that basic story was cut.

Post: Performing *Memory Tricks* in New York was a turning point for you in terms of professional recognition. Can you describe how that came about?

Gomez: George C. Wolfe was curating the Festival of New Voices at the New York Shakespeare Festival. I was recommended to Wolfe, who called and asked me to send him a videotape. He said it was one of the best things he'd ever seen and then told me several things I had to cut out of the piece. I said, "Sure," because I figured he must know what he's talking about.

After I performed the piece at the festival, it got picked up for a run at the Public Theater. I got reviewed by *The New York Times*. *American Playhouse* commissioned me to write a screenplay. *Vogue* magazine did an article about me—not something I'd ever expected, but you don't have to read *Vogue* to be in it. The *New Yorker* did a caricature of me. After that you can just die, you know? You can watch TV for the rest of your life. You got your caricature in the *New Yorker*.

That's what it's all about. It's just media attention and approval, and then suddenly all the people who dismissed you in the past show up.

Post: You've been successful doing both theater and stand-up. What role does humor play in your theater pieces?

Gomez: Humor is my main survival mechanism. Everyone I've been close to has had a sense of humor. People I know who've faced tragedy have used humor to get through. When you're dealing with a hard subject, I don't know how you could get through without humor, and love.

Sometimes, for me, funny is a bit of a crutch. Before I rewrote *Memory Tricks*, there was a lot more humor in it that was there just for the sake of entertainment. There's one line about Michael Jackson that I couldn't bear to cut, even though it's just a cheap shot. I'm talking about how my mom got in a car accident and while she was in the hospital she took the opportunity to get some plastic surgery on her nose. I say, "She always wanted a Caucasian nose like Michael Jackson's." The audience laughs every single time. What can I do? Every night I'd go up there and I'd say, "I'm not going to say it tonight." Then I just couldn't help myself.

With that joke I crossed the line with the theater purists. It's stand-up.

Post: How would you define your humor?

Gomez: I try not to have any artifice. I try to be real. Some stand-up comics are slick and impersonal. They're just technicians—joke machines. What I'm trying to do is really be present with the audience. I'm not trying to control them. I'm sort of vulnerable and I'm very honest. I'm not a political comic, in that I don't follow the world news and comment on it, although I admire comics who do that. I use my own life.

Post: How do you develop new material?

Gomez: When anything comes up that's bizarre or ridiculous, I make a note of it. Then I expand on it. I think all comics do that.

Post: What happens when an idea you've come up with doesn't work?

Gomez: I pretty much believe everything I try onstage is good. If it doesn't work, I develop it. You're always cutting as much as you can in order to get to the laugh. If it doesn't work, it's not the idea, it's me. I just know there's a way to sell it. After you do this for a while, even if you don't know how to explain what you're doing, you've instinctively figured out how to deliver material so that the audience might not even be laughing at what you're saying as much as how you're saying it.

If something doesn't work, I'll just keep trying. I won't use it in a high-pressure situation, where I could cause damage to my career. But where I've already done fifteen good jokes that they like, I'll put in the one that maybe they'll like this time. Then when they do like it, I try to remember how it came out, so that I can repeat it.

Post: What does it feel like to be onstage doing stand-up and have people laugh at what you're saying?

Gomez: Sometimes I'm surprised. There are things the audience laughs at every single time and every time I'm surprised. Sometimes I forget why the material was funny in the first place.

Post: Do you pay attention to your audience's response when you're performing a solo piece like Memory Tricks in the same way that you do when you do stand-up?

Gomez: No. It's a different way of being with the audience. I'm taking them with me, but it's really important that I don't leave the story or the characters. It really shouldn't matter how they respond as long as I'm being true up there and I'm being focused. If I'm giving it a hundred percent and I'm opening myself up, then they can be laughing during the saddest parts or quiet during the funny parts. It's different every time and I think that's the way it's supposed to be.

Keeping track of the audience response to something like *Memory Tricks* is the director's job. She'll find things that weren't working or weren't clear for the audience. What you're mostly trying to do is make sure that it's clear for the audience. Not that it's funny for them or sad for them, but just that what happened is clear. She'll give me notes afterward, and we'll get to the bottom of any problems with the piece.

With stand-up, I'm my own director. It's not really life or death, you know. I do want to hit some important themes, but it's also just something for people to do while they drink a beer. I mean how serious can you get about it? It's comedy.

Post: What do you think about the current explosion in mainstream visibility of lesbian comics and of women comics?

Gomez: It's great that Lea Delaria and Kate Clinton went on "Arsenio." I guess my problem is that a lot of comedy clubs will do Gay Night instead of trying to integrate queer comics into their regular lineups. I worry that they're doing Gay Night as a money-making idea and that's all. And when the queers stop coming, what will happen to the queer comics?

It's really a lot more fun playing for an audience that has a queer presence than an audience that's all straight people.

When you say there's an explosion of women comics—I did *Comic Relief* last January and that was great. But there were three female stand-ups and how many male stand-ups.

Post: True.

Gomez: The numbers are still pretty bad. The comedy scene is suffering now. A lot of the clubs are closing. The whole business is changing again. I think women will carve out their own scene, their own market, and their own audience base. But all those clubs we were trying to break into are going out of business. I think it's because of the sameness of the comics they were hiring.

Post: What impact will the clubs' closing have on the comedy scene?

Gomez: There won't be as much opportunity. People who aren't really original and who are stealing shit will have to go and get another job. The people who are really artists are going to do it whether or not they're going to make a ton of money or get a sitcom from it. They're going to do stand-up comedy because they have a passion for it and a need for it. Those people will continue, and they'll either make it or not, just like they did in the fifties and sixties. The difference being that it won't just be the domain of straight white men.

Post: Those are all good changes.

Gomez: The advantage that I've had and a lot of my peers have had is that we've had the women's festivals and feminist producers and an incredibly strong network that's not based on money but is based on politics and sisterhood. It's based on ideals. And that network has gotten better and more organized over the years. So we're probably in better shape than someone like Andrew Dice Clay.

Post: You said earlier that you want to break into films and television. Do you want a sitcom? A talk show?

Gomez: No, I don't want a talk show. I want a game show.

Post: You want a game show?

Gomez: Yeah. Maybe "The Divorce Game." Something with dysfunctional families.

Post: What vision do you have for yourself in the next few years?

Gomez: I hope to be working in film.

Post: In more dramatic roles or ironic, humorous roles?

Gomez: Erotic mysteries! [*Laughs*] No. What kind of roles? Anything with a decent part. I don't want to be vacuuming somebody's rug, you know.

Post: Would you take a role like that if you felt you could do such a stellar job with it that it would help your career?

Gomez: I guess if the maid, let's say, killed the whole family, you know, or if the story was about the maid, I could do the maid. But if the maid is just there as a piece of furniture, I cannot do the maid.

Post: What impact do you want your work to have?

Gomez: I'm really just trying to make a living for myself. I just want to be honest about who I am and not lie. I want people to leave the evening feeling satisfied that they got their money's worth.

karen Haber

by Andrea L.T. Peterson

"Every time I mentioned the fact that I wanted to be in the movies, it provoked such laughter and derision from my family—and not just my nuclear family," says comedian Karen Haber, about why her desire to get into show business took her from New York to California. "My aunts, my uncles, my cousins—it was the scream of the Passover seder: 'Oh, Karen's going to go be in the movies!' It was the funniest thing they'd ever heard."

So Haber headed for California. "I was naive enough to think that there weren't another million billion girls wanting to do this," she comments.

"Who would leave their families and the safety of all that just to be in the movies?"

When she got off the plane there were no Hollywood agents waiting to sign her up, and the competition was fierce. "No one," she says, "could have been less interested in me."

While getting into the movies might not have been as funny as her family had thought, it wasn't easy. She took acting classes and made lots of friends. Her friends thought she was funny. "At some point," she explains, "everyone would say to me 'Why don't you just try to be a stand-up?' "

A monologue she wrote for an acting class turned out to be the perfect vehicle. After wearing out the sidewalks and herself, Haber finally arrived at the Comedy Store, where owner Mitzi Shore "just opened up the door wide. She was fabulous. She just said 'Welcome to show business and come on in'."

That was ten years ago. Since then Haber has been performing steadily.

"I found myself through comedy," Haber says. "I'd never really had to think about it, but because my act is about my life, I found out who I was." Haber's comedy career has also affected her relationship with her family. "I got in an incredible relationship with my mother. She loved my act—half of it was about her. She was just thrilled about it. Our relationship changed. We became adult friends, and we had incredible discussions about being women—all the hassles, what a pain in the ass and how fabulous it is."

At first, comedy was just a way to get into show business. Now, says Haber, "comedy is the best thing that ever happened to me."

It's great to be doing work that she loves. And it's great to have the opportunity to be a role model for her one-year-old daughter, Lilly, whom Haber hopes will learn that "a woman can both be a mommy and have a life, be independent and all that stuff." Haber feels that her act, "even though it's really goofy and funny and girlie, girlie," is also very feminist. "It happens to be about my life, but it's really about any woman's life."

That would seem to be the essence of successful comedy—universal truths grounded in personal reality—whether it's growing up, moving away, marrying, divorcing, working or not having a job, having kids or living life without them. And Haber knows a bit about all of those things. "My perfect man," she says, "is smart, funny, good-looking, a good dresser, sensitive, and he won't chase other women. So what I figured out is that my perfect man is gay." Hence, her husband Michael "is not my perfect man … but it's just fine."

Michael may not be her perfect man but he seems pretty good-natured, opting not to take her punch lines personally, as when she tells audiences: "The first time I saw my husband naked I was so excited, I closed my eyes and thought, Here comes my Chippendale poster boy … and I opened my eyes and it was the Michelin man."

The couple tried really hard to have a baby, "including sex," but nothing ever happened. So they went to one of those "nightmare fertility clinics where they charge you twelve million dollars every time your husband jerks off into a jar," but he was too uncomfortable to give a sample. Finally, Haber explains, "to get the sample I had to fly him back home to his old room in his mother's house." After all that, they just decided to adopt.

Now, Lilly Belle, as Haber calls her daughter, "is a woman—a total woman. My girlfriend's baby is a year old and he's not a man, he's still a boy. And I'm sure that's like life: men are always little boys, and my baby is a year old and she's a woman."

Getting into show business has always been her first ambition, but Haber, who has appeared often on TV as well as half a dozen feature films, also harbors a desire "to open a whorehouse for women so we can get it the way *we* really want it. Like, we pay our money and guys pretend they like talking to us and they care about our lives, then they have to hold us real tight and say, 'Oooo, you're so thin'. Even if they've never seen us before, they have to say, 'Have you lost weight?' "

And then we have sex, and right before that fabulous moment, they have to shout, 'I can't believe how great your shoes match your dress!' "

Rhonda Hansome

by Susie Day

Raised by her mom in the tough Bedford-Stuyvesant section of Brooklyn, Rhonda Hansome graduated from Brooklyn College of Performing Arts with a B.A. in speech and theater, fully expecting —and deserving —to sign on as an actress at the Public Theatre, the Negro Ensemble, or La Mama. But offers were few and far between, and when they did come, they were for bit parts: hookers and maids.

"When I came out, everything was all singin', all dancin', all grinnin' for black women," says Hansome. "I just got tired of waiting." She turned to comedy, getting her material from what she saw around her: newspapers, overheard comments, bathroom walls. Hansome worked the streets of New York City, played comedy clubs and learned puppetry from the Muppets' Jim Henson. Over the years, she's opened for superstars Diane Ross, James Brown, the Pointer Sisters, and Anita Baker, and appeared on "Arsenio," "Joan Rivers," and "Caroline's Comedy Club."

Hansome's act, like her life, is about being talented and black. She works off of black culture from an insider's perspective, predicting, for example, that by the year 2000, "calisthenics, aerobics and Nautilus will just be names that black folks call their children." Or she'll fantasize about being at a Michael Jackson concert on the night his nose falls off. Hansome also gets in plenty of zings at the opposite sex. A favorite line is: "A man's got to do what a man's got to do. A woman must do what he can't." She's currently working on *Last Stop Before Dreadlocks*, a one-woman show about her life.

Day: How long have you been doing comedy?

Hansome: Forever.

Day: Are you tired of it?

Hansome: Well, now, I like comedy. Sometimes you can get tired of *doing* comedy. It's a lot of work. One of the things that's exciting about comedy, but is also a downside, is that you never know how it's going to go. Right now, I happen to be very excited about doing it, but sometimes you get tired.

Day: What about it makes you tired?

Hansome: A while back I got tired because I'd lost connection with my sense of creativity and expression. I was doing it for reasons that had nothing to do with that. It was like I was chasing after something that had nothing to do with the reason why I started.

Day: I'd think that the pressure to make people laugh is anti-creative, in a way.

Hansome: That depends on where the pressure comes from. I was leaving my son's school—I'm copresident of the PTA—and a kid saw my jacket with "Comic Strip Live" on the back and said, "Say something funny!" I looked at him and said, "Your grades." It was incredibly funny, to me. The kid looked stunned. It was a variation on that stock line where someone says, "Tell me a joke," and you go, "Look down." I was laughing the whole day over that little interchange.

Day: When did you decide you wanted to be a comic?

Hansome: I'd graduated from Brooklyn College with a B.A. in speech and theater but I couldn't get work as an actress. I got tired of waiting for auditions, then waiting to be cast in things that didn't pay or where I was the hooker or the maid. Then I saw a woman comedian on a cable show, and I thought, I can do that. And I don't have to wait for someone to choose me to do that. I can start doing that. And that's what I did.

All I wanted comedy to do was get me jobs as an actress. But I got waylaid by comedy. Because I got appreciated in it. I also got paid. And it was a chance for me to express myself.

Day: A lot of the material in your act is very political.

Hansome: I talk about what interests me. Some people used to tell me that it frightened them that my act was very racial. And I felt like asking, "When I'm talking about Catholicism, exactly how was I racial? When I'm talking about sanitary napkins, exactly how was I racial?" I'm a multidimensional, multifaceted person. I talk about topics that interest me, from my own perspective.

Day: What's the toughest audience for you?

Hansome: That's hard to pinpoint. I've been promoting Southern Comfort, which has been great. It's like a little "chitlin circuit," promoting it in black bars and nightclubs. Last Thursday, I was in this little bar with a very small audience. They had difficulty with the microphone. Finally I said, "I'll do it without a mike." They had no stage. I was standing on a chair in front of the bar, yelling down the bar. And I had a great, great time. The next night, it was a more upscale audience but I didn't enjoy myself. It's so mercurial. I call it the X-factor. You just don't know when it's going to be bad, when it's going to suck, when you're going to wish you'd never even started.

I can't say it's one type of audience. I have nights in the Catskills where I kill, where there's no one under forty in the audience. Or I could be with teenagers and have them not know what I'm talking about.

Day: Do you try out your material on your friends or family?

Hansome: My son's a good audience; my husband is a terrible audience. I'm not the kind of person who is always "on," but if there's a line I'm particularly excited about, I might throw it into a conversation and see what the reaction is.

Day: Comedy is still pretty much a male-dominated field, right? Do you get much support from other women comics?

Hansome: Recently I was in the middle of a writing session with my writing partner, and I started talking about having been a member of the Friars Club, about how weird it was being a woman in a male-dominated context like that. It was one of the few places I've been that I haven't taken a leadership position. I was telling him about going in there and sitting around and being overcome by the scent of Polident, stuff like that. And he looked at me and said, "Do you talk about this in your act? The women in your audience would probably like to hear this."

That struck me because very often men comedians don't recognize that a woman has said something funny. But I'll be with women performers and say something funny, and they'll say, "Do you say that in your act? I like that." That's support! That's the kind of support that's basic, you know?

Day: Do men approach humor differently than women do? A woman can be on the floor laughing at something, and it will be almost embarrassing for the guys. Is there such a thing as "women's humor"?

Hansome: No, because when I look at someone like Ellen Degeneres or Paula Poundstone—I mean, I could not go on for twenty minutes about a cat. I'm sorry, no, thank you. Especially since I'm allergic to them. I think the best use for a cat is a doorstop or something. So it's not "women's humor," it's just a different approach. Ellen also does a bit about waiting for an elevator that I love, because it's part of my experience.

Day: Roseanne said recently that comedy is the last free-speech art form. What do you think about that?

Hansome: Well it is, if you've got your own show. [*Laughs*] If you're the biggest producer on the network, sure. When I do a TV shot, I'm censored. I don't think I could talk about masturbating on the road on the "Caroline's Comedy Hour" I'm about to do. What you can say depends upon your venue, your audience, whether you're network or cable, which cable station. It's so many things.

Day: So what do you end up performing, then, when you go on a show like "Arsenio"?

Hansome: Some kind of homogenized, censored version of my act that's just recognizable enough that I can take it off the TV and send it out to people and say, "This is what I do."

When I went on "Arsenio"—this was a very important event for me—I had a great time and I killed. I mean, I absolutely killed. Then I got the report back that I hadn't "surprised" them.

But I wasn't going to start out on my first late night foray experimenting: "You know what happened to me on my way to the studio tonight, Arsenio?" I didn't want to take that risk, and be sitting there with people saying, "Why is she on the show? She ain't said nothing funny yet."

Day: What's your idea of success?

Hansome: When I started out, my idea of success was that I'd be doing comedy for maybe four to six months, then I'd be on Carson. Now I'm just trying to take things a step at a time. Right now I'm excited about writing my one-woman show, *Last Stop Before Dreadlocks*. I'm talking about my life.

I'm trying to get closer to my own truth and what I'm about. It's been hard, accepting who and what I am, but more and more I'm starting to like me, with all my warts and flaws. And the beauty, too. I used to keep wanting to get to a place where everyone would give me what I need. I expected to get a certain kind of recognition and a three-picture deal and my own TV show, whatever. But the truth of the matter is that I'm the only one who can give me what I need.

Day: Who has inspired or influenced you as a comic?

Hansome: Gene Shepard, a radio personality, was very influential during my childhood. We didn't have television, and I listened to him all the time. Lily Tomlin and Lucille Ball. And Joan Rivers. It's frightening—there have been times in my life when I've been onstage in the Catskills and I've, like, felt her spirit or something.

Day: You've channeled Joan Rivers! You've been on her show, right?

Hansome: Yeah. She's been very sweet to me. I did the movie reviews on her show for a while. It was wonderful. I liked working with her a lot.

Day: Do you get tired of being alone onstage?

Hansome: Oh, *no!* I love it. I just did a show at a university, and having that big ol' stage was just wonderful. I love a big stage. When I was at Radio City Music Hall, it was like, "Hey! I am in *show business*!" You know? I love that big stage.

Day: You've opened for some very big stars: Aretha Franklin, the Pointer Sisters, Smokey Robinson, Anita Baker. What's that like?

Hansome: It's wonderful! I love it. I'm a part of something that's huge, that has its built-in audience. I get to do my little thing, and then I can watch someone like Diana Ross or the Pointer Sisters, people I used to pay to go see when I was a child. To work with them and talk with them—I love that. It's fun, and nice money. They all treated me very well.

Day: What do you do to inspire yourself as a comedian?

Hansome: I read. I read magazines, tear things out of the paper. I listen to the radio a lot. I look and listen to people a lot. I read bathroom walls. I just absorb, and when something hits me, I go, [*snaps fingers*] "I got a bit!"

Day: Do you worry about being too "anti" anything in your comedy? Antimale, antiwhite, antirich?

Hansome: No. I've got fifty-five, sixty more good years left, and if people don't understand me, fuck 'em if they can't take a joke. In my act I say, "I don't believe in male-bashing, because hitting a man below the belt just diminishes his mental abilities." I *love* that line. Why should I worry about how people might take it? Whether I worry about it or not, somebody will always think I'm racist or antimale or antiwhite, ageist, sexist, whatever. So what's the use of worrying about it? I used to focus on how people were going to take it. Now I try not to censor myself. I'm trying to enjoy myself a lot more because, hey, if I don't, that X-factor could get me at any time.

Geri Jewell

by Janet Wollman Rusoff

In 1981, Geri Jewell, who was born with cerebral palsy, made show business history as the first disabled person to land a recurring role on a television series. That show was NBC's popular "The Facts of Life," and Geri played rich Blair Warner's cerebral-palsied cousin, Geri.

At twenty-four, Geri was carving out a career in stand-up comedy, when "Facts" producer Norman Lear caught her act and hired her for his highly rated show. Geri stayed four years and went on to costar in the movie *Two of a Kind* with George Burns and Robbie Benson, and be booked as the opening act for the likes of Robert Goulet and Judy Collins. She's also a busy lecturer and motivational speaker on attitudinal change in the workplace.

Geri can make spontaneous comedy out of anything—from trivia to tragedy—and never be cruel or mean-spirited. It isn't that, as a professional comedian, she's always "on." It's just that she views the absurdities of life from a marvelously humorous perspective, and she's creative, quick and articulate enough to turn her sharp observations into funny, witty stuff.

Rusoff: Where have you been appearing lately?

Jewell: I've been doing stand-up in L.A. at the Improv and the Ice House and also in New York. My husband and I are moving to Las Vegas in January, and I intend to do more stand-up there, at the hotels. But this month is Disability Awareness Month, and so I am booked solid. [*Laughs*] I'm doing a lot of training seminars.

Rusoff: You have an extremely active lifestyle. Having cerebral palsy hasn't stopped you from reaching out and experiencing life to the fullest. What are the positives to having CP?

Jewell: It's taught me tolerance, and patience with other people. It's allowed me not to be judgmental of others. Because I have CP, I get mistaken for being on drugs, having mental retardation, having mental illness, being under the influence of alcohol. It's taught me not to be so quick to assume things about anybody. People assume also that because I'm well known I'm probably stuck up and conceited.

Rusoff: For example?

Jewell: I remember once in Chicago, these kids who recognized me from "The Facts of Life" were chasing me down the street. They thought I didn't want to have anything to do with them. But the fact is I'm hearing-impaired—a lot of people don't know that because I don't advertise it—and it was pouring that day, so I didn't hear them calling my name. I got frightened when they started running after me, and I kept running faster— I didn't know why they were after me. Finally they caught up with me at a red light, and they started yelling how stuck up I was and what a snoot. All they wanted was my autograph. They kept yelling my name, but I couldn't hear them.

Rusoff: You wear hearing aids, don't you?

Jewell: Only 60 percent of the time. In some situations, like with background noise, they don't help. I'm reading your lips. You have a nice, low voice, and that's easier for me to hear. I do pretty well, but occasionally I screw up.

Rusoff: Did anything funny ever happen because you misunderstood someone?

Jewell: Oh, boy, yes. Kathy Buckley—a hearing-impaired stand-up comic—and I have something called "deaf lunch." We've done this several times. We'll call each other on the phone and set a place where we're going to meet, and it ends up that we're each sitting in a different town waiting for the other person—because she heard one restaurant and I heard another. We think that we're being stood up. But then we'll call each other later and ask what the other had for lunch: "Well, it was real fun. Nice if we could get together again sometime." So, yeah, I screw up.

Rusoff: What was your comedy act like when you first started doing stand-up?

Jewell: My first routine was in October of 1978. I walked out onstage, and it was very quiet. I'd been introduced as a man. With a name like Geri, there's a fifty/fifty chance that will happen. So I walked onstage, and number one, I wasn't a man and, number two, I looked highly under the influence. You can imagine how tense that moment was, and the first thing that came out of my mouth was: "I'm not sure about you people, but I've heard an awful lot about gays coming out of the closet lately. What you probably haven't heard is how these CP people have been coming out of the closet. But let's just keep that between you and me. I don't want Anita Bryant to hear about it; she'll get on another bandwagon and say, 'We can't allow these CP people teaching our children. They'll influence them, and before you know it, all our kids will be walking around like this'." That was my opening line back in 1978.

Rusoff: Were you nervous?

Jewell: Oh, just slightly! You could hear a pin drop when I got up there. Being so nervous made my CP 100 percent worse. I had major CP. [*Laughs*] So much involuntary movement. And I was wearing a T-shirt that said "I Don't Have Cerebral Palsy, I'm Drunk."

Rusoff: When Norman Lear hired you to be on "Facts of Life," it was unheard of to cast someone with a disability such as CP in a TV series, wasn't it?

Jewell: It was similar to African-Americans in the sixties. They weren't cast unless it was specifically a stereotypical African-American role. The whole concept of my coming on the show was basically to kick off the International Year of the Disabled, in 1981. The first episode was probably the best; all the following ones didn't have nearly the impact. It was about Blair's cousin with CP coming to visit. She didn't want her to, and everyone thought it was because she was ashamed of having a cousin with CP. But it really wasn't that at all: she was jealous of her cousin with CP because of all the attention she got. There was nothing she could ever do to compete with me, which I thought was very insightful.

Rusoff: Did the succeeding episodes focus on your having CP?

Jewell: They tried to get away from it, but I don't think they did so successfully. I was before my time. There was no such thing as having a person with a disability on TV every week, like today with Chris Burke on "Life Goes On" or Marlee Matlin in "Reasonable Doubts." It just wasn't done back then, and there was the fear that every time I was on the show it would take the attention away from another scenario. They underestimated the fact that over a period of time, if you look at something often enough, you eventually don't see it. [*Laughs*] If you see every week that I have CP, it's not going to be any big deal.

Rusoff: So taking the focus off your CP wasn't accomplished?

Jewell: It was their attempt to accomplish it, but they didn't do it completely. The full-blown risk was something they took with Chris Burke, but not with me. They chose not to. But Chris was still sort of a token "super person with a disability who made it." It's integration into the entertainment industry, as opposed to being mainstreamed. There's a big difference.

Rusoff: Have you now been mainstreamed into the entertainment industry?

Jewell: Most of my mainstreaming has been in nightclub work, not the entertainment industry as a whole—not in acting. Basically, all that clubs care about is, Are you funny? If you have CP, if you're African American, whatever you are, they don't care. All they care about is if you're funny.

Rusoff: In these days of X-rated comedians, you do a pretty clean act, don't you?

Jewell: I'm one of the cleanest comedians in this town. I can't even get work at some nightclubs because I'm too clean. The only racy material I've done is an orgasm joke, and that wasn't for shock value. That was because there's an assumption that people with disabilities are asexual. I thought if I can incorporate some kind of sexual material without being dirty and communicate that people with disabilities are sexual beings like everybody else, my work is done. [*Laughs*]

Rusoff: What's been the roughest time for you?

Jewell: Coming home from appearing at the White House and having no money. From 1985 to '87 were such incredibly painful years. I was so disillusioned and lost. In l985 I was asked by Nancy Reagan to appear at the White House. At the time, I had no money. I was on my way to the White House but I couldn't pay my rent. [Laughs] I was in a lot of pain, my career wasn't going well, and I couldn't understand for the life of me why I was going to Washington. But I was the most visible person with a disability in the country at that time, so my appearance was important, because then they could say, "See, disabled people are succeeding." And I thought it was very hypocritical of me. I was angry for their not wanting the truth, and the truth was that I wasn't successful materialistically.

Rusoff: When was the last time you worked in Hollywood?

Jewell: I didn't work here from l984 to '89.

Rusoff: What do you think has been the main problem in getting acting jobs?

Jewell: There is not much opportunity for an actor with a disability. And practically every audition I've ever been on has been for a role where the person has mental retardation. I accepted one, the made-for-TV movie "Two of a Kind." But nine out of ten times when I go on these auditions, I do not get the part, and usually they'll say something like, "Well, she has too much intelligence. You can see it in her eyes; she's too bright!" What a slap in the face! The point I'm making is that because I have CP—and so many times people with mental retardation do have CP—they think this is a wonderful role for me to play. Now, if I worked hard enough at it—I'm an actress—I could wipe that intelligent look off my face. [Laughs]

Rusoff: Your mother died of cancer recently. Has her death brought any insights or changed your attitude about life?

Jewell: It's made me realize how precious our life span is. I know that I'm here for a reason and that I have a lot of work to do. That's one of the reasons I do attitudinal training in the employment of persons with disabilities. And I've written a lot of things about attitudinal change in the entertainment industry, which I'm trying to sell. I don't sit by a phone waiting for someone to call me for another disabled role. I don't have time to play that game. I used to, for years, and almost died because of it. I believe I'm here in part to try to unify people and eliminate prejudice and discrimination. Maybe I couldn't have gone on this mission without having CP.

Rusoff: You were very close to your mother.

Jewell: Yes, and I miss her tremendously. Two of the things my mom gave me was a sense of purpose and a sense of humor. If I didn't have a sense of purpose, or a sense of humor, I wouldn't have been able to survive Hollywood. It's so limited in how it perceives people's abilities. But I decided, instead of letting it destroy me, to become tougher, get all the skills under my belt, learn what the issues are about disability, and go out into the world and help change people's minds. And if I was meant to have a TV series, do another film, or whatever, it will happen. But I'm not sitting at home waiting for someone to hand me something. I'm out here trying to make the world a better place.

Rusoff: But that started before the death of your mother.

Jewell: Yes, I was doing it to one degree or another. But when I was on "Facts of Life" I was only in my twenties and emotionally a little kid. I didn't have the maturity to realize that "Facts" wasn't going to transcend me to nondisability. I thought, My god, I'm on a national sitcom, I'm known by millions of people, and I can be accepted socially in the real world. How naive. How young. What I failed to realize was that being in that situation was only going to make me a super disabled person! You don't have CP; now you have Super CP! So it gave me the opposite of what I thought it would, which led to despair and disillusionment. Finally, God hit me on the head and said, "Geri, do you get it yet? You have to stop denying you have cerebral palsy and start being a real person. Don't be phony." And that saved my life.

Nancy Kennedy

by Roz Warren

Nancy Kennedy is a Los Angeles television reporter and producer turned comic. She's also tried her hand at screenwriting, activism, and acting (she appeared on "General Hospital" for two years). Comedy is a tough profession, but for Kennedy it's even tougher. Because she's in a wheelchair, getting onto a comedy club stage can be a major challenge.

When Kennedy finally makes it up onto the stage, she'll confront the audience, growling, "All right, who's the asshole who parked in my spot?" It gets a big laugh, and it sets the tone for her set, which is acerbic and uncompromising. "Yeah, it's me," she sneers, "that courageous inspiration. Do I sound a little bitter? You should have seen me before the accident. I've mellowed!"

"A lot of disabled comics are self-effacing," says Kennedy. "They think that'll put the audience at ease. Me, I'm tired of reverence. I want them to see me as my friends see me: an ordinary schmuck who can be nice and nasty just like everyone else." Her comic persona, Kennedy says, is "Bitter Woman." And she's got plenty to complain about, like all the stereotypes and assumptions she battles daily. "When I tell people I was married for seven years, they always assume my husband was disabled too, which he wasn't," she says. Because people often think of people with disabilities as sexless, Kennedy makes sure to joke about her sex life: "I like to be on top—and for that I have to rent a crane. So for all you women who complain that it's unwieldy to carry a diaphragm on a date …"

Kennedy also jokes about girl stuff, like bras, visits to the gynecologist, and L.A. hairdos. But she gets the most mileage out of mocking the insensitivity of the nondisabled public. "I love it when people come up to me on the street and say, 'So how'd it happen?' " she says. "What other stranger do people go up to and ask, 'Excuse me, could you please tell me all about the most traumatic thing that's happened to you in twenty years?' " She continues: "People ask me, 'Were you depressed?' Nah—I did it for the preferred parking!"

Kennedy's act can make people uncomfortable. That's the point. "A rabbi told me that when the Messiah comes, I won't be in a wheelchair," Kennedy observes. "I said, 'When the Messiah comes, you won't need me *not* to be in one;.'"

Lisa Kron

by Roz Warren

We've all had moments of acute embarrassment, moments when we've said or done something so truly awful that we long to forget about it forever, instantly. Lisa Kron has done just the opposite: she's remembered every single one of those excruciating episodes and turned them into a heartrending, hilarious performance piece, *One Hundred and One Humiliating Stories*. (Actually, the show includes only seventeen stories, the comic admits up front, "but each story has several humiliations!") It's a show that captures the joy of discovering that you've been walking around the office of a snooty corporate law firm with the back of your dress hitched up over the elastic top of your panty hose so that your rump is exposed. Or the experience of dropping a sanitary pad in a high school hallway on the way to the bathroom. ("Nobody picked it up—not even the *guidance counselors*.") Kron also celebrates what she calls "geeky celebrity encounters," including an awkward meeting with Sigourney Weaver at a cocktail party.

The piece is structured around Kron's thoughts about being invited to appear at her tenth high school reunion in Lansing, Michigan. Kron, a self-described "Big Lesbian," shares with the audience the various ways she might reveal (or conceal) this part of her identity, including the possibility of beginning her address with the words: "Members of the class of 1979, beloved faculty, honored guests—I am a Big New York City Lesbian." *New York Newsday* said about the show: "The tension between the bold performer and the frightened Midwest teenager inside is pungently and poignantly revealed."

Kron, who is also one-fifth of the performance group Five Lesbian Brothers, has been working as a solo performer since 1984. Her other comic monologues include *All My Hopes and Dreams* and *Facing Life's Problems*.

Maxine Lapiduss

by Deni Kasrel

Many comedians cite a saga of having had a tough childhood, in which some important aspect of their personality was squelched. Somehow the experience led them to the comedy stage, where they could laugh at life and also gain empowerment as the center of attention in front of a large crowd.

Maxine Lapiduss enjoyed many years as a stand-up, but she has no woe-begone tale to tell. She had a happy childhood, and her parents raised her to have high self-esteem. Comedy for Lapiduss was just something she enjoyed and was good at. It was fun to be funny, no big psych-out going on here.

This doesn't mean the content of her humor is all happy talk. She may be well-adjusted, but the world at large sure isn't, and like many comics, Maxine is plenty pissed about this predicament. She's angry that the society we live in is fraught with injustice, poverty, and crime in the streets. Of course, she acknowledges, no one wants to hear a bunch of ragging about all that stuff. So she takes these topics, wraps them with laughter, and *voila*, people listen.

The daughter of two entertainers, this funny gal knows what it takes to hold a crowd's interest. She did so as a stand-up for many years, and she's been an in-demand comic writer for some time. Lapiduss's talents have been tapped by Roseanne, Lily Tomlin, Sandra Bernhard, and Tim Allen. Her witty words have been used on numerous television shows: she was story editor for "Dear John," a producer for "Roseanne," and co-executive producer of "Home Improvement." She's currently based at Warner Brothers Television, where she is engaged in several projects.

Kasrel: I hear that you're currently working on two sitcoms.

Lapiduss: I've sold one, "Doing Life," to CBS. It's about a female parole officer in New York City. Rhea Perlman is interested in doing it, and she's my first choice. I've also signed a two-year deal to create a sitcom called "Salad Days" for Warner Brothers. I'm collaborating on "Salad Days" with a young comic from Minneapolis, Colleen Kruse. She's only twenty-five, but she's been a stand-up comic for quite a few years, and she's doing great. The show is loosely based on her stand-up and on her life. She got pregnant when she was nineteen and the father was seventeen, and she had the baby. She went on welfare and she worked at a diner. There are so many young women in this country right now in the same predicament.

Kasrel: Whoopi Goldberg was a welfare mother.

Lapiduss: Yeah, exactly. The characters in this diner where Colleen worked were hilarious. It's this pit of a place in Minneapolis called Mickey's. We sort of based it on them. Hopefully, it'll get picked up by NBC, and we'll do a pilot for a series.

Kasrel: How did you come up with the concept of the show about the parole officer?

Lapiduss: Reading the newspaper. All the crime is just overwhelming. I thought, How can I really say something with this stuff? In real life, a parole officer is in charge of people who've come out of jail, everyone from petty thieves to mass murderers. It's the parole officer's job to try to help them assimilate back into society. There are groups called Lifers Groups that parole officers are in charge of. There are endless comic possibilities in this. I had a Jean Harris-like woman who's shot her lover come into the group. I had a postal employee who chopped up his supervisor and UPSed him to thirty locations worldwide. I had all of these different ideas that aren't really that far off from what happens in the news every day.

It's very dark humor, but it's really funny. What's unique about the show is that we're dealing in a comedic way with all this stuff that's actually happening right now. The reality of it is so much more bizarre and strange than you could ever dream up.

Kasrel: Do you feel that doing this show enables you to say something constructive about the topic?

Lapiduss: I was always socially aware as a comic, although I was never out to make a point; I wasn't a "woman homemaker comic" or a "lesbian comic" or a representative of any other very particular viewpoint. But I did try to illuminate some of the struggles of everyday living. That's what I'm attracted to writing about. That's why I worked on "Roseanne" for two years, and why I put up with a lot of what I had to put up with to stay there.

I'm drawn to writing things that have a consciousness to them, but of course the most important thing is that it's funny. Otherwise, who's going to listen?

Kasrel: When you write for someone like Roseanne, do you have to write differently than when you're writing for yourself?

Lapiduss: Sure. I'd write a different line for Roseanne or for Lily Tomlin than I'd write for myself, and I've written for both of them. It's like playwriting. If you're writing for different characters in a play, you write in the voices of those characters.

Kasrel: Is your comedy based pretty much on your own approach to life?

Lapiduss: Quite frankly, in the past several years my stand-up has taken a back seat to my writing. But certain things just happen to you. I get fueled by the injustices of life, by all the insanity involved in just trying to function. I feel a lot like Charlie Chaplin in *Modern Times*, dealing with mechanized modern society. I'm overwhelmed with what you have to deal with. You walk in your house and your alarm goes off. The phone is ringing and you're disconnecting people, and then you're trying to turn the TV off, but you can't find the remote control—it just takes over your life.

Kasrel: Is looking at the insanity of trying to function a key to your own comedy?

Lapiduss: It's about one woman struggling against the injustices of society, one person looking at society and how it's changing. The other big influence is money, because what most people struggle with is that they can't keep up financially.

Kasrel: Are there comics whose work has influenced you?

Lapiduss: Growing up, I was influenced by Joan Rivers, certainly, and Alan King. I thought Flip Wilson was incredible, because he was really talking about his life experience. I still think Richard Pryor is brilliant, and I love Roseanne. Roseanne filled a void for women that was so enormous. Before she hit, there was nobody telling it like it is from that point of view.

Kasrel: Do you consider your work political or feminist?

Lapiduss: Some of the "Roseanne" or "Home Improvement" episodes I've written are very much from a feminist's point of view, or a humanist's point of view. It's very tough at times for women to have a certain amount of respect or equality in the workplace, but *everybody* encounters a lot of injustices during the course of their day.

Kasrel: Can you give an example of a "Roseanne" episode you worked on that you'd consider feminist or humanist?

Lapiduss: We won an award from the Gay and Lesbian Anti-Defamation League for an episode of "Roseanne" I wrote with Martin Mull about his character, Leon, who was Roseanne's boss. Leon came out in the show, but we did it in the last three pages of the script. The show wasn't about "Oh, my God, Roseanne's boss is gay!" Instead it focused on a lot of things happening in Roseanne's life, and as a side issue everyone was wondering why Leon wasn't going to go out with a woman they all really liked. They couldn't figure out why *he* didn't like her. Then at the very end of the show his boyfriend came and picked him up. It was never really commented on, it just happened. If you blinked you missed it.

That's how life really is. Sometimes things get a bit overdone in sitcoms. We feel we only have twenty-two minutes to tell a story, so we have to do it really big so people will get it. But the better shows are still the shows that are very subtle in the way they present their topic.

Kasrel: You've been both a stand-up comic and a comedy writer. Can you compare the two?

Lapiduss: When you're performing stand-up, you take on a different persona. You're more "out there." You have to be more confident, to have some bravado. You feel as though you're prizefighting every night: "I'm going out there and I'm going to do a good show and I'm going to be tough." That's great, and that's a lot of fun. But as a comedy writer—well, one big thing is I don't have to wear lipstick when I go to work. I don't have to get dressed up. I sit around with a bunch of people all day and we try to crack each other up. It's a pretty good way to live, to make a lot of money to sit around and crack jokes.

Working on a sitcom, though, you tend to work twenty hours a day. As a stand-up, you work an hour or half an hour a night. I had a much freer existence as a performer.

Kasrel: But you had the pressure of being in front of people.

Lapiduss: That's the trade-off. One reason I went into stand-up was because you have some control over your own destiny. You can work solo. You can book yourself for gigs, and you don't have to depend on somebody else to cast you in a show. So if what you want to do is perform, stand-up has advantages over acting.

For years, I was both writing scripts and doing stand-up. But I didn't really need to perform, and I knew if I focused on my script and TV writing and film writing I could say what I wanted to say and get my voice out that way. Part of it is about how to make a living. As a stand-up you make a certain amount of money, but unless you start really hitting huge, you don't make a lot. You can make more money as a writer.

Kasrel: You have a B.F.A. in acting. As a child did you think you were going to become an actor, or a comic?

Lapiduss: My mom is an actress and a stand-up. She's great. Before I was born, she worked for many years at the Concord, and she did the borscht belt. She's very much like Bea Arthur—tall, and sort of imposing, with grey hair. She's got a great face for takes, and she tells great dialect stories. I got an ear for that from her. I was a mimic and all that stuff when I was a kid. My father was a bass player and a drummer. When I was growing up I really thought I was going to be a singer and a musician.

Kasrel: How did you start performing stand-up?

Lapiduss: When I was fifteen there was a great comedy club in Pittsburgh called the Portfolio. That's where Dennis Miller started. This was in the mid-seventies. I went down there one night. I was broke, and I was very tall for my age; I had a guitar, and I sang some songs. Dennis was hosting. He thought I was great, so he booked me on a local kiddie show he had in Pittsburgh. I did some little bits on his show, and I started to think, Well, this is cool. I could really do this.

I put myself through school at Carnegie Mellon doing one-night gigs around Pittsburgh. By the time I left school, I had a two-and-a-half-hour act. I was pretty well established, so I went to New York and tried out at the Improv, and I got on. They had a house band and I knew I could sing, so I got on there, and at Catch, and at all these clubs as a singer.

Kasrel: Were you singing serious songs? Funny songs?

Lapiduss: I sang ballads, but I'd introduce the songs with comedy. People started saying, "You should do more comedy." Eventually, the act evolved to where it was was 90 percent comedy with one song. And that was that.

Kasrel: Your act includes a lot of funny material about mothers, and both the sitcoms you've developed are about mothers. Do you have a particular interest in motherhood, or family?

Lapiduss: I wouldn't go that far. Most TV is based on a family unit—that's what you can sell. There are two kinds of shows on TV: family shows and workplace shows. My shows have both elements going for them. They're mostly workplace shows, but family life is there as well.

What's unique about the family unit in my two shows is that the fathers aren't involved. In "Doing Time," there was a very bitter divorce, so this woman is living with her mother and her kid in her mother's apartment in Queens. "Salad Days" is another unconventional family, because this girl is a young, single teenage mom. There are no men in that situation either. She and her friends form the family unit, and the people who work at this diner are also a family unit.

I had a wonderful family life. My parents have been married for forty-five years. They're very together, and they were a wonderful influence on me. But the reality is that very few people have that now. What's important to put out there is that you can still have stability. It doesn't matter how many parents you have; what matters is who the parent is.

Kasrel: And the shows are based on reality, as opposed to something like "The Cosby Show," which is rather idealized.

Lapiduss: I like comedy to come from a clearly realistic point of view. I want to see stuff on TV that relates to my experience. Some people watch TV to escape; they'd rather see an ideal family. Part of the key to the success of "Home Improvement" is that it isn't a reality-based show. When I went there to work, I tried to write stories for them that would be a little more hard-hitting, about solving problems that families actually have. But they really didn't want to do that kind of show. On "Roseanne," that's all they want to do.

Kasrel: You can't say "Roseanne" avoids real issues.

Lapiduss: There are very few shows that are smart and funny and deal with life as it really is.

Kasrel: Your primary focus these days is on writing for television, but you came up performing live comedy. What do you enjoy about doing stand-up?

Lapiduss: Just knowing you can make people laugh. That's a very powerful thing. I got hooked from a very young age. You're up onstage and you say something funny and you see five hundred people with their shoulders moving up and down at the same time because they're laughing. Just seeing rows and rows of teeth and different shoulders going up and down—It's very odd. People are very vulnerable when they laugh. They're very open and relaxed. Most of the time when you meet people, they're very tight and closed. Their arms are folded. Then you say something that they feel they can open up to, and that's a very powerful experience. That's what gets you hooked. It certainly did for me.

Kasrel: Does it have something to do with the fact that they're paying all this attention to you?

Lapiduss: The attention isn't what's important. It's getting people to be open to what I'm saying. I've been doing this for twelve years; you reach a certain level of expertise. You start to figure out a rhythm. You time your material so there's a real ebb and flow. You start with a joke that isn't a huge joke, then you do a nice joke. Then you do a little bit bigger joke, and then you do a huge joke, and then you do a little bit smaller joke. It's really like waves and waves of laughter. You try to get to a point where it's well orchestrated and people have a great time. But what's powerful for me is just getting people to a relaxed, open place where they will take that information in.

Kasrel: Are there things you say or do that are designed to help get people in that frame of mind?

Lapiduss: I didn't mention Bette Midler, who also is a very big influence on me. I saw her show when I was fifteen. She sang a ballad called "Hello In There." Her introduction to that song was the most perfect, perfect bit I've ever seen anyone do. She tells this whole story about walking down Forty-Second Street in the middle of July and meeting a homeless woman with a fried egg on her head. It goes on and on, and it's *really funny*, and you laugh and laugh, and it has all this pathos in it, and you laugh and it has more pathos, and then all of a sudden she hooks you in. Then she starts singing the ballad. And my heart just stopped.

To be able to manipulate an audience that way, from complete laughter to complete tears, is truly brilliant. Very few people can do that. I wanted to be able to do that, too.

Kasrel: It's interesting that you were aware of what was happening. A lot of people wouldn't necessarily recognize what she was doing.

Lapiduss: I certainly recognized her artistry. It was brilliant.

Kasrel: You have a bit in your act that's very critical of the song Madonna sings about keeping her baby.

Lapiduss: The problem I have with that song is that it's so irresponsible. So many of the images that television puts out are so irresponsible. If your audience is twelve- or fourteen-year-old girls—wake up and have a brain when you're putting stuff out there.

Kasrel: I've heard comics say, "It's not my responsibility. I can say whatever I want because it's just a joke. It's comedy. It's not real."

Lapiduss: Anybody can get up on a stage and say "shit" and "fuck." Anybody can get up on a stage and say "blow me" nine or ten times. It's one thing if you're using expletives or being aggressive to make a point. But most of them just get up there and think, Richard Pryor is dirty, so I'm going to be dirty, too.

Kasrel: What's the difference? He's using the profanity to make a point?

Lapiduss: He's brilliant, and he's insightful. There are still times he says things about women that I'm not thrilled about, but he deserves to talk, and I think he's very, very aware. Also, when Richard Pryor's movies came out, they had R ratings and X ratings on them. Now we're putting that kind of material on MTV and twelve-year-old kids are seeing it.

Kasrel: Do you really think that television has an impact on kids? Some people don't think art can really make people change their minds about anything, or make much of a difference.

Lapiduss: Oh, I think it makes an enormous difference. Watching "I Love Lucy" completely changed my life.

There are images from that show that I saw when I was eight years old that are still so strong. Like when Lucy first told her husband she was pregnant with Little Ricky. They're dancing and Ricky is singing "We're Having a Baby, My Baby and Me." The real emotion that they felt as a very loving couple was great. There were also just the most hilarious comedic moments from that show. I still think it's the best sitcom ever.

Kasrel: What funny moments do you remember?

Lapiduss: Remember the candy episode? Lucy was going to get a job, and Ricky is making rice and he's making fifty thousand cups of rice per person. The whole thing is about putting a value on what your wife does. A lot of people don't realize that housework is really hard. Making the little things big is what we tried to do on "Roseanne" and on "Home Improvement." You make the little victories big. That's what stand-up is brilliant at: to take the underdog and say, "This happened to me and isn't this insane? But look how I dealt with this situation and isn't this funny? And you can deal with it this way, too, if you're smart."

Kasrel: A lot of the humor in your act is about being Jewish. Why do you choose to focus on that?

Lapiduss: I think Jewish humor is brilliant. Just the rhythm of it and the storytelling aspect of it fascinate me. And my mom was a great storyteller. That's really a unique talent, to be able to tell a five-minute story. The punch line isn't even that great. It's getting there; it's all the little laughs along the way to the punch line.

Being Jewish is just a part of who I am. It's not like I think, I'm going to do a Jewish joke now. It's part of me, so if I'm presenting myself then that's obviously in the mix.

Kasrel: What's your take on the current stand-up scene?

Lapiduss: One thing that interests me is that the whole way of telling a joke has completely altered over the last fifty years. With Jewish humor, or any humor that was a story kind of a joke, you'd tell the story and then the punch line made you laugh because it was unexpected. You took a left turn when you got to the punch line and it wasn't where you thought you were going, and that's why you got the laugh.

Now, with the Velveeta-ization of comedy, where everybody does five minutes on a comedy-club stage, it's all about "Does this ever happen to you?" "Don't all men do this?" "Don't all women relate?" It's completely changing the basis of the humor. Now you want people to relate to your experience. People aren't doing jokes that take left turns. They're doing jokes that are completely dead-on. Which to me are not funny, because you know exactly where they're going. They're going to do a Seven-Eleven joke. Then they're going to do a joke about the Indian guy working there, you know?

A big reason I stopped doing stand-up is that I didn't want to do that kind of fast food comedy—doing topics that everybody can relate to. I love to tell stories. But it takes time to weave a good story.

Kasrel: Instead you're writing for sitcoms so that you can tell a story?

Lapiduss: Even though that story time is shorter and shorter as well, from thirty minutes down to twenty-two minutes, you can stay on one topic, and you can take side trips. You just haven't got the time to do that if you have to get the big joke out, get the big laugh, and move on.

Kasrel: I loved your Jewish-mother rap.

Lapiduss: Thank you. Everybody loves that bit—Protestants, Catholics, blacks. You don't have to be Jewish. Everybody has a mom who drives them nuts.

Kasrel: Is getting that kind of positive feedback from your audience part of the appeal of performing? You've said the audience is able to relax and that it's a release of tension. As a performer, do you get a similar release?

Lapiduss: I think that's the biggest reason why you do it. I have a lot of things to say and that's a great way to let off steam.

Kasrel: But I wouldn't characterize you as an angry comic. There are some comics who clearly come across as angry people.

Lapiduss: I'm not an angry person, but there are a lot of things that anger me about society and about the way we deal with each other. If I can have the opportunity to talk about it, I am going to talk about it. In fact, I'll probably go back to performing soon because I have a whole new crop of things that are pissing me off. It's always good to get to the point where you're kind of flipping out because you are so nuts about stuff that you want to talk about it. For me, that's the only way to do it.

Lynn Lavner

In a world where "going mainstream" has become the end of the rainbow for many performers, Lynn Lavner happily remains a minority of one. "My songs and humor are drawn," she says, "from my own experiences as a short, left-handed, Jewish lesbian from New York, which are considerably different from the experiences of an average person from, let's say, Columbus, Nebraska." To say nothing of the fact that the quick-witted Lavner, who stands only five feet tall, performs in black leather.

Billed as "America's most politically incorrect entertainer," Lavner has taken her original brand of music and comedy to forty states and five foreign countries ("six, if you count Provincetown"), bowling over audiences and critics alike. While her act is gay in content, her appearance is aimed at playful parody of stereotypes, and the material is universally appreciated by anyone with an open sense of humor. ("They say that opposites attract. If that were true, I'd be out of work.")

Lynn Lavner has been playing the piano and writing songs since she was seven years old. "Jewish people from Brooklyn are expected to do this," she claims, "and it is preferred that they be self-taught and unable to read music." After an apprenticeship served in the piano bars of Greenwich Village ("My hero is anyone who wrote a song between 1911 and 1943"), she made her debut at the Duplex Club in New York, earning glowing reviews (and a description as a "pint-sized Tom Lehrer") with such tunes as "Shelly, You've Gone Nelly On Me." Appearances followed across the United States and Europe, with Lavner taking time out to record for Bent Records, which has released her albums, *Something Different, I'd Rather Be Cute, You Are What You Wear, and Butch Fatale*.

Truly a crossover act, Lavner has performed at events as diverse as the twenty-fifth anniversary gala of the National Organization for Women and the International Mr. Leather contest. Her irreverent wit has served her well at pride celebrations, political and AIDS fund-raisers, women's festivals, college campuses, and special events throughout America and abroad. She's the recipient of the 1991 Christopher Street West Award for extraordinary creativity in gay and lesbian music and entertainment.

Carol Leifer

by Deni Kasrel

Had Carol Leifer not had a boyfriend who wanted to be a stand-up comic, who knows what she'd be doing today. As an undergraduate at State University of New York at Binghamton, she majored in theater arts. Her guy at the time was trying to break into the stand-up scene. One evening, she accompanied him to an open-mike night at Catch A Rising Star. Carol soon found herself bitten by the comedy bug. Next thing you know she was auditioning her own act at New York's Comic Strip.

That was in 1978. The boyfriend in question was Paul Reiser, star of TV's "Mad About You," but back then just another struggling comic on the scene.

The evening Leifer auditioned at the Comic Strip the emcee was Jerry Seinfeld. Others there included Dennis Miller and Rich Hall.

Those were the days, Carol recalls. There was a lot of tough competition to contend with, and there was also a tight camaraderie among the comedy crowd. "I started at a good time," she has said. "There wasn't the pressure of a million comedians. People got a lot of stage time and there was a community spirit." Her being a freewheeling, freethinking woman on the comedy podium made for real novelty, too.

Doing humor that was off-the-wall yet fully grounded in truth made for a different style of female stand-up. The notable precursors in the trade—Joan Rivers and Phyllis Diller, for example—had gotten into live comedy in times when the prevailing notion was that women should stay barefoot, pregnant, and in the kitchen. To break into what was pretty much a man's scene, these ladies had to make sacrifices and, in particular, they had to be self-deprecating. Diller berated her homely looks; Rivers bemoaned being flat-chested.

Carol came up when the mood of the day was more feminist. Routines based on the self-put-down dwindled, while women of Leifer's ilk—those whose bits were based on wry observation of the general state of human affairs—emerged to command a stance on a par with their male counterparts. So much on a par that Leifer eventually became a story editor for the hit TV program "Seinfeld."

The television gig is recent. To get it, Carol had to prove her mettle for several years on the circuit, performing at umpteen comedy clubs. She's also worked as a staff writer for "Saturday Night Live," and she made and starred in several cable TV specials.

Leifer's humor draws on real-life incidents and experiences. Travel, something she's done a lot of, is one of her oft-used topics. Once when she was in London, she bought a box of chocolates. The cashier said, "That will be ten pounds." Leifer found this the perfect set-up for the retort, "Rub it in, why don't you!"

Sly and dry, Carol's brand of comedy is fairly harmless and generally clean. Racy for her is this reflection on going to the gynecologist: "They always ask what was the first day of your period. I'm like, 'I don't know, ask my dry cleaner'."

A notable exception to the clean routine is her Showtime special "Gaudy, Bawdy, and Blue," a mock documentary in which Leifer plays a fictitious female comedian, Rusty Berman, a raunch-mouth who came up through burlesque houses. Leifer used the show to stretch her own brand of satire as well as to draw attention to comedic groundbreakers of yesteryear: women like

Rusty Warren, Belle Barthe, and Pearl Williams, all of whom enjoyed thriving yet underground careers in comedy. "I've always been intrigued by forerunners," Leifer explained. "These women weren't as cerebral as Lenny Bruce, but there was something heroic about them. Things were so uptight then, doing 'dirty' material was a way to be daring."

This comedian has exhibited her own type of daring. She grew up on Long Island and hails from a nice Jewish family of doctors. Her parents had hoped Carol would chose to pursue a mainstream professional occupation, as did their other two children. Instead, this daughter turned into a comedian who makes fun of her mother, the psychoanalyst: "It's weird that I have a parent who's a shrink. It's hard to think of my mom solving other people's problems when she's the root of all mine."

Leifer is a divorcee, and she incorporates this ordeal into her routine, approaching the subject with a healthy attitude. One of her jokes on the topic: "Some people have their marriages annulled, which means they never existed. Boy, talk about denial! What do you say when people see your wedding album? 'Oh, that was just some play I was in'."

Her real-life split-up wound up proving a gold mine of laughs, which Leifer made maximum use of when she cowrote and starred in the TV special "Carol Doesn't Leifer Anymore," which takes a humorous look at the first eighteen hours after divorce papers arrive. The special was produced by David Letterman, a longtime Leifer fan on whose show Carol has guested more than two dozen times. She also appears on "The Tonight Show."

Coming up in comedy is far from easy. Looking back at her early days, Carol recalls sending for law school applications just in case she didn't make it in stand-up. "At the beginning you always have those feelings, at first you have to suck. It's inevitable." But if you've got what it takes, which Leifer does, persistence pays off. Whatever turn it takes next, her career is likely to stand on solid footing. She hopes to use her roles as writer and editor for "Seinfeld" to one day have a hit show she can call her own.

Sabrina Matthews

by Roz Warren

Sabrina Matthews isn't wild about the name her mother gave her. "My mother really wanted me to be this nice, girly-girl kind of ... girl," says Matthews. "She was hell-bent for leather on having, well ... a daughter. She named me Sabrina. Sabrina Wilhelmina, that's my name. She put every feminine syllable that she could into my name. You look at me, you don't think, Sabrina. You think, Chip.

You betcha. Sabrina's a short-haired, freckle-faced, flannel-shirt kind of gal. *Deneuve* magazine said she looked like "the quintessential dyke-next-door." Her good-natured, freewheeling act involves spinning stories about daily dyke life, extended riffs on topics like trying to meet women, getting a good haircut, or the ordeal of wearing panty hose and pumps to work. She also touches on current events. Reading a news story concluding that scientists had discovered "Evidence of Difference in Brains of Gay Men," Matthews comments: "We got a bunch of guys walking around that think that 'salmon,' 'mocha' and 'champagne' are colors, and we need to cut their heads open to find out they're different?"

Matthews' very best material is about her relationship with her mom, a woman, says Matthews, with a "tenuous grip on reality. Like for my birthday this year she gave me Chanel cologne, some lesbian pulp fiction, and a Harley Davidson T-shirt. At the same time, my mother thinks that Georgia O'Keeffe was actually painting flowers!" Another favorite Matthews story is the one about her mom's insisting that she unplug the microwave at night, fearing that one of her cats will climb in there, punch in a cook cycle, then get the other cat to hit the Start button as part of a suicide pact they've arranged beforehand.

Matthews also focuses on the nature of friendship. She defines a true friend as "someone you don't have to talk to anymore when the food is on the table."

"Everything I say onstage is true," Matthews revealed recently in a *Deneuve* interview. "It's all happened to me—I just shape it into a storytelling format. My style is, I'm just up there talking—I'm not one of those in-your-face performers."

Matthews, who's held jobs as a child-care worker, bartender, and tofu-maker, jokes that she got into comedy to avoid "the last two lesbian professions left open to me: UPS carrier and massage therapist." She loves her job, appearing frequently at San Francisco Bay Area gay and lesbian clubs, and she has recently begun doing "out " material at straight clubs, as well.

Beverly Mickins

by Roz Warren

Beverly Mickins has performed at clubs, including Catch a Rising Star and Caroline's in New York, the Comedy Store in Los Angeles, as well as performance spaces P.S. 122 and Highways. She's also appeared at benefits in Nicaragua, at colleges, women's music festivals, at NOW's twenty-fifth anniversary, and at benefits for GLADD and AIDS Project Los Angeles. Her TV credits include "thirtysomething," "Sirens," and "Square One Television."

Mickins's material is sharp, uncompromising, and political. She began a recent year-in-review piece for a popular magazine with "When [this magazine] suggested I write a year-end wrap-up, I agreed ... but only if I could wrap it up and heave it through Bob Dole's window." Scanning current events, Mickins provides her audience with a much-needed reality check. How does she develop material? "I look through the paper and watch the news, trying to keep up with all the absurdity," she says. And there's plenty of absurdity to notice. On the gays-in-the-military flap, for instance, she comments: "Conservatives are worried straight men might become targets of sexual overtures. In other words, men in combat might have to face the same hell that's confronted secretaries and waitresses for generations." On sex education, she says: "They say teaching sex education in the public schools will promote promiscuity. With our educational system? If we promote promiscuity the same way we promote math or science, they've got nothing to worry about." She also defends Hillary Clinton, commenting that "forces in the White House want Hillary to 'tone down'. From what? Did I miss her crazed-leather-biker-chick period?"

How did Mickins come to comedy as a career? "After being unceremoniously fired from a number of office jobs," she offers, "I realized I had to choose between being a performer or a disgruntled former employee. Actually, I've always felt very alive and joyous onstage; it's always felt like home." Her comic influences include her dad, Bugs Bunny cartoons, and Whoopi Goldberg ("for her truth and intimacy"), as well as Carol Burnett, Dick Gregory, Richard Pryor, Lenny Bruce, "... and my boyfriend, who makes me laugh out loud!" Mickins loves her work, "especially on those magical nights where everything is right, it's all working and I feel like I understand my mission on earth."

She's currently working on a one-woman show.

Bette Midler

by Samantha Rigg

Bette Midler, "the Divine Miss M," is a classic, a performer who can, and does, do everything. To her fans she's something between a dear old friend and an adored legend. Midler began her comedy career in 1971, working in New York at the Continental Baths, a gay men's hangout. They loved her outrageous sense of humor and style: she dressed in black lace corsets with gold high heels, strutted across the stage as an exaggerated Bette Davis, winked, leered, smiled seductively, and belted out Sophie Tucker songs. Never once did she put herself down. Never aspiring to be a conventional beauty, Midler always assumed that she looked fabulous. "I am a living work of art!" she told her audience, and they shouted their approval.

From the baths, the Divine Miss M sauntered onto the Broadway stage, selling out the Palace Theater. Her debut album went gold. Just two years after she first began performing, she was awarded a Grammy for Best New Artist of the Year. Next came the world tours, more albums, concert films, and in 1979, her stunning performance in *The Rose*. But when her next film, *Jinxed!*, came out in 1982, it lived up to its title and flopped. Bad-mouthed by Hollywood colleagues, Midler became depressed enough to stay in bed for the next six months.

After some years of time off and therapy, Midler made a big comeback in a string of successful comedy films, including *Down and Out in Beverly Hills*, *Ruthless People*, and *Big Business*. Since then, she's done a little bit of everything, from playing Woody Allen's neurotic wife in *Scenes from a Mall*, to a witch from Salem, Massachusetts, in *Hocus Pocus*, to nailing the part of Mama Rose in the TV broadcast of the musical *Gypsy*. In 1993, she toured the States for the first time in ten years, and people came out in droves to see her.

Midler is an enormous talent, but Hollywood often doesn't seem to know what to do with her. "Sometimes I think I'm in the wrong era," she once told a reporter, harking back to the thirties and forties when so-called women's pictures like *Stella* and *For the Boys* were the rule, not the exception. "Yet I know I'm lucky to be where I am, because then I would never have made the cut. I don't have the face for it, and I don't have the body. I don't have anything they required except the enthusiasm and the drive."

Midler's comic talents are enormous, as is her emotional connection with her audience. She's famous for her ability to move people from laughter to tears and back again. "I'm always on the edge between laughter and tears," she once said. "I'm very emotional. I'm not happy with a performance, even acting, unless I feel I have been through something myself. I have to have a catharsis in order to be satisfied. And onstage, if you don't phony it up, if you don't disguise what you're feeling, then it's mesmerizing."

Anita Milner

by Roz Warren

Comic Anita Milner was once mentioned in a Supreme Court opinion. But Justice Byron White wasn't quoting one of Anita's acerbic one-liners about married life. ("In August my husband, Morris, and I celebrated our thirty-eighth wedding anniversary. You know what I finally realized? If I had killed that man the first time I thought about it, I'd have been out of jail by now!") Instead, he was citing from one of Milner's law review articles.

Milner is both a stand-up comic and an attorney. A former housewife, the self-described "Change Of Life Lawyer," graduated from law school at age forty-nine and passed the California bar at age fifty. The pressures of law

157

school, she jokes, both brought on menopause and inspired her to finally try stand-up. During a family vacation on a cruise ship after Milner's second year of law school, she volunteered to perform on amateur night and was hooked. "It was great!" exults Milner. "I did a snappy four minutes. It was more fun than sex—and lasted a little longer."

Milner practices *elder law* in Escondido, California, performs comedy at local clubs and is frequently booked as a "luncheon humorist" for business and banking association meetings. She's also appeared on "America's Funniest People."

Milner's act focuses on marriage, motherhood, menopause, and middle age. She finds that women, especially older women, are usually on her wavelength. "I do okay with mixed crowds," she says, "but with groups of women I really do well. If I have an all-woman audience, I know I'm going to get applause." They can relate to observations like: "Scientists say you can get cancer from the radiation thrown off by your electric blanket. I'm so depressed. Here I am, fifty-six years old, and the most dangerous thing I've ever done in bed is turn on the blanket." Milner is also comfortable ad-libbing with this crowd. In the middle of a story about coping with her hubby's snoring, an audience member vocalizes agreement. "You've slept with him too?" Milner jokes.

Milner, who cheerfully describes herself as "old enough to personally identify every object in antique stores," gets plenty of good material from the experience of growing older. "Lately," she jokes, "I'm starting to worry more about getting Alzheimer's than AIDS ... but for the life of me I can't remember why." Naturally, her act also features lawyer jokes. About a state bar opinion finding it unethical for a lawyer to have sex with a client, she quips, "And I was so close!"

Milner's comedy career helps balance the often grim reality of her law practice, which, being focused on senior law, frequently brings up issues of death and dying. After an afternoon spent drawing up wills, Milner welcomes the opportunity to take the stage at a comedy club and make jokes. Humor is healing, she says. "When you make people laugh, it does you just as much good as it does the audience."

Lynda Montgomery

by Roz Warren & Laura Post

Like many comics, Lynda Montgomery first learned humor skills within her family. "My dad's an alcoholic, my mother manic-depressive. It was definitely a dysfunctional family, but funny. We laughed about everything."

A distant cousin of Alfred Hitchcock, Montgomery's first ambition was to be a writer: "I always wrote stories. I also had some relatives who published their own book of poems, called *Snatches from Everyday Life*. They didn't know how funny that was. *We* all did, though."

Montgomery was an Air Force brat. Her family relocated frequently, and she honed her funny bits in order to fit in. As a kid whose family had moved

159

thirteen times before she was in the eighth grade, she quickly learned that "comedy is one of the quickest ways to connect with people.

"Every time I went to a new school, I'd have to do a little opening monologue. They'd say, 'Tell us a little about yourself'. I'd remember the things that kids laughed at, and repeat them at the next school."

After a five-year stint in the Air Force, Lynda got into the health club business. She currently owns a fitness center. Her comedy career happened by accident. "My ex-girlfriend was living with Judy Carter, who teaches comedy classes. My ex wanted me to get to know Judy, so I took her comedy class. I thought I was terrible, but I got obsessed with getting better, and that's how I got into comedy."

From the start, Montgomery knew what she wanted to talk about onstage: "I wanted to talk about being gay. I was an activist, and I wanted to do jokes about that. But I'm still trying to find the balance; I don't want to be a shock comic." Her current act is a wealth of sharp observations about lesbian life that amuse but don't offend, such as: "I'm a little bit femme and a little bit butch. I wear makeup ... but I keep it in a tackle box." Or: "I'm out to everybody in my family, except my aunt. She's agoraphobic, and I figure if she won't come out for me, why should I come out for her?" Montgomery's vegetarianism also leads to some great lines, like: "Why does Sea World have a seafood restaurant? I'm halfway through my fishburger and I realize, Oh my God—I could be eating a slow learner."

Although she is concerned with keeping her audience at ease, Montgomery isn't afraid to aim her wit at the occasional political Neanderthal who turns up at mainstream clubs. "I was doing some material about gays in the military," she recalls. "There were some military guys in the front row. They all got into a little flap. Actually I had a good time with it ... I got a lot of jokes about them ... they looked stupid. As you get more confident onstage, you can deviate from what you were going to talk about. If I get a heckler, I can go on a little tangent and then come back to my material."

Montgomery draws her material from her own life: "When it's true, it's easier to remember!" But she doesn't try out material on her friends. "That's why I *have* friends." She doesn't even like to be introduced to people as a comic. "They expect you to be amusing right off the bat. I can't stand it when comics don't turn it off."

How does she develop her act? "One joke at a time—starting with the ones I told in kindergarten." She's disciplined about her comedy writing. "I force myself to sit down with my word processor at least a couple hours a day."

Montgomery was recently interviewed by *People* for a feature on Bobbitt jokes. (For instance: "They're going to do a movie about John Bobbitt. It's going to be called *Dickless in Seattle*.") "Bobbitt jokes just about write themselves," observes Montgomery. She demonstrates: "The news is so depressing, and I just don't even like to listen to it sometimes. But every once in a while, there'll be a heartwarming story that'll make you feel all warm and glowy inside. Like when Lorena Bobbitt cut off her husband's dick and threw it in a ditch." She pauses, "That gets a laugh." She continues: "But Lorena did do the right thing. She did tell them where to find it. Which is good. He won't have to wait forever for an organ donor."

Montgomery makes fun of straight people, but she also mocks some of the mores of the lesbian community: "It's really hard with lesbian relationships to know when your anniversary date is. Is it your first date? The first time you go to bed together? Is it the day you move in? Lucky for my girlfriend and me, all those things happened at the same time."

Montgomery can also laugh at herself. "When I did Provincetown, I was billed as a 'tasteless comic', because they'd read on my resume that I'd won a contest at a comedy competition that was specifically designed to be tasteless. So my opening line at that gig was that I was offended that they'd said I was tasteless, and I'd actually asked a couple of my girlfriends—they said I was hygienic but not totally tasteless."

Montgomery is so scrupulous about not stealing material from other comics that she once actually negotiated with comic Suzanne Westenhoefer to divvy up the territory in which they did a joke. Independently, the two comics had come up with the same line: "My only fear about being a lesbian comic is that the *National Enquirer* is going to write an article saying I'm really straight." Montgomery explains that "since Suzanne didn't steal it from me, and I didn't steal it from her, we agreed that she could use the joke on the East Coast, and I could use it on the West Coast."

Montgomery's goal is fame within the gay community. "I want to make homosexuals laugh. I wouldn't turn down opportunities in the heterosexual world, but I'm not obsessed with getting on 'Comic Strip Live' or 'Caroline's Comedy Hour'." Her dream, she says, is "for everyone to come out of the closet in Hollywood so that as an out lesbian I can sleep my way to the top!" But for now she'd settle for a more immediate goal: "to qualify for a mortgage as an out lesbian comic."

kathy Najimy

by Toni Armstrong, Jr., interview by Deni Kasrel

When Kathy Najimy was filming *Hocus Pocus*, Disney officials asked her not to wear the fake teeth that went with her witch costume—they wanted to be sure people would know it was her. "I couldn't really imagine a dilemma where people would be sitting there in the dark thinking, Hmmm … is that Kathy Najimy or Michelle Pfeiffer? she says. But eventually she chose to lose the snaggle teeth and was presented with a copy of Madonna's book, Sex. "I thought that was a kind of cool gift from Disney," says Kathy.

The award-winning actress brought authentic radical feminist culture to the mainstream with *The Kathy and Mo Show*, a two-woman extravaganza about women's lives and issues. The show, which People magazine called "a blitzkrieg of cutting-edge skits," ran for six years, playing venues in New York, San Francisco, Los Angeles, Baltimore, and San Diego. Kathy and writing partner Mo Gaffney wrote and starred in this hard-hitting, side-splitting production. It was made into a one-hour special on HBO ("The Kathy and Mo Show: Parallel Lives"), which earned two Cable Ace awards in 1992 (Best Special of the Year and Best Performance in a Special).

Najimy's film credits include *Soapdish* (as Sally Field's costume assistant), *Hocus Pocus* (as the sister of two other witches, played by Bette Midler and Sara Jessica Parker), and Nora Ephron's *This Is My Life*. Her most famous performance to date is, of course, as the relentlessly cheery Sister Mary Patrick in the 1992 box office smash *Sister Act* (with Whoopi Goldberg and Maggie Smith) and in the sequel, *Sister Act 2: Back in the Habit*.

A native of San Diego, Kathy's early theater days included directing the New Image Teen Theater (which she founded for Planned Parenthood), the Rainbow Repertory Theater, the radical feminist Sisters on Stage troupe, and a one-woman show called *It's My Party*. In the early days, she supported her theater habit by doing odd jobs, which included delivering singing telegrams. Once, dressed in a rabbit suit, she delivered one from herself to her idol, Bette Midler.

Najimy has won a variety of awards, including an Obie for acting (for *Kathy and Mo*) and an American Comedy Award for Funniest Supporting Female in a Motion Picture (for *Sister Act*). She has appeared in most of the major entertainment magazines and on many TV shows. Never one to mince words, Kathy's opening compliment to Jay Leno on one of her "Tonight Show" appearances was, "You're one of the only talk-show hosts who isn't racist, sexist, homophobic, and doesn't think with your penis."

Kasrel: How did you first get into performing?

Najimy: It was one of the things I was good at. You know, doing drama club with my friends, acting out characters, lip-syncing to songs. I did all that stuff early on, and it just seemed the natural way to go if the business would have me, and sooner or later it did.

Kasrel: Did you have your doubts at the time about whether the business would have you?

Najimy: For a long time I was comfortable with the fact that I'd just be doing little projects on my own to have a creative outlet. Being accepted by the masses was nothing I really thought was ever going to happen to me. Which was fine with me.

Kasrel: You didn't aspire to be a big star?

Najimy: I was a big star in my own world, but I never thought I'd be nationally recognized. I did political theater up until just a few years ago, when I started doing movies. My performing wasn't for everyone; it was for a very specific audience.

Kasrel: Yet somehow you ended up becoming a very famous person. Does it surprise you that you're famous?

Najimy: Yes and no. In a way I always thought it was what I deserved. When I was little, in my mind, even when I was putting on Ronald McDonald carnivals in my backyard to raise money for … I think it was muscular dystrophy—even back then, those were huge productions which I produced and directed and starred in. So I thought I was a big star. Did I ever think it would overflow into, you know, actual stardom? No.

Kasrel: What attracted you to the idea of performing?

Najimy: Performing isn't my favorite thing, but it's a great outlet, and it's fun. Doing something like Sister Act was just silly and fun. If you feel enough for the character, you can really have a good time. With a show like *Kathy and Mo*, the great thing is getting to make your vision happen.

Kasrel: If performing isn't your favorite thing, what is?

Najimy: Directing. It's what I did for a living before I was a professional actress, which is funny because it's usually the other way around: first you're an actor, and then you aspire to be a director. But I was a director before I became an actress.

Kasrel: What do you like about directing?

Najimy: You get to create your vision and be in control of it. I enjoy working with creative, talented people.

Kasrel: And you've worked with some of the top talents of our time. Do you find that this helps you with your own craft?

Najimy: Being around really funny, interesting, talented people keeps your juices going. I certainly am who I am today because of all the people I hung out with. In eighth grade, we did drama club. We just sort of organized ourselves and every Wednesday and Saturday night we'd put on costumes and run around town in character like lunatics. I got my first taste of doing characters and being able to be free and uninhibited and going as far as I could and trying things out. And I loved it.

Kasrel: What kind of comedy most appeals to you?

Najimy: The comedy that attracts me is comedy with substance and point of view—not only being funny but also having something to say that I'm passionate about. The challenge is to take something with substance and make it theatrically appealing. Everything I've done hasn't been like that. I've been in movies that have no point of view at all. But the political comedy is what I prefer.

Kasrel: That can be tough to pull off. How can you make it work?

Najimy: It has to be true to you. Even if it's something tiny, like how you feel about your aunt, if it's true to you and you feel really passionate about it, then it has substance and can be interesting. It can be something as general as how you feel about abortion rights or as specific as the fact that someone looked at you wrong when you were in the fourth grade.

Kasrel: Are there attitudes or trends in humor that you're uncomfortable with?

Najimy: Recently it's become hip among certain celebrities and comics to say that they're politically incorrect. A comic will stand up and say, "I'm politically incorrect and I'm proud of it." And everyone cheers. And I think to myself, Boy, *that* was hard. It's the easiest, most wimpy, weak statement in the world! Being politically correct just means respecting different kinds of people and groups of people. It's a lot more difficult and courageous and hip to be politically correct *and* funny. To be politically correct and still be funny— now there's the challenge!

Kasrel: Are there topics—like homelessness or AIDS—that you just can't joke about?

Najimy: With *Kathy and Mo* we dealt with topics like abortion rights and racial harmony. We didn't make fun of these things, but we did make points about these topics with humor. One of the reasons I wanted to do *Kathy and Mo* was that I couldn't stand up at a podium for forty minutes talking about feminism without people being really bored. But if I could do it in this funny skit with this funny character people would listen.

Kasrel: *Kathy and Mo* did have a lot of impact, particularly with feminist audiences.

Najimy: I'm very proud of it. Of course, we were only able to do it because of the women who came before us. Another thing that's happening in Hollywood now is many famous women directors saying, "I'm not a feminist. I did it myself. I've never come up against any sexism, and I didn't need the women's movement." Which is such bullshit. There's no way these women would be successful if it weren't for the women's movement. I'm proud of *The*

Kathy and Mo Show. We really did good work and I take credit for that, but I attribute a lot of our success to the work that Lily Tomlin did, and Ruth Draper and Bette Midler.

Kasrel: How did you start working with Mo Gaffney? I've read that you saw her in a theater group and felt that she was funnier than everyone else and wanted to direct her. What made her stand out?

Najimy: I just knew that she was funny; she made me laugh. Comedy has to have a certain honesty to really get me, and there has to be something unexpected. She just was very surprising to me, and honestly funny.

Kasrel: Was she doing feminist material?

Najimy: Actually, when I first saw her she was doing improv. I was running a cafe for women performers called Wing Cafe, and I called her up and said, "Get together a group of women improv artists and we'll put you on." She got together a group called Hot Flashes. We started hanging out together and doing characters and talking about my directing her in a one-woman show. Because we were both doing the characters, we decided to write *Kathy and Mo.*

Kasrel: Did each of you write your own part or did you write it together? Did you write for each other?

Najimy: We did all of that. Sometimes you'd write things that you thought were going to be for yourself and they'd turn out to be for the other person. There's one piece I wrote with Mo about an aunt who discovers her nephew is gay. Mo did it for a couple of years, then we switched and I started doing it. A lot of times we improv-ed into a tape recorder. We improv-ed "Sister Woman Sister" into a tape recorder and to this day, ten years later, we perform it exactly how we improv-ed it into the tape recorder.

Other things went through really painful and crucial writing and rewriting over the years and don't resemble the original at all. The show got really different as the years went by. By the time we were off-Broadway, we were writing in a very different way. We knew exactly what we needed to write. There was a lot more pressure; we knew we'd be reviewed by critics.

But in the beginning we were free and didn't give a shit. We just wrote about whatever we thought was funny that day. As the years went by, the writing changed, but in the beginning it was me and her sitting on her roof with candy bars and diet soda and Mo smoking cigarettes and the two of us just writing. As time went on and circumstances changed, the writing got a little more deliberate and actually a little less fun.

Kasrel: Was that why you ended it?

Najimy: We ended it because it was over. We never intended to be "Kathy and Mo" our whole lives; we just wanted to do our play. It was a total of eight years, and then a year and a half off-Broadway, eight shows a week. And we were both onstage the whole time. Whoever thought up eight shows a week was a sadist. It was grueling. It was just too hard to keep doing it.

Kasrel: I want to ask about some specific parts in *Kathy and Mo*. There's a section where you're just by yourself talking about choice.

Najimy: The abortion monologue is forty-five seconds long, and it's the only forty-five seconds in the show that isn't funny. We couldn't find a way to make that statement about abortion be funny. It was really a challenge for me, and kind of scary, because here people are laughing and laughing and then all of a sudden for forty-five seconds there's no joke. It's serious. It was very different from anything else in the show. But I felt it was important to do it. A lot of directors and producers disagreed and tried to talk us out of it, but it was important for me to say that, so I did.

Kasrel: In contrast, the skit in which the aunt is talking about her gay nephew has some serious things, but every once in a while you toss in a joke.

Najimy: That's more in true Kathy-and-Mo form: bring up something of substance, but then right away make people laugh.

Kasrel: I've read that you were concerned at first about whether your audience would enjoy "Sister Woman Sister."

Najimy: We both had big gay followings, and we thought for sure that the lesbian faction of the community would just hate it.

But they loved it. They realized it was like a tribute. You can't make fun of something until it is something. They felt the lesbian feminist poetry movement must be something if someone's mocking it. And Mo and I had been heavily into women's culture. We could make fun of it because we'd experienced it.

Kasrel: The audience could accept the humor coming from one of their own, an insider. You weren't laughing at them from the outside.

Najimy: We got some of the lines from a lesbian friend of mine. She said, "Oh my God, Kathy, I fell in love with this woman last night at this bar. Look at this letter!" She showed me this letter, and some of the lines made me laugh so hard that later on, when we were improv-ing "Sister Woman Sister," I just threw them in. Like, "you are Venus mound" and about "her champagne flowing …"

Kasrel: Oh, that poor woman, if she ever saw the show ...

Najimy: I'm sure she wouldn't recognize herself. So many people wrote like that then.

Kasrel: You said that because you were part of the movement the audience was able to laugh at the piece, because they understood that your heart was in the right place. Where is the line between mocking in a fun way and really being deprecating?

Najimy: It comes down to whether you still have respect for the person or the movement. Humor becomes offensive when you lose that respect. I know it sounds very Hallmark card-ish, but I don't believe that in order to be funny you have to hurt people's feelings, or hurt a group. I can't really explain what the line is. I only know that you can tell there's no respect when Andrew Dice Clay does it and there is respect when Lily Tomlin does it.

Kasrel: You and Mo are working together on a screenplay, "Bus Plunge." Can you tell me something about that?

Najimy: Hollywood Pictures commissioned us to write it when *Kathy and Mo* ended. We've been slow with the rewrites, which is why it's still ongoing. I'm hesitant to talk about it because we've been talking about it for four years and everyone is like, "Yeah, well, where is it?" It's about a group of people who are in a bus plunge and reunite five year later. It's along the same lines as *Kathy and Mo* in that we deal with issues of substance and, hopefully, it's funny.

Kasrel: You began your acting career performing feminist, political material. In contrast, a movie like *Sister Act* isn't hard-hitting political material and doesn't have any particular social value.

Najimy: I didn't write *Sister Act*, I just acted in it. It was a good opportunity and good money. I never said everything I do has to have some big meaning. It's great when it does, but a project like Sister Act is like drama club in the eighth grade. It's just fun.

Kasrel: Does the fame that results from appearing in high-profile movies like *Sister Act* give you some kind of platform for speaking about the political issues that you care about?

Najimy: I'm basically the same political being that I've been since I took my first women's lib class in the eighth grade. I've been saying the same things for twenty years. The only difference is that more people listen now, because they've seen me in movies like *Sister Act*. When I was in San Diego directing teen theater, I had strong feelings about abortion rights, but it just went as far as me and my ten friends. Now, if I express the same views in *People* magazine, it affects a lot more people. I'm sure some people hate it and want to kill me, and some people think, Hmmm, she might have a point. And some people think, Oh good, there's another person out there who thinks the way I do. It has a bigger effect. I hesitate to say whether this effect is negative or positive; I just know that it has a bigger effect.

Kasrel: You've always been political but not everybody knows that.

Najimy: They know me as the funny nun.

Kasrel: Do you think your political beliefs influence whether people will cast you in a particular role?

Najimy: Well, I used to be pretty naive. Up until about the hundredth reporter asked me if being a political activist hurt my career, I'd always say, "Oh no, I'm sure it doesn't affect it at all." Then it dawned on me that maybe it is hurting my career. There's probably a group of people in Hollywood who think, Why doesn't she just keep her mouth shut? She's an actress; we don't need to hear what she thinks. We don't agree with what she's said, so we're not going to cast her.

I'm sure it is hurting me but I don't really care. I can't care. I became an activist because I have a really low tolerance for things that are offensive. My feelings get hurt for myself and for other people. I'm sensitive to homophobia and racism and misogyny. I've come to the conclusion that maybe my career is being hurt horribly by my saying what I feel, and that's sad and unfortunate, but I don't know what I could do about it.

Kasrel: Do you think your political views affect the kind of scripts that people send you?

Najimy: Not really. I still get all kinds of scripts.

Kasrel: Are you disappointed with the kind of scripts people send you?

Najimy: People always say they're shocked about the lack of good scripts with roles for women, and the fact that the roles that do exist for women are stereotypical and shallow. I'm not shocked at all. Hollywood just reflects the rest of the world. If women are second-class citizens everywhere else, why wouldn't they be in Hollywood? I'm a realist; I don't expect any more of Hollywood than I do of the rest of world.

A couple of years ago, I'd consider any script that wasn't offensive and would be funny and fun to do. Now I'm at the point where I'm turning a lot of things down, because the next movie I do has to be really different, or else I'll just be the funny nun my whole life. I'm in negotiations now for a serious film, a thriller. It's dangerous and romantic, the kind of thing that people haven't seen me in.

Kasrel: You're also working on a one-woman show?

Najimy: It's called *My Body's Not My Instrument*. It's based on my experience here in Hollywood with how actors behave, and actor lingo. The title came from an article I was reading about a Hollywood star, and she said, "I go to the gym because my body is my instrument." It cracked me up. *My body is good for having sex and taking a shower, you know? It's not my instrument. It's not as if it's a saxophone.*

It cracks me up when people say things like "I love your work." That phrase is so "actor" to me. Or when actors say, "I really love the choices you made on that." It sounds so serious, and this can be such a silly business.

Kasrel: You don't take Hollywood that seriously?

Najimy: Hollywood can be so full of shit. If people only knew how some of these people make decisions and what their qualifications are, they'd double over in laughter. I mean, some of these clowns are just cartoon characters.

Kasrel: Who in Hollywood do you respect? Whose work has influenced you over the years?

Najimy: Bette Midler was a huge influence. Her live shows were so awesome and so honest and so funny and so unique and so great. I don't know whether she considers herself a feminist, but her early concerts were so freeing. Just by her sheer being, she was saying, "You don't have to look the way they think you should look. You don't have to behave the way you're supposed to." That really inspired me.

Kasrel: She was a feminist by her actions rather than coming out and saying certain things.

Najimy: Right. Lily Tomlin was inspiring because she did so many different characters, men and women and children. She rejected the stereotypes of how you're supposed to be. And she dealt with issues that had substance, things she was passionate about. Susan Sarandon is an influence. She's like a goddess to me; she can't do anything wrong. How she conducts her life is so inspiring. She's politically outspoken, and she's designed her personal life without caring what convention is. She's just so fucking right-on, you know? She's great. She's beautiful. She's sexy. She's proud of her age. I love her. And also Linda Ellerbee, Roseanne, Lillian Hellman, Ntozake Shange, Jane Campion and Debra Winger.

Gloria Steinem has also been a huge influence. You know how sometimes you'll get into a situation and you'll ask yourself how someone you respect would handle it? I'll think, What would Gloria do? What would Lily do? Then, ultimately, I just do what I want and I'm usually wrong. [*Laughs*]

Kasrel: You've had a chance to work with Bette and Whoopi and other great comic actresses. Did you learn from that experience?

Najimy: You learn something working with anyone—even the extras on the set, if you talk with them. With *Soapdish*, I hung out with the extras and learned a lot. It's not so much different from what you learn from the stars. You're always learning things, even if it's "I don't want to behave like that." What I picked up from Bette Midler was how successfully she incorporated her personal life and her professional life. Her husband and daughter were on the set. She showed that you could be a superstar and still maintain some kind of a healthy balance.

Kasrel: What about Whoopi Goldberg? Did you two interact when you weren't on the set?

Najimy: Oh yeah, we've known each other for fifteen years. We toured together for a year in the seventies, with a political four-person musical group. I knew her before she was famous. I hung out with her. I took her daughter to day care.

Kasrel: What was it like to work with Maggie Smith?

Najimy: Maggie Smith is a legend, and when you work with her you realize why. At the table reading of the first *Sister Act*, her performance was so good they could have filmed it. She was so brilliant, so funny, and so dry. She was great. It was like being with royalty. Then when it was time for me to film my first big moment in the film—where I'm talking about my mother saying I was either going to be a nun or a stewardess—she sat off on the side, and after every take she laughed out loud. I can't tell you how much confidence that gave me. I ran and grabbed a cellular phone and called my friends in New York and said, "Oh my God, Maggie Smith just laughed at me."

Kasrel: Do you think she did that on purpose?

Najimy: I don't know. She either truly thought I was funny or she did it just to be supportive. Either way, it changed my life for that moment. It gave me confidence. I thought, Okay, maybe I can do this movie stuff.

Kasrel: What's the difference between being in a movie and doing a show like *Kathy and Mo*?

Najimy: When you're acting in a movie, you're only performing in short, little spurts. You never have to concentrate for longer than two or three minutes. It's easier than something like *Kathy and Mo*, where I had to be onstage every minute of the full two hours. It's exhausting. It's like working out for two hours. With filming, you do a scene for a couple of minutes, then you go off for an hour and wait around while they reset the lights.

Kasrel: Because you're perceived as a comic actress, do you ever find that people expect you to be hilarious offstage?

Najimy: Sometimes people will invite you to a dinner party to be the comic element and you don't feel comic that day. I can be funny when I'm with my friends. I can be witty, but it's not as if I'm always funny. Most funny people aren't funny. Some say comedy comes from pain. The funniest people I know aren't comic actresses—they're just funny.

Rosie O'Donnell

by Deni Kasrel

You wouldn't think that Rosie O'Donnell would need to work on a laugh—she heard so many of them doing stand-up comedy. Even so, O'Donnell had to put in a lot of time to perfect the laugh she used for her role as Betty Rubble in the live-action feature film of the popular cartoon show *The Flintstones*. Of course, that role called for a special sort of giggle, so you can forgive her for having to practice at getting it just right.

Then again, maybe she has forgotten what the world of laughs sounds like since in the last few years O'Donnell's career has had little to do with stand-up, unless you count standing up in front of a movie camera. Rosie is currently riveting her way into Hollywood, where her recognition factor has come swiftly.

This speedy fame is perhaps not terribly surprising when you consider that for her silver-screen debut, in the movie *A League of Their Own*, O'Donnell was cast as the tough butchy pal of one of the all-time biggest pop stars, Madonna. She was next seen as Meg Ryan's good-hearted, wiseacre best friend in Nora Ephron's 1993 smash hit, *Sleepless in Seattle*.

She's appeared in several subsequent flicks, including John Badham's Another Stakeout (where she held her own opposite Richard Dreyfuss and Emilio Estevez), James L. Brook's *I'll Do Anything*, and Carl Reiner's *Fatal Instinct*. None did boffo box office, but that hasn't taken any blush off of O'Donnell's rosy prospects in Hollywood.

She belongs to the comedy club that includes Lily Tomlin, Whoopi Goldberg, Billy Crystal, Roseanne, and Kathy Najimy. All gained fame on the live laugh circuit, then used their notoriety as a vehicle to shift into an acting career. In O'Donnell's case, that includes stage musicals—she did the ol' song and dance routine as Rizzo for a theatrical run of *Grease*. She's into stretching herself artistically in more ways than that, too, having taken on more challenging material in a cinematic adaptation of Anne Rice's *Exit to Eden*.

Playing the comedy circuit as a means to move into more lucrative television and movie opportunities isn't novel. Plenty in the stand-up trade will tell you that one reason they got into doing live humor was so that they could be seen by casting agents—many of whom make rounds of the clubs in search of new talent. If you're good at it, comedy can offer one of the few steady sources of income for someone building a career in the entertainment trade, as club owners are always rotating acts, and the pool they have to select from is far less crowded than is the gushing torrent from the never-ending flow of aspiring actors.

O'Donnell was bitten by the acting bug early on. When in first grade, she once sang "Second Hand Rose" for show and tell.

She idolized Barbra Streisand, imagining the star as a replacement mom. (Rosie's mother died of cancer when she was ten.) She's always loved sitcoms, and the funny women she liked best as a kid were those who projected a strong presence and who added a manner of physicality to their routines, such as Lucille Ball, Carol Burnett, and Bette Midler.

Losing her mother at a young age was traumatic. Humor offered an outlet to release some of the pain. A strict and stoic Irish Catholic upbringing at home put the clamps on outward displays of emotional expression, so O'Donnell had to go elsewhere to express repressed feelings: "I lived all my emotional truths in the movie theaters or in Broadway shows. I got all my pathos and catharsis through that—not through my actual real life at home."

In her late teens, O'Donnell began hitting the comedy houses. After a few false starts, she developed a saleable shtick, putting on a persona that's essentially an exaggerated version of herself: a wisecracking, no-nonsense babe who doesn't mince words. Early on she snagged a job emceeing and introducing comedians. From this position, she saw how other comics structured their acts.

She traveled the club circuit for years. Her first big break was in 1984, when she won several preliminary trials on Ed McMahon's "Star Search." Using her prize money, Rosie headed to L.A. "If you want to surf, you have to go to the water," she has wryly observed.

It was rough riding at first, then came slow but steady progress. As it turns out, her decision to do stand-up to attract attention to her talents as an actress proved a prescient ploy. One night when she was doing her comedy routine at a West L.A. venue, two producers of "Saturday Night Live" were in the audience—they'd come to check out another comic, Dana Carvey. O'Donnell impressed the TV men so much that they signed her to the role of Nell Carter's upstairs neighbor in the sitcom "Gimme a Break."

She did a stint as a VJ on cable's VH-1. At the time, this sister network of MTV was in the fledgling stage. It was low-profile, and the monitoring of programming was lax. O'Donnell took advantage of this by having fun on the air, mocking her own role of video jock and trashing rock stars. Once, when she came on the air following a Paul McCartney video, Rosie quipped, " 'Maybe I'm Amazed', a song he wrote the day Linda sang on key." Another stunt she'd pull at her VJ post was to introduce herself as a famous has-been celebrity.

When this gig ended, Rosie persuaded the network to let her host and executive-produce "Stand-Up Spotlight," a comedy series that handily suited her sensibilities and talents. Then began her movie roles, and as her star rose on this horizon, she set down her stance in stand-up.

She's heavy into films now, and from the looks of it, she'll enjoy a bountiful career as an actress. Just as she used stand-up as an entree to acting, she is parlaying her clout as an actress to find opportunities to write, produce, and direct.

In Los Angeles Magazine *Buzz*, O'Donnell clarified where she'd like to see herself go in the entertainment industry, declaring that if she had her druthers she's shirk off playing a part for a full-time seat in the director's chair. "Not because I don't respect it," she says of the craft of acting, "but creatively it doesn't fulfill me as much as I would like it to. When you're an actress, you're not selling the character. You're selling you … I'd like to have the piece of art I make be something I can hand to someone else. And have it not be me."

Ellen Orchid

by Roz Warren

"You ever heard of Freud airlines? They have two sections—guilt and non-guilt. The seats go all the way back ... to childhood." Jokes about Freud come easy to psychiatrist-comedian Ellen Orchid. By day, Orchid, an M.D. and Ph.D., treats patients at a mental health clinic specializing in posttraumatic stress disorder. At night, she performs stand-up at comedy clubs around New York City. In a city with more than its fair share of analysands, audiences can truly appreciate jokes like: "Sigmund Freud and Carl Jung broke up over the concept of penis envy. Freud thought that every woman wanted a penis. Jung thought that every woman wanted *his* penis."

Naturally, Orchid's act is full of jokes about her profession. "Is anybody here in therapy?" she'll ask the audience. "Is anybody in therapy but ashamed to admit it?" [*Pause*] "Is anyone hearing so many voices, they don't know what I just said?"

Even in the nineties, being in therapy can still carry a stigma. Orchid feels that jokes about psychiatry help counter that, because they "make people more comfortable with the topic." Orchid's act is also popular with her psychiatric peers; she performs often for medical association meetings and conventions, wowing them with lines like: "I had a very confused patient once. He thought that Darth Vader was a Jewish holiday."

When asked if she ever plans to abandon her therapy career for show-biz stardom, the comic again refers to Freud. "Freud was so ahead of his time," she smiles, "he even gave advice to young comics. He said '*Kündigen Sie nicht Ihre Brot-und-Butter Stelle*', which means, "Don't quit your day job.""

Janice ("Gal") Perry

by Roz Warren

    Janice Perry has been performing what she calls "stand-up theater" or "one-woman cabaret" for over a decade, both here and in Europe. Born and raised in Vermont, the daughter of a country doctor, Perry holds degrees in English and philosophy. It is not surprising, then, that her comedy is both literate and philosophical, not to mention provocative and political.

    Onstage, Perry comes on strong and subversive. *In World Power Sex Control*, a one-woman show about "the interrelationship between war, censorship, and tango," she dons a muscled, gold lamé breastplate to recite the subtext of the United States Constitution: "We, the white, rich, heterosexual old men ..." Strapping on a gigantic plastic phallus, she performs a living tableau of some of Robert Mapplethorpe's erotic photos. She describes being drummed out of the U.S. mainstream during the Gulf War when *her* tree was discovered to be the only tree in North America without a yellow ribbon.

Perry rarely traffics in one-liners. Instead, she takes off on inspired, extended riffs on favored topics, which she dramatizes with the use of eye-catching costumes and, often, musical embellishments. "It's no longer safe to be a woman in the United States," she'll declare. "It's no longer safe to be a woman anywhere in the *world*. And that is why, after thinking about this very carefully for a very long time, I have decided that from now on I, Janice Perry, will no longer be known as a woman. From now on., I, Janice Perry, will be known as ... Elvis!" (With this statement, "Love Me Tender" is cued-in over the theater's sound system.)

Perry also makes powerful statements about sexual freedom, abortion rights, and censorship, including a memorable monologue about the price of the use of the word *fuck* in comedy.

"When I performed at the University of Utah," Perry reminisces happily, "one audience member called me the devil and ran screaming from the room."

Warren: How would you describe your humor? What kind of comedy do you most enjoy?

Perry: I think everything we do is based on fear, ultimately, fear of death. Especially humor. I like comedy about real things, comedy that addresses issues we struggle with individually and collectively and that encourages the audience to stand up and fight back. Comedy has the ability to transform fear into power.

Warren: What kind of comedy don't you like?

Perry: Comedy that wastes time. Jokes about nothing, that you laugh at and forget immediately. I hate self-deprecating humor and so-called jokes about classes of people. Throw-away humor. I resent that misuse of energy and power. I don't like most jokes. I don't like most stand-up comics. I see them and can only think how fabulous it would be if they were actually *saying* something, addressing real issues like the imbalance of power and social injustice. Instead they're saying "I'm so ——- nobody will fuck me" or "She's so ——- nobody will fuck her." What a waste.

Warren: When did you first realize that you could make other people laugh?

Perry: My parents would put me in my high chair and turn on the electric eggbeater. I would stick out my tongue, vibrate my whole body, and shake my head side to side. This was apparently the only form of amusement that my parents could afford in the early fifties.

Warren: Were you aware of or influenced by TV comics when you were a kid?

Perry: Last year I saw a Carol Burnett special, and I realized that I'd stolen her act! I mean the form. Come out, talk to the people and fool around, sing some songs, wear fabulously ridiculous outfits, and perform social satire. As I watched her, I realized that she had an incredible influence. She was so *smart* and *sexy* and *funny*. Growing up, I watched her every week. I also liked Lucy's work, but she made me sad because she was so jerked around by Ricky all the time.

Warren: Are there any other comics whose work you admire?

Perry: I like Richard Pryor, but it must be noted that his attitude toward women stinks and always has. Robin Williams makes me laugh but also repulses me. Victoria Wood, Dawn French, and Jennifer Saunders in England have moments of brilliance that cheer me up tremendously.

Warren: How did you first get into performing?

Perry: I was singing with rock and cocktail bands and got sick of traveling around with five boys all the time. I stayed home and wrote fiction and songs. I made weird tapes, with overdubs of songs and poems and soliloquies to my cat. A friend sent one of my tapes to the first New England Women's Musical Retreat. My first solo performance, at age thirty-one, was in front of two thousand women. They liked it, and so did I. I thought, Why do anything else?

Warren: How does it feel to make people laugh from a stage?

Perry: Performance is a state of grace.

Warren: Describe your audience.

Perry: Americans. Germans. Norwegians. The Swiss. The Danish. The Dutch. The English. The Scottish.

Warren: Who would you like to be your audience?

Perry: Everybody else.

Warren: What kind of impact do you want your work to have?

Perry: I'm getting more and more serious in my work. I'm not babying the audience anymore. I want my audience to go home from the performance and start changing things.

Marilyn Pittman

by Roz Warren

"Dang funny but about as demure as a rattlesnake" is how the *Anchorage Daily News* described San Francisco comic Marilyn Pittman, who has made a name for herself both on the queer comedy circuit (she's a star of the first gay comedy video, *All Out Comedy*) and as a featured act in mainstream clubs.

Pittman actually has two thriving show-biz careers—when she's not doing stand-up she's a leading voice consultant for National Public Radio. She's produced and hosted many radio shows, including several nationally syndicated shows for NPR. In demand for voice-overs, she narrated Debra Chasnoff's 1992 Academy Award-winning film, *Deadly Deception*.

Pittman's solo show, *Thank You For Sharing*, makes use of both her comedy and broadcasting skills. It's a fast-paced mix of stand-up, improv, and character sketches interspersed with prerecorded radio commercial parodies. (Like the one for S and M Banking at Naughty American Savings and Moan: "I applied for a loan. They turned me down. I was humiliated ... I loved it!") Pittman's show also features mock newscasts in the manner of "Saturday Night Live." (One news item: "In response to the antigay fundamentalist video *The Gay Agenda*, gay activists are producing their own video, *The Heterosexual Agenda*. It features tailgate parties, wedding receptions, date rape, child abuse, and Spring Break.")

Pittman's style is smart and exuberant, combining professionalism with an enormous sense of fun. She takes contagious delight in cutting through the bullshit of contemporary life, targeting inner children, self-help books, fundamentalists, politics, therapists, the New Age, and J. Edgar Hoover. Her radio experience has made her alert to the absurdities in the way we express ourselves: "What do people mean when they say, 'The computer went down on me?' " she queries.

In contrast to many contemporary TV-oriented comedians, books and reading are central to Pittman's act. She knew one relationship had soured, she jokes, "when one night we were reading in bed and I looked over and she was reading *Healing Through Grief* and I was reading *Living with Joy*." In fact, three of Pittman's best bits involve reading books onstage, including *How to Marry the Man of Your Choice*, which advises "Say hello to any man you are reasonably sure is not a felon." Pittman also gleefully reads aloud from lesbian personal ads, injecting some reality into the writer's fantasies. Funniest, however, is Pittman's dramatic reading from the infamous toe-fucking section of *The Joy Of Lesbian Sex*.

"I'm trying to talk about taboos, the things we're not allowed to talk about," explains Pittman. This she does in bits like her catchy rap song for white people that mocks being Caucasian ("I'm White ... and I'm Pale!" goes the refrain).

Performance comes naturally to this comic. "My grandmother was in vaudeville, and I was always encouraged to perform." She feels at home onstage, "To make people laugh," she says simply, "is bliss."

A lesbian comic faces a double dose of discrimination—sexism and homophobia—but Pittman never considered staying closeted. Being out, she feels, only enhances her comedy. "Queers aren't bound by societal norms. We're free of the pressure to conform. We queers have something to teach."

Pittman wants her comedy to transform anger into humor, shed light on misunderstanding, and initiate change. "It's a spiritual act to find humor in life," she says. "Comedy relieves us of the burden of taking ourselves too seriously."

Spirituality aside, however, she says her real goal in performance remains "to make people laugh until their faces are about to blow up."

Reno

by Deni Kasrel

Watch out for Reno. The one-named wonder of political comedy. The mouth that roars. Rants. Raves. When fully revved up, she's a furious ball of kinetic energy. A woman of high intelligence and voluminous vocabulary, she can wax on, most loquaciously, about a slew of topics; however, the word *inertia* is likely unknown, and incomprehensible, to her.

Don't call what she does an "act." Reno rejects the term—it implies something that's "contrived."

"It's not my favorite word for what I do," she clarifies. "That word sounds fake. What I do is reality-based. I don't look in the *Reader's Digest* for ideas, I've got way too many of my own."

Sam Cohn, agent to the stars, briefly took her on as a client. No go, though. He saw what Reno did—*her presentation*—as something merely to establish her position in the "industry." What he wanted, for this peripatetic, peroxided performer, was that she become a movie star. "That's so they can make a million dollars," Reno deadpans.

If it worked for Lily Tomlin and Whoopi Goldberg (two prior Cohn prizes) why wouldn't it work with Reno? Maybe because Reno didn't *want* to be a movie star. "My work is my work, and that's what I wanted to do," she emphasizes.

She wants to get in front of audiences and talk about the dilution of the Declaration of Independence, the obfuscation of the Bill of Rights, what a farce the Federal Reserve Bank is, the depth of social inequality. She is not interested in getting dressed up in wardrobe attire and futzing around on a film set all day. She and Cohn parted ways.

Reno has created several one-woman shows. Her first full-fledged program, *Reno In Rage and Rehab*, played off-Broadway and was adapted for an HBO special. *Reno Once Removed* opened at Lincoln Center, played New York's Joseph Papp Public Theater, then made a national tour. *Reno Besides Myself* begat *Citizen Reno*, the working title of a recent project.

What she does has been described as *stream* of consciousness. But stream is too timid a term. Reno's routine is more like a whirlpool, or grand rapids, of consciousness. Twisting, spewing, and rushing out gale-force wit with fervid ferocity. "Input is a big problem for me. I don't know how to screen. Which is one reason why what I do is stream of consciousness. Because everything is as important as everything else," she says.

This poses a personal difficulty, admits Reno: "If I were anything else, in the real world, except for what I'm doing, I would not be able to function well. I don't know how to shut up."

Having no shut-off valve works well for her in some respects: it allows for a fast flow of content. Then again, audiences have a problem relating to too many tumbling concepts, and sometimes, if ideas come up and out too fast, they don't always make sense. The danger of this was most apparent when Reno was first developing onstage, in the mid-eighties, back when she did her thing at grungy, punk/alternative performance spaces, where audiences didn't expect much in the way of "entertainment." "I would go up there and talk off the top of my head," she recalls. "I was saying stuff that didn't necessarily mean something, because I was never clear. Sometimes it would be just completely off-the-wall."

As was the artist herself. Reno makes no bones about admitting her time as a substance abuser. Self-medication to quell disquiet that took refuge in her soul.

As she began to channel her energies into comedy, Reno's existence took a turn for the better. "The professional career choice was not a choice but a godsend," she says in a contemplative tone. "It was luck. A lot of people pushed me toward it. Had I been out there on the street one more moment, doing what I was doing, I would be in prison or in a mental hospital by now."

Her troubled times made for material in her performance. She told about being a dark-skinned Hispanic child adopted into a Long Island WASP household. The neighbors were not impressed. She related true stories of being arrested. Tough luck stuff. Reno kvetched about her lousy life with high-minded hilarity.

That is her gift. There is excruciating angst and anger in what she puts out. And while she's made a concerted effort to rein in her torrent of thoughts, so as to offer a more cohesive presentation, there are still moments when she leaps far off, cruising past the cutting edge on out to the bleeding edge. Where it hurts. So bad you want to cry. But Reno makes you *laugh*. And wonder, Why is this funny?

Female circumcision, not knowing whether to put the names of friends who are dying of AIDS into a new address book—this is not the usual shtick of stand-up. Reno isn't a stand-up comic. Even in that world, which teems with misfits, Reno doesn't fit in. Comedy houses aren't her milieu. She doesn't do *jokes*. There's no punch line. Nonetheless, plenty of her lines land with a punch.

So what is she? "I suppose it would be better if I did know, but I don't. I don't have one word for it," she responds matter-of-factly. For the sake of simplicity, she has at times settled on referring to herself as a "comedic performer."

What she definitely is, is alienated, anxiety-ridden, and disgusted at the sorry state of affairs that we allow our world to be in. Very little is spared from her penetrating probes that pierce and pummel to a pulp. Playing it safe isn't worth the trouble. When interviewers annoy her, she lets them know it. Cursing at their obvious idiocy. Not everyone is up to Reno's snuff.

Her realm is reality. What it is. Her show gives us the world according to one very smart, critical woman who is both mad and maddening. This is scorched-earth style humor.

She's aghast at the notion of considering homosexuality a choice. Queers get beat up, disowned, cursed, and hated for no other reason than their choice of lover. "Oooh, sounds great!," she screams sarcastically. "Where do I sign up?" Her words gush. She looks like she'll explode. Her arms flail, her body twists. We were so flipped out by Watergate that "we were too flipped out to care about Iran-contra!" she bellows. And what of the Constitution? Its amendments have been upended! Yo, out there. Are you aware? Reno is sounding a wake-up call.

She's movement-oriented, though less now than before. She used to be majorly mobile onstage, prowling about like a crazed, caged panther. She'd spin, pace, careen, writhe on the floor—a radical approach for a radical rave. Part of this was the offshoot of nervous, unfocused energy, Reno now thinks. As she's become more at peace with herself, her performance is less jittery. Still, she sometimes can't help herself from letting loose with a jerk or spasm. "I do it by default. It's what comes out. I don't know where it's coming from; it's just who I am," she says. "I can't completely articulate how I feel about something with just words. So my body just sort of gets into the act and explains what's going on. It's just another dimension."

She used to just leap onto the stage and start to ramble. When the media started paying attention to her, Reno realized, Oh, Jesus. Somebody's *listening* to me! I better know what the hell I'm saying.

In an effort to reach out and touch a wider audience, Reno has toned down her antics. She's hired people to help her hone a "formalized" show that develops in a more logical fashion than pure stream of consciousness. Hers is not a middle-of-the-road product. Even so, she wants to speak to the mainstream, so they might hear what she has to say. There's some real awful shit happening out there—maybe she can help wise a bunch of us up.

Citizen Reno is a kind of a stylized playlet. It opens with its sole performer sitting on a couch talking to her dog, Lucy, whose coat is dreadlocked. There are a few props, some audio effects, sort of a storyline, and she "acts" a little, putting herself into different situations and altering her persona. In other arenas, she's gone further to infiltrate the mainstream, by really *acting a part*. She is the voice of Edith Ann's psychiatrist in Lily Tomlin's and Jane Wagner's animated Edith Ann series, and she did a cameo in Robert Redford's movie, *Quiz Show*.

Time to get back with Cohn, perhaps? Get real. Reno still wants to do her own work. Her program goes on as planned. Even if she does stem the screeching some, she will not shy away from incendiary political content.

Reno can't help but express her consciousness. "Whoever you are shows up in your humor, and if it doesn't, if you are contriving to be something that you are not, then your humor will suck."

karen Ripley

by Laura Post

Karen Ripley grew up in the early fifties in Richmond, California, an area north of Oakland known for its industrial architecture and petrochemical haze. "When you drive through Richmond, you can smell Standard Oil," she says. "My dad was a truck driver. We were your basic white, working-class, dysfunctional family." She discovered her future career at age four, when her family got a television. "I started seeing Lucy," says Ripley, "and I wanted her job."

At fifteen, Ripley acquired a set of drums and took a musical detour from that earlier ambition, playing in a number of Bay Area rock bands.

When the women's music era dawned, she joined the all-lesbian "Klondike Country Express."

In high school, Ripley was active with the drama department and was labeled "Senior Class Character." She tested out her stand-up material at the lesbian bars in San Francisco and the cabaret Valencia Rose. "It was really steady work," says Ripley, "and before you knew it, people began to know my name." She became known for deadpan one-liners like "Is it okay to hate men but dress just like them?" and "In San Francisco there's a bar on every corner; in Oakland, there's a bar on every window." Along the way she took a class with Whoopi Goldberg, who advised her, "Some will like you, and some won't. Just keep doing what you do."

However, for many years, Ripley's stand-up took a back seat to what she calls "my drinking and drug career." She was finally able to get sober in 1977, and then refocused her energy on her comedy. She studied improv at the Pacific School of Religion, believing that comedy has "a real spiritual element." She explains: "You have to surrender to the moment. You have to trust who you're with. You can't deny anyone's reality. You've got to go with stuff that might scare you."

Ripley cites Lily Tomlin as an example of the kind of comic she admires: "Lily Tomlin did a disabled woman. She didn't offend anyone because she was coming from her gut and because she studied her characters first. See, there's a way in which you can do anyone on the planet without hurting anyone. But it's a thin line in stand-up. You don't want to offend anyone. Especially in Berkeley—the dykes will let you know, okay?" Very popular with the Berkeley crowd are such Ripley lines as "Why do they call it menopause and not menostop? And what do men have to do with it anyway?"

In the past two years, Ripley's parents have both died. A few years before that, Ripley suffered a life-changing ruptured disk. Bedridden for weeks, she was forced to reevaluate her day job as a cook. "It was obvious I couldn't stand eight hours a day anymore. So I thought I'd better give it all to comedy. Because my mouth still works!"

Ripley is featured in the video *All Out Comedy* and recently cut a cassette, with Teresa Chandler, called *I Survived A Femme*. She's also a member of the improv quartet Over Our Heads and teaches improv to kids at summer camp. About a fourth of Ripley's gigs are benefits. "It's not about fame and fortune," she explains, "it's about love."

Joan Rivers

by Roz Warrren

Joan Rivers has come further against tougher odds than anyone else in this book. It's impossible to overestimate her impact, both because she redefined what was possible for women in comedy and because she's been a role model for so many.

When Rivers started out, there were few women stand-ups. There was, however, a long tradition of women comedians who hid their intelligence or attractiveness to court audience acceptance. Rivers, in contrast, took the spotlight as a chic, well-dressed woman who was up front about being both smart and funny, not to mention gutsy, irreverent, and outrageous. Rivers did something revolutionary: she spoke the truth onstage about women's feelings. For the first time, a woman comic revealed what women really thought and felt. Rivers talked about all the secrets women usually kept hidden, making audiences laugh at such taboo topics as having an affair, going to the gynecologist, having a baby, and faking orgasms. Tame by today's standards, a joke like "When I had my baby, I screamed and screamed. And that was just during conception," both shocked and delighted sixties audiences.

Rivers talked to her audience the way you'd dish with a close girlfriend. That included dissing other gals. Who can forget her infamous quip that in a *People* magazine cover a fat Liz Taylor looked like she'd devoured her previous husbands. It was mean, it was shocking … and it was hilarious. Because it was exactly what we were thinking ourselves, but were too timid (or too kind) to express.

While Rivers has been criticized for putting down other women, if you examine her material, you'll learn that she always plays fair. She's just as tough on herself as she is on others, she never picks on anybody who can't defend herself, and she only mocks upward. The rich and celebrated are fair targets for her wit; the underdog is not. Before putting down Rivers for putting down women, consider too her reputation for generously supporting other women comics in what is often a cutthroat business.

An early feminist, Rivers' material challenged the gender stereotypes of the time. She mocked the requirement that women be perfect little housekeepers with jokes like: "Don't cook. Don't clean. No man will ever make love to a woman because she waxed the linoleum—'My God, the floor's immaculate. Lie down, you hot bitch!' " Rivers didn't put herself down because she couldn't cook and clean; instead, with her wit, she celebrated her indifference to these tasks.

Rivers has cited Lenny Bruce as an inspiration for comedy based on a bold telling of the truth. Perhaps because the basis of her act is sharing with her audience the kind of truths women tell when we're alone with a best friend, she's always evoked a strong, personal audience response. She, in turn, respects and connects with her audience, comparing her onstage role to that of a support-group leader: "This is a very, very angry country," she wrote in her second autobiography, *Still Talking*. "Women are thrilled to hear another woman articulating their rage."

She also makes it clear that she needs us: "The ultimate high, the ultimate happiness," she's also written, "is when the audience is standing up at the end of the show and they won't let you go."

We love Rivers because she works hard for us. She takes nothing for granted. She courts us relentlessly, never resting on her laurels and never putting on airs. In fact, part of the appeal of her self-deprecating material may be that we're convinced by it that no matter how rich or famous or celebrated she becomes, in her heart she doesn't see herself as superior. She'll always thumb her nose at the snobs; she'll never become one.

We love Joan because throughout an emotional roller coaster of a career, she's never lost her irreverence, her ability to delight and shock with her wit, or her belief in herself. Most important, she's never lost that magical ability to "think funny"—to always, no matter what, come through for us with a joke that kills.

Roseanne

by Kathi Maio

How can I say this as unequivocally as possible? Roseanne—née Barr, formerly Arnold—is the most important woman in the universe of popular culture today.

Do you scoff, gentle reader? Think about it. In the last ten years, this fierce, funny female has (while retaining a large, enthusiastic following) broken almost every taboo and exploded nearly every myth about American womanhood.

Start with body size. The "average" American woman may be a size 14, but how often have you seen the American norm on your television screen?

(No, the weepy self-haters on diet commercials don't count.) Oh, there have been a few larger gals in supporting roles on situation comedies, but they've mostly been self-haters, too. In fact, the ample females of sitcomland seemed to exist for the sole purpose of providing the show's writers an opportunity for a few fat jokes.

Women of substance led a shamefaced, completely secondary existence in our culture. Until Roseanne. When she entered our living rooms via our television screen, she was like an invading army (of Amazons). She took no prisoners. And she made it clear that she wasn't going to put up with any bullshit about her jeans-size—or anything else.

"I ain't got nothing to fuckin' hide," she has told interviewers. And that is the essence of her appeal. Roseanne's career in show business has been one long, unrelenting Speak Out. In interviews, in her stand-up routines, in Annie Leibovitz photo spreads, on her brilliant top-five sitcom, and in the merciless light of tabloid headlines, Roseanne has exposed the female experience by exposing herself. Overexposure, many have long called it. But I see it as a noble, if often brutal, brand of honesty.

It has been fascinating to watch her over the last decade. During that time, Roseanne became famous—later infamous—and learned to cope with her new wealth and power. Simultaneously, she embarked upon a painful voyage of self-discovery. And she has shared that journey with all of us.

Most of us first became aware of Roseanne Barr sometime in the mid-eighties, when she was America's "Domestic Goddess" (a subversion of a term from the right-wing best-seller *Fascinating Womanhood* that exhorted women to Stepford-Wife submission). Roseanne's Domestic Goddess was as far away from submissive as you could get. She was, instead, an enraged working-class homemaker, temporarily escaped from the trailer park.

The sarcastic feminism of that routine won her club headliner status and a crack at the big time via venues like "The Tonight Show." And it's been preserved on videotape in her 1987 HBO special, "The Roseanne Barr Show." She's come a long way since, but that comedy hour is still a fine piece of revolutionary art.

Unlike earlier women comics who did marriage material, Roseanne's routine wasn't about telling jokes; it was about telling the truth. And, even then, the truth could be a little uncomfortable. Especially if you were a man. Her attitude toward the American husband was merciless. And as she so aptly observed, "We're all married to the same fuckin' guy."

She should know. In a real "Twilight Zone" touch, her then husband and her future one both played her spouses in her 1987 special. Bill Pentland portrayed her "real" husband in the opening and closing domestic scenes, while Tom Arnold took the part of her mate in the staged skits that punctuated her stand-up routine.

It is an interesting illustration of how blurred the lines between life and art become when you watch Roseanne. And when you compare that special with the situation comedy series that succeeded it a year later, it becomes an even more significant illustration of something else. And that is Hollywood's refusal to give Roseanne credit for her many achievements.

With her growing fame, and the success of that HBO project, Roseanne was offered a shot at a network situation comedy. It came from the Carsey-Werner Company, the folks who gave us the sanitized sainthood of "The Cosby Show." The executive producer of the show was Matt Williams.

It was Roseanne's big break, and she didn't want to blow it. Nor did she want the powers that be to blow it for her. From the get-go there were fights over the content of the show. As Roseanne told *TV Guide* in January 1989: "I want a portrait of working folks with a little warmth and dignity, not buffoons." It was a struggle to maintain that vision, when the show was produced and written by people Roseanne felt understood little of working-class women and their families.

The fight for power at "Roseanne" was dirty—and painful. In 1989 and 1990, while the show was riding high in the ratings, the press often reported that Roseanne was proving to be a difficult star. Word (from production company and studio execs) was that Roseanne was ruining "Roseanne" by throwing meaningless tantrums.

In retrospect, the truth of the matter is apparent. Roseanne was fighting the good fight for the integrity of the show that bore her name. "They'd attack me, then ignore me, treat me like I was stupid," she told *TV Guide* in 1991, after the smoke cleared. "It was a class thing and a women's thing. I wanted them to write more from the woman's point of view and they thought it meant putting in tampon jokes and castration jokes."

Roseanne knew better. And she fought Williams to the point of ultimatum: him or me. Williams left, but got a permanent credit as the "creator" of the show. It's balderdash, of course. Matt Williams is no more the creator of "Roseanne" than is Mahatma Gandhi. All you need do is look at those early Domestic Goddess routines and that first HBO special to see that Roseanne is the show's real creator. (This is *her life*, after all!)

But this media compulsion to deny Roseanne her due continues to this day. Look at all the stories from the early days of her second marriage. Tom Arnold wasn't a fellow comedian she fell in love with and married; he was, the press reported, a Svengali who held Roseanne's life and career in his total (sinister) control.

Yeah, right. You know what they say about Anonymous being a woman. It applies, even to the most famous woman on television. But while Roseanne doesn't get formal credit for creating her show, she is most certainly behind its continued success. For although "Roseanne" was good from the start, it has never been better than in the last couple of years. Just consider, for a moment, the topics this prime-time network show has tackled.

First there are the economic issues. Rosie has toiled as a factory worker, a fast-food peon, a beauty parlor sweep-up girl, and a lunch-counter waitron, to name but a few of her many exciting occupations. Watching her struggle (and that of her husband, Dan) to pay the bills and support the three kids tells us more than any politician's "jobs" speech ever could about the eroding financial security of the American worker.

And as for Dan Quayle's favorite topic, family values, "Roseanne" abounds in them. At the same time, the show hides nothing of family dysfunction and misery. The two shows devoted to getting Roseanne's sister, Jackie (Laurie Metcalf), out of an abusive relationship represent the best television treatment of family violence I have ever seen. And the show has given us an unblinking look at everything from teen depression to the pubescent discovery of masturbation, from fertility problems to unexpected pregnancy, from mother-daughter angst to the death of an abusive father. And, yes, even homosexuality and bisexuality.

And the most amazing thing is that, with Roseanne at the heart of every episode, the show is still very, very funny.

But it's the honesty that really blows me away. And the social realism of "Roseanne" is only the beginning. In the last couple of years, Roseanne the woman has, in violation of all the rules about the pitfalls of fame, become even more radically candid about her personal life.

Roseanne divorced, and she and her lover saw each other through recovery programs for substance abuse. She remarried, was reunited with a daughter she gave birth to as a single teen and gave up for adoption, and has dealt with the various crises of her other teenaged kids. She has been denounced by a president of the United States for her rendition of the national anthem, has had breast reduction and plastic surgery, and dumped a second husband. Most importantly, she remembered and broke silence about the incest she suffered as a child.

All this material (if I dare call it that) has shown up in Roseanne's comedy. Some has provided grist for the writers of her sitcom. More of it has shown up in her stand-up. Call it kamikaze comedy. Call it a life as performance art. Roseanne's unflinching humor is, I think, a large part of her recovery process.

In June of 1992, Ms. Arnold, resplendent in a copy of a gold suit once worn by Elvis, did another HBO comedy special. It was filmed live at the Guthrie in Minneapolis, and it was the most sharp-witted, frightening, socially-conscious hour of comedy I have ever witnessed. There was political commentary. (On women going into combat: "Yeah, I wanna go over there and die for your sexist, racist country that I ain't even a fuckin' equal member of!") But most of the commentary was scathing, scatological ... and profoundly personal. She spoke of, among other things, her sick family, Barbie dolls, obsessive compulsive disorder, Barbara Bush, and being fat. And in between bits, she would mutter, "It's all bullshit and lies," or, "Got to stop the lyin'—goddamn it!"

That's what it's all about. Fearlessly, Roseanne aims to strip away more and more of the lies and bullshit until the essential truth of her life illuminates the lives of all of us.

So of course she would write another autobiography now that the ugly memories of her childhood have all come flooding back. And why would she deny any aspect of her life to a magazine like *Vanity Fair*? Yes, she's experienced lesbian sex. Yes, she supported her kids, during her early days in the comedy clubs, by turning tricks in the parking lot.

For many, these were shocking revelations. But Roseanne never denied any of it. In fact, the truth behind all of those tabloid headlines is right there in her comedy routines, if you listen carefully enough. For example, her experiences with sex work (and the Hollywood machine) provided the brilliant bit with which she closed her 1992 special. In an annihilating analysis of power politics, Roseanne compared the relative advantages and disadvantages in deciding whether it is better to "kiss the ass" or "suck the dick."

Sucking the dick, a straightforward business proposition requiring payment up front is—when done right—a finite act. It is, she therefore concluded, much preferable—if a choice *must* be made—to kissing ass, which goes on forever and is never rewarded.

Rough stuff. Over the top, some would say. Hell, yes! Roseanne is over the top. She is storming the barricades. Which is why the backlash that is often leveled against her (e.g., tabloid claims that Saddam Hussein has a sexual obsession for her) can be so absurdly vicious. No matter. This is one woman who won't back down.

Hey, she can eat these guys for lunch. The media feeding frenzy doesn't frighten her. From time to time, she even takes pleasure in playing with their (sick, pin-)heads.

What fun it was, watching the press scramble when Roseanne and Tom announced that they were marrying their assistant, Kim Silva. (The best touch, I thought, was when the happy trio registered at Ben & Jerry's for six flavors, including Chocolate Chip Cookie Dough.)

How can you not love it—and her?

As with many of Roseanne's tabloid brouhahas, you later wondered what pain she might have been hiding beneath her bravado. But that's what makes her humor so complex. And that's what makes her life seem like such a risky, valiant endeavor.

Roseanne used to call herself a Domestic Goddess. You were selling yourself short, sister. To me, you are Aphrodite, Medusa, Cassandra, Athena, Hera, Artemis, and all of Demeter's Furies rolled into one. You are to be worshipped. (So, pardon, gentle reader, my idolatry.)

I like to think about that cover of *Vanity Fair* from February 1994. Roseanne was sitting above a handful of broken cigarettes and a toy train, with a knowing look on her face and a grapefruit in her hand. She was wearing the briefest black lingerie and silk stockings. Her legs were spread fully apart. She was plump and très sexy.

I don't, however, like to think of the reactions of many men (and some women) to that photo. I remember one guy, a psychology professor at the Boston university where I work, picking up the issue and spouting off in outrage. "She's a pig," he exclaimed. (As if you had room to talk, prick.) Then he said: "Has she no shame?"

And I say to that guy again now: "No. Roseanne has *no shame*."

Roseanne is fat. She is loud. She is angry as hell. And she is the funniest woman that ever told the truth, the whole truth, and nothing but the truth. That is not a matter of shame. It is a reason for pride and celebration.

And if you can't deal with it, buddy, then, crawl back under your rock.

Flash Rosenberg

by Deni Kasrel, interview by Roz Warren

Flash Rosenberg is a gentle-voiced flyweight with long dark hair, boundless energy, and a childlike, springy step. A photographer, cartoonist, and multimedia artist, she has more recently packaged her provocative, perceptive, and wholly humorous thoughts into a stage show featuring absurdist monologues, slides, videos, intellectual yet amusing musings, playful props, and helpful household hints. "It's like making the avant-garde suburban," she says.

Flash enjoys working on such a diversity of projects, since once she learns something she wants to learn something else. "It's what I loved about photography," she comments. "I was going to be a cartoonist or an illustrator, but I loved being out in the world to collect information about how it all worked. I always wondered, Why are we here? and What are we doing?"

Prior to putting a concerted effort into developing as a performer, Flash (formerly Susan) ran a business that provided photographers who were more than mere snapshooters, but served as active entertainment as well. She and her staff came to functions wearing outrageous costumes. On the spot, they created wacky photo-inspired party favors. Her performance pieces expand on this concept of using the visual arts as a basis for the creation of something that's zany, unusual, and unexpected.

Ardently curious and cleverly cerebral, Rosenberg constantly ruminates on what's extraordinary in the seemingly ordinary. Wordplay gives her great enjoyment, and she loves to concoct shrewd, sometimes subversive observations of how scientific concepts apply to everyday life.

Possessed of an endearingly impish spirit that belies her forty years, Rosenberg has developed a stylized stage persona that's a heightened version of herself. Flash the performer is a smart, inquisitive woman with a demeanor that's sweet-hearted, sentimental, and sprightly. Her presentation is sometimes clownish and her humor bridges genuine befuddlement and braininess. She's the child that will never grow up, who is nonetheless a wise old soul.

Warren: What inspires your comedy?

Rosenberg: I have a fluency in misunderstanding things. I see everything in stereo. I understand the general consensus about the way things are, but I also understand them surrealistically. It's like speaking two languages. Humor is also my way of coping with the world. The world is so confusing and complicated and disappointing. Making it funny makes it bearable.

Warren: Yet your approach isn't particularly angry or judgmental.

Rosenberg: I don't think I'm bitter about a thing being as it is. I'm just trying to get to the truth about how things really are, because so much of what's presented to you as what you should feel or should be or should do isn't what's really happening with anyone.

I've also found that by being nonjudgmental more people have told me deep, dark secrets or comic secrets or unbelievable things that have happened to them. They trust that I'll believe. This gathering of information is the base and core and inspiration for my humor.

Warren: Gilda Radner once said, "Comedy is the truth, only faster."

Rosenberg: Humor is a way of boiling down something that sort of dithers and blathers and spatters, of making it concise and understandable.

Warren: Many comics are actually very serious people. You're aware of life's injustices, but your approach is playful and lighthearted rather than angry.

Rosenberg: I used to let the audience in on my own nervousness; I thought that was honest. But people don't really come to a show to be scared; they come to see what you're thinking about, and what you've learned. If I feel miserable, why project that on my audience, when they have their own load of misery? I'd rather try to help everybody do that kind of weaving that turns straw into gold, by taking what's bad and retelling it in a way that makes it funny.

Warren: A lot of your material is a retelling of setbacks you've encountered. Do you have to achieve a certain amount of emotional distance from something before you can start to use it as material?

Rosenberg: If it still hurts too much, I don't sound funny, I sound wounded. In some ways my work helps me accelerate getting emotional distance from certain things.

Warren: Where do you think your interest in humor comes from?

Rosenberg: I was involved in photography for many years because I like making the negative positive. My humor involves doing the same thing verbally. I come to comedy not from wanting to be an actress, but from visually observing things and doing that kind of inside-out game.

I'm very interested in inverses—in turning things around and twisting them, not for the goofiness of it but because it's interesting. I love to sew, and sewing to me is exactly the same as making a good joke, because you turn things inside out. *You* see how a thing is constructed, but from the outside it just looks like an outfit.

Warren: How do you create your comedy?

Rosenberg: I'm constantly asking myself questions. Some people wallow in feeling miserable. They'll say, "How do I feel? I feel awful." And the next thing they ask themselves is, "How do I feel?" Again, the answer is, "I feel awful." Well, you can build yourself into feeling really awful by the end of the day if you don't change your question.

Instead, I ask myself, "What's making me feel awful? Is it because it's grey and I have to go out? Or is it because I don't feel loved?" I keep changing the question, getting more specific.

There's a game my mother used to play with me. I was a very poor eater. She'd serve me something and I'd say, "I don't like it." She'd say, "You can't just say you don't like it; you have to be more specific." So if I didn't like peas, for instance, I'd say, "I don't like the way the skin is kind of tough and the inside is kind of mushy. I just don't know how to get my teeth ready." And she'd say, "That's a good reason," and I wouldn't have to eat peas.

My way of getting out of doing what I didn't want in life was to be funny and to notice things more sharply.

Warren: Does your family still encourage your comedy?

Rosenberg: Oh yeah. In my family it's considered bad form to be a grump. When you talk about some ill that's been visited on you, you always try to tell it in a funny way. It's a way of not worrying those around you. In fact, your impression of me being upbeat is this real deep wish not to worry those around me. I've always had that kind of Jewish way of putting things in perspective: "It's not so bad. I have my health. I have a home. I have friends." I try to be grateful for what I have even when I'm really upset about what I've lost or been denied.

Warren: Do you consider your material gender-based? Do you consider yourself a "woman comic"?

Rosenberg: Because I don't come to comedy from the theater, I think I'm less likely to think of myself as a woman comic. Actors are taught to be aware of how the audience perceives them. I'm a photographer, and as a photographer you feel invisible. You forget you even *have* an appearance.

That isn't to say that the audience doesn't perceive me as a "woman comic." I did my show at the North Star Bar recently and got twelve calls the next day, six from men and six from women. All the men complained that the material I did about having trouble with romance wasn't believable. They said, "You seem attractive. Anybody would want to be with you. You're just whining for no reason." But all the women said the material was right on. How I came across was based on whether I was viewed as a compatriot or as an object of conquest.

Warren: But I assume that onstage you don't consciously assume either of those roles?

Rosenberg: I think of my demeanor as one of being a sister. That's my best role. What I say is relevant to everyone. For instance, when I say: "I don't understand the speed of light. What does the speed of light have to do with daily life? What I want to know is the length of matter. If someone breaks up with you and it hurts, how long will it matter?"

That's not about being male or female—it's about being human.

I'm trying to sort out what I've been through as a person. Comedy gives me a structure. I can put things into topics and categories and groups and themes. Otherwise, it's this just disorganized, frazzled blurt.

Warren: Much of your material deals with people—men in particular—who have given you a hard time. Yet your humor is very kind.

Rosenberg: I really believe that people are doing the best they can. I don't have an elaborate sense of what's right and wrong; I just focus on what is. My response to all these divisions of people into gay, straight, black, white, women, men is to try to get into a zone that's beyond that, without negating any of that. Instead of having to declare that I'm this component of ethnicity and gender and sexual orientation, I want to get to the root of what's universal about all of us being here.

Warren: Do you think humor in general is evolving in a positive, or more progressive direction?

Rosenberg: There's been a century's worth of humor at others' expense, and I'm hoping that's becoming unacceptable. Also, in terms of the way it's structured, I know that my own humor evokes laughs at a different point than a traditional joke. It's not an ejaculative "Ha!" Instead, it sort of brews.

Warren: Can you give us an example?

Rosenberg: I'll say, "I've brought my diaphragm to the show tonight." There will be some laughter. "Because it doesn't have a chance to get out much." More laughter. Then I say: "I dreamt I was holding my diaphragm up to the light to check for holes. And all of a sudden it turned into … a giant diaphragm planetarium!" Third wave of laughter. "With sparkly dots of light everywhere!" A little more. "And just like anyone who has ever been in a planetarium I was wondering …" (Stop. Let everybody in their own heads think of what they're wondering.) "Where's the Big Dipper?"

The joke comes like a woman.

Warren: A lot of women got into comedy because they grew up watching Lucy or Carol Burnett and said to themselves, "I want that job." That's not the case with you.

Rosenberg: No. I'm just trying to figure out all the things that I pay attention to, whether it's pop music or poetry or people that I've met. I read recipes to figure out structure for jokes. Right now, I'm reading a book on logic and possibility in order to get more jokes. I buy goofy books and goofy records: books like *Fortune Telling for Fun and Profit*. Those are my comic influences.

Warren: You seem to enjoy, even welcome, new situations and challenges.

Rosenberg: I'm a photographic personality. Wanting to be a photographer and wanting to be a comic come from the same impulse, which is to go somewhere you haven't been and take a look around. If you have a camera, you have a license to go there and do it. If you have a show, you get to go up onstage and see how that works.

I'm very comfortable with not being comfortable. In fact, part of the delight of performing, for me, is the kind of fear you feel right before you go on.

Warren: You enjoy stage fright?

Rosenberg: I think it just means that you really care about your audience. It feels like the fear you have when you first fall in love, in that romantic phase when you're not really sure it's going to work out, but you want it to so much.

Warren: If you bomb and you just can't connect with your audience, does it feel like a failed love affair?

Rosenberg: I don't bomb very often, but when I do I guess it just means that we just weren't really meant for each other. If you put yourself out there, it's bound to happen. What I do isn't going to work for everyone. Sure, there's always someone who will hate it. I call that the whale theory: if you come to the surface and spout off, you can expect to be harpooned.

Warren: But, in fact, your work has been very well received. You just won a Philadelphia City Paper Reader's Choice award. You were named Local Comic Most Likely to Make You Laugh Until It Hurts.

Rosenberg: The part about it hurting has me a little concerned.

Warren: Your act is very clever in that it involves a lot of wordplay, but it's also very accessible.

Rosenberg: What I do isn't that highbrow, although I've had editors and producers tell me, "I like your stuff, but you're a little over the heads of our audience."

I want to reply, "Hey, *you're* not that smart and you get it." But I'm a diplomat, so I say, "Hey, *I'm* not that smart and I get it."

In fact, one of the nicest things people have said about my show is, "We laughed and we left feeling a little smarter."

Warren: You were turned down recently for a TV gig; they said you were "too old and too ethnic." An evaluation that has nothing to do with your wit and everything to do with your appearance.

Rosenberg: I'm not impressed with television, and perhaps that goes both ways. Maybe I just don't belong there. I don't say that in order to condone closed-mindedness. It may take someone with more imagination or courage or insight or all three to see where my place might be. I wanted the job, of course, but we all have breaks, and the breaks get broken, and you get more breaks. It's all part of the adventure. All you can do is put all of your lines out and see what happens. You can spend a lot of time promoting yourself; I'd rather spend a lot of time doing the work. Then spend some time trying to figure it out. Then spend some time earning money. And then spend some time complaining, carousing and trying to forget the whole thing.

Warren: How did you start working with props?

Rosenberg: When I started performing, props were like my training wheels. Instead of feeling that I was up there all alone in the middle of a sea of nothing, gasping for words, I had something onstage that was comfortable that I could immediately begin to talk about. I wasn't all alone—I had my toys. I don't use them as much now, but they're powerful if used as punctuation.

Warren: You perform in cafes and art centers more often than you do in comedy clubs. Is there a reason for that?

Rosenberg: If you're in an art center, people are relieved that it's funny. But if you're in a comedy club, no one is going to be relieved that it's art.

Warren: Many comics are very career-oriented. Everything they do is part of an overall game plan meant to get them onto television or to Broadway or into the movies. You don't seem that driven about your career path.

Rosenberg: Advancing my career isn't the focus of my life. I'm having a ball with humor, rather than being on a career mission. An agent once told me that there are two kinds of people. There are people who want to publish a book. They come in every day and, oh, they want to publish a book so bad. But they don't want to *work* on a book. But I actually like working on this stuff, so I'm working on it. I'm having a wonderful time developing my material. And when the opportunity comes, I won't be caught short.

Warren: You don't want to be a movie star.

Rosenberg: I always like the house lights up a bit when I perform. I don't like everybody to be in the dark and me to be in the light.

Rita Rudner

by Deni Kasrel

The voice is the first thing that throws you off: it's soft and airy, nearly naive. Her hair is a wavy, ruddy tress. She wears a wide-eyed gaze that suggests this person is not all there. And then there's the dress—always some sort of long-length gown that's stylish but not too flashy. That's Rita Rudner— a ditz with glitz.

Don't you believe it. The coy routine is just that—a routine. Rudner is nobody's fool. To the contrary, she's got a razor-sharp awareness of human nature that's incredibly on target. The woman hits the bull's-eye with such ease that she's the sharpshooter of stand-up.

Like many in her trade, Rudner is a perceptive observer who finds mounds of material in the experiences of everyday living. Take the drawback to feeling well: "Health basically gives you the freedom to agonize about things that have absolutely no importance," she wryly notes in her book of collected essays, *Naked Beneath My Clothes*. Riding in the car with her mate presents a curious circumstance: her husband insists he's the better driver of the pair, yet he's been cited with a few moving violations, and Rita's record is clean. She knows why women hate shopping for bathing suits: They must be tried on in tiny dressing rooms whose interiors are flanked by mirrors that accentuate body flaws. "I think after you leave those rooms they should offer some kind of counseling," she writes. "Or at least have a sign on the mirror that says, 'Caution: objects in mirror may appear larger'."

The jokes that Rita writes are constructed masterfully. She employs a standard though subtly complex formula: set up a premise, go off on a few tangents, elaborate and embellish some of the seemingly unrelated topics to create small jokes along the way, draw it all together, and then end with a zinger laugh line. It's a scheme that must be done just right to work. If the audience can tell where the joke is heading, or a line goes astray, then it all falls flat—there goes the oomph out of the punch line.

Rudner's jokes hit you squarely on the funny bone. These aren't hard hits, mind you—they're not assaultive chop-busters. These are sharp hits with soft edges. Just the type of thing you'd expect from a demure, ladylike woman whose mind just happens to be sharp as a tack.

Perhaps this ability to be so *en pointe* derives from the performer's background as a dancer. Prior to stepping up onto the comedy platform, Rudner's feet were busily stomping away on the theatrical stage. As a child, she studied ballet, and she's transferred aspects of this training to the crafting of her routine: "You can't possibly dance a ballet step until you break it down and know what you're doing and why in every little teeny moment. That's the way I do comedy."

Her dancing career had been successful—she'd landed a supporting role in the Broadway production of *Annie*—but Rudner disliked the tiresome auditioning process, and roles she did land were confining. Eight times a week, Rita repeated the exact same steps. Performing stand-up, on the other hand, was liberating: "To be able to think of what you want to say and say it, however many times you want to do it … was much more satisfying to me."

A winning act didn't come easily, but Rita had learned from dancing that practice makes perfect. That, plus knowing your subject inside and out. She immersed herself in a self-styled course of study in comedy, going to New York's Museum of Broadcasting and poring over tapes of successful comics.

She paid special attention to clips of Jack Benny and George Burns, noting their knack for understatement and use of few words to get the big laugh. She listened to albums by Woody Allen and Bob Newhart, and even examined psychological studies on humor. The intricacies of voice and phrasing intrigued her: "I was fascinated by the craft of comedy: How if you said something one way they laughed, but if you added a word here, they didn't. The choice of words is so important. You've got to be so specific. People don't know how hard it is."

Like her icons Benny and Burns, Rudner has determined her best bet is to go with a less-is-more shtick. Jerry Seinfeld described her act as akin to haiku, and it's true her work is the product of distinctive simplicity.

Rudner is one of those rare comics who headlines in major theaters. She no longer does comedy clubs and is more likely to be seen playing a casino showcase. Credit for this goes to her husband/manager, Martin Bergman, a British theatrical producer who first saw Rudner's act back in 1984, at Catch a Rising Star. He polished up her presentation and packaged the performer as an entertainment product, giving her direction on how to do interviews, work out publicity campaigns, and perk up her onstage wardrobe.

Along the way the two married. As a working duo, the pair cowrote the movie *Peter's Friends* (1992), an ensemble project centering around a ten-year reunion of English college chums, in which Rudner plays a neurotic, bitchy, self-absorbed American actress.

She'd like to do more acting, preferably in major motion pictures, as opposed to television. Another book is said to be in the offing, plus she and Bergman have suggested they've got other projects up their sleeves. It seems the pair have found the secret for success in both their careers and their marriage is not to let failure stand in one's way when striving for ultimate success. "We're relentless," Rudner has stated. "People say to me, 'You're always working.' I'm always getting rejected, that's why I'm always working."

Betsy Salkind

by Roz Warren

Betsy Salkind graduated from Massachusetts Institute of Technology with a master's in management science, but she soon became restless with her sensible future as a bank examiner. "I'm going to die some day," she told herself, "Is this what I want to do with my life?" It wasn't, so she quit her job to begin working with comedy groups, like the Terrorist Bridesmaids. Since then, Salkind has performed stand-up in comedy clubs, on television, and even in a women's prison. Her movie roles include the head flight attendant in the lesbo soap *Two in Twenty* and the lead Barbie in the cinema epic *Barbie Graduates*.

Salkind's stage show features an almost too convincing rendition of a cat throwing up a hairball, a Sapphic version of "Cagney and Lacey," and characters like The Godmother, a send-up of the Marlon Brando character as a powerful, matriarchal cat-nurturer. Salkind's wit ranges from wry, political one-liners ("I recently became a Christian Scientist. It was the only health plan I could afford") to longer, more poignant observations about gender and culture. ("In high school my girlfriends and I gave each other hickeys and then made up fictitious male lovers who gave them to us," she observes. "It never occurred to us that we were real.")

In 1989, Salkind premiered "The Emperor's Getting Fucked," a ten-minute piece about misogyny, racism, and viciousness in the comedy clubs that had quite an impact on the Boston comedy community, marking the end of Salkind's comedy club career and the beginning of her shift to performance art.

Her first one-woman performance piece, *Master of Science*, combined cooking as a spectator sport with a feminist critique of the military-industrial complex. Her next solo piece, *All My Life*, described as "the darkest comedy this side of hope," was an autobiographical work inspired by the comic's rediscovery of her own "baby book." After exploring the pages devoted to baby Betsy's first words, early friendships, and the like, a blank screen appears on the overhead projector. "This is the page for abuse," Salkind comments.

Salkind characterizes her philosophy as "Ask not what the world has done to you, but what you can do to the world." She is currently working on *Come Here, I'm Not Going To Hurt You*, a comic/surreal documentary film about child abuse, and is also penning her next performance piece, *Anne Frank: The Comedy*. She's well aware that her comic message is unconventional: "When I tell people I'm a comedian, they say, 'Are you funny?' I say, 'No, it's not that kind of comedy'."

Claudia Sherman

by Deni Kasrel

An emcee introduces stand-up comic Claudia Sherman, saying she just got married. The 5 foot 3 inch comedian steps to the stage wearing a puffy-sleeved, satin wedding gown. Audience members might suppose they're about to hear the shtick of a nice-genteel lady.

Guess again, guys. The dress, she tells us, cost two thousand dollars. "And you're supposed to wear it only once? *Bullshit!* I wear it to work, I wear it to the toilet, I wear it to the supermarket."

The bit gets a big laugh, and Sherman's act is off and running, as is her mouth, which motors along at a fast pace. The jokes come quick. There's a barrage of barbs. She takes hard and fast swipes at male behavior. "It's a penis thing!" she's fond of saying, or more accurately, yelling, as a way to come to terms with otherwise inexplicable behavior that appears related to testosterone levels.

The institution of marriage is raked over the coals: "Why can't we be honest with wedding invitations and have them printed with fifty dollar cover, two-drink minimum?" Claudia wonders. She drills into the ridiculousness of various nuptials' conventions—a point made all the more glaring as she delivers her missive in an expensive, yet usually intended to be worn only once, wedding gown. She skewers her husband, who wants sex at inappropriate times—like when he's all sweaty and dirty, meantime she's just come out of the shower.

Her mother-in-law, Mona, merits no mercy, either. Mona once asked Claudia if her son was a good lover. "He's got a big schlong," replied Sherman, who reports that Mona responded, "He gets it from me."

There's a level of absurdity to be reckoned with here. Still, the material rings true. And that it is: Sherman claims her act is autobiographical: "I exaggerate—but it's all based in truth."

During her time onstage, Claudia insults audience members, pulls at toupees, and slaps people's heads. She's hostile, on the edge. You'd think she'd scare patrons off. To the contrary, her behavior elicits large laughs. Not everyone can get away with such stunts. She figures her ability to "act like an animal" and have folks love her for it, is because all that she says and does is drawn from heartfelt sincerity, and people pick up on that.

"It's almost like Don Rickles," says Sherman. "He sees someone short and he says, 'When you were born, what'd you do, come out and hit the wall?' He's not personalizing it. I don't know what it is."

People sense a vulnerability about her, she surmises. "I have a very good heart. You know people pick up energies. Supposedly, Don Rickles is one of the nicest people. He's very shy and cordial."

We live in an angry world filled with problems, she declares. People enjoy watching antagonism because they can't let out their own frustrations. When they see someone enraged, they experience a vicarious release of pent-up emotions. "Didn't you ever see somebody on the street that you didn't like and they had a bad toupee or something?" she asks. "Wouldn't you just love to go over to them and pull it off and say, 'Get a life!' You can't do that. But on the stage you can."

Claudia says that expressing anger as part of her act makes her less angry in real life. No stranger to hostility herself, Claudia was raised in a household of constant screaming and bickering. Her parents got divorced when she was young, and she lived with her grandmother for a while. "It wasn't the most pleasant childhood," she comments, "but I was always allowed to express myself. Everyone in the family expressed themselves."

Growing up in New York's borough of Queens turned her into a tough street kid. "I'm a rebel, I defy authority," she boasts. "The kids I hung out with were not on the honor roll. I'm not saying they weren't smart, but they'd flip you the bird."

New York-style street talk added to her attitude. "It was like, if you thought someone was ugly, you said, 'You're ugly.' If someone is fat you call 'em a fuckin' whale."

High school meant ongoing rank-out sessions. The nonstop one-upmanship there, on the level of "Your mother!" "No, *your* mother!" "No, your mother!" lends itself to the kind of humor Sherman has built into her routine. "It's almost like starting a fight, but you know you don't really mean it. It's just kidding around with friends," she says.

She hopes to form a similar kinship with her audience: "When I perform, what I would like to achieve is that if I'm in front of a group of 10 people or 350, I would like to make friends with them all on that stage and to make it feel like we're sitting around the dinner table all having fun, just laughing."

Camaraderie aside, Sherman says one of the things she likes best about doing stand-up is that it affords her an opportunity to command strict attention. Her ranting offers her catharsis. "The way I do it is out of control, but by doing it, I gain that control back again," she explains. She acknowledges, for instance, that telling Mona that her son has a big pecker is a bit over-the-top, but at the same time, by telling that to her mother-in-law the comedian slyly articulates a personal commentary: "I make it funny. But I'm also making a statement. Because it's asinine. But the question she *asked* me is asinine!"

Claudia's coming to comedy was accidental. She was a drama major in college and had hoped to become a director. Just out of school, she found quick yet short-lived success as an actress, landing a part in John Sayles' movie *Baby It's You*. After that glimpse of stardom, she bounced around Manhattan, going to various auditions. She took a few classes to stretch herself artistically, one of which was in comedy. It seemed like a fun thing to do, and besides, doing stand-up might get her seen. She sparked a romance with the comedy instructor, who encouraged Sherman to try stand-up, and with his help, she edged her way into what was then a burgeoning comedy-house circuit.

Stand-up and acting aren't all that different, observes Sherman. Both require performance skills and both are forms of entertainment. Claudia claims innate comedic timing and sensibility: "The way I say things, I just know how to make something funny."

She's studied what it takes to make a good joke. That's how she came up with the wedding gown. There's the gimmick factor—it's hard to forget someone who performs while wearing this dress—and it's unexpected, which makes for laughs. "If you read any book about writing a joke, one of the main things is you write a premise and at the end you give it a twist. That's exactly what I'm doing … I wear sneakers, too. High tops. And if a guy says, 'What's with the sneakers?' I say, 'So I can run away from you.' And that's that."

She can be nasty, but she's not mean-spirited. She knows having a commanding role in front of a crowd permits her a privileged vantage point. She won't misuse her position of power to promote ill will, and she considers comics who do so to be socially irresponsible. "Andrew Dice Clay. Here's a guy who gets up, he calls women cunts, he talks about pussy, pussy … he totally disses women and minority groups. And the people that listen to him take that stuff away with them. So when they go home they call their women cunts."

The stage provides a platform for this rebel, and when her audience responds to her heartfelt, albeit kvetching, performance, something special happens: "The stage is the most magical place in this universe. There are so many possibilities. When you're onstage—even if it's an empty stage and no one's on it and you're just looking at it—it's magical … It's like you're a fairy godmother; you can make anything happen."

When she's up there, is she a magician or is she part of the magic?

"Part of the magic. Yes, part of the magic. And that's the most wonderful feeling."

Judith Sloan

by Laura Post

Meet "performance activist" Judith Sloan and you're introduced to a whole cast of characters: Sophie, the old Jewish woman, a survivor and shrewd observer; Rheba, the hip hairdresser who aspires to rock-and-roll stardom; Muriel, the outrageous feminist; and the precocious, wise, and irrepressible kid, Jennifer.

See Sloan's show and you encounter an activist's political consciousness expressed through a funny, poignant collage of one-liners, sketches, dramatic characterizations, and clever doublespeak. From her analysis of the Persian Gulf War ("Operation Desert Schlong") to her hilarious "history of silicon" (from sealant in Navy ships through Silly Putty to breast implants) and her feminist take on popular culture ("If gentlemen prefer Hanes, why don't they wear them?"), Sloan's world-view, expressed through the voices of her many characters, is politically aware, topical, and on target. "I talk about world peace, relationships, sex, and laundry ... all the important things," notes Sloan.

Sloan's wry, conversational commentary, written with husband Warren Lehrer, combines stand-up with "serious" theater; her show also makes use of slides, tapes, and music. Sloan, a character actor who is also a comic, describes her approach as "humor in service of a serious message": "I want to provoke people to think and question what's going on."

Sloan began acting at age fifteen as one route out of her inner-city New Haven high school. She trained as a beautician ("the perfect profession for a radical feminist," she cracks), which gave her stable income as well as daily contact with a number of interesting customers. A stint in street theater inspired her to pursue a career in performance.

In 1984, Sloan began research on what was to become one of her most powerful characters: Sophie, the Holocaust survivor and "quintessential Jewish grandmother." Interviews with residents of New Haven's Jewish Home for the Aged soon grew into a much larger project, which received grants from the Connecticut Humanities Council, the National Endowment for the Arts, and various private foundations. The resulting show, *Responding to Chaos*, which Sloan has toured throughout both this country and Israel, preserves through the powerful medium of oral tradition the memories and truths of a culture that nearly perished in European concentration camps.

"Researching and fleshing out Sophie has been very important to me," says Sloan. "I spent three years interviewing old people, listening. I learned a lot about understanding people who are different from myself through Sophie." Sloan learned even more about the power of Sophie's voice during the Persian Gulf crisis: "I called several radio talk shows, and no one listened to me. Then I got the idea to call as Sophie. I was very surprised that they listened to her; they treated Sophie with a lot of respect. Through Sophie, I got to speak my mind about the war and about Bush's policies."

Besides performing, Sloan also teaches acting, voice, comedy, and character creation in university theater departments and high schools. In 1993 she released her first recording, *The Whole K'cufin' World ... and a Few More Things*. When asked where her politics fit into her work, Sloan replies, "Anywhere I can squeeze them!" Her material includes a hilarious send-up of George Bush's State of the Union Address and an extended critical riff about the Gulf War ("Peace Is Just Another Word for Nothing Left to Kill"), including her remark about the standing ovation once given to the wives of President Bush, General Colin Powell, and General Norman Schwarzkopf: "Oh great, a new support group—men who kill and the women who love them!"

Sloan and cowriter Lehrer are currently working on two shows. *Denial of the Fittest* is a serio-comic play about family secrets, politics, nervous breakdowns, and beauty school. *A Tattle Tale* is based on an ex-deputy who blew the whistle on her supervisor in Mississippi.

Margaret Smith

by Deni Kasrel

Before finding her calling as a perpetually pouty comic, Margaret Smith tried out a number of trades that weren't terribly well suited to her talents, one of which was working as a dental assistant. This was a short-lived job—she got fired for never smiling.

Nowadays, still a grinch about grinning, Smith makes a living from her unsunny disposition. She's chronically cranky and happy to tell us all about it. Apparently this trait runs in the family. Margaret claims her Uncle Swanee's tombstone bears the inscription "What are *you* looking at?"

Her various relatives are frequently used as fodder in her comedic material. For years, much of her repertoire drew on the despair she felt as the third of six siblings stuck in a demented, dysfunctional Middle American family, where mom was a misguided smotherer and pop a gambler and a drunk. Not a happy-go-lucky circumstance; however, Margaret has managed to make the best of it. Her displeasing circumstances served as a catalyst for her to foster a career in a field that welcomes misfits with open arms.

Her tough childhood has left Margaret defiant but not bitter. She attacks not to scratch or maim but rather to chew on the quirky morsels that life comprises. She's accomplished personal triumphs, not the least of which is the ability to present her humorous, cranky self to large audiences. She has done this so successfully that she has been nominated for best female stand-up comic at the American Comedy Awards.

Scathingly sarcastic, Smith is a shrewd, sophisticated satirist who takes no prisoners. Recalling her mother asking if she remembered to send her dad a Father's Day greeting, Margaret relates, "I hate this occasion; I can never find the right card, because they're all too nice." Sounds pretty spiteful, and it could well come off as such, except that the comic dispenses her dark-humored lines in deadpan fashion and punctuates her jokes with a wily smirk. As Steven Wright has proven, donning a blank-faced demeanor can be explosive. And the smirk, well, that just reminds us that, hey, it *is* comedy, folks. Besides, bleak as it sounds, you gotta laugh at lines like: "There's a light at the end of the tunnel. Yeah—it's a train."

Kasrel: You've called yourself "the anti-comedian." Do you think of yourself as an outsider, as a comic who doesn't fit in?

Smith: I'm not a traditional comic. It always bothered me to see comics beat people over the head with the punch line. As an audience member, I'm happier when a performer leaves something to my imagination and doesn't do all the work for me. It's more engaging to let the audience participate and interpret the work, and the more you indicate, the less they participate.

Kasrel: Your comedy addresses some very difficult topics.

Smith: Some of my material could be disturbing if you thought about it that way. I talk about my dysfunctional family, and if I were talking about it in therapy, a therapist might say, "Boy, that's sad." But my intention isn't that my audience think it's sad, or I'd be out of business.

I intend it to be funny. And people can say, "Yeah, my family is like that," or, "I've got a cousin like that."

Kasrel: The things you talk about are universal, or at least things that everybody has seen or known.

Smith: People can relate to it, although I don't think they come to a comedy club expecting to hear about it. I think they go to a comedy club and expect to forget their problems, not to have someone up onstage talking about them.

Kasrel: And as you say, you're talking about not just your problems but what are probably their problems, too.

Smith: Everyone comes from dysfunction; there aren't a lot of healthy families out there. I mean, what else would we do in life if we didn't have unfinished family business?

Kasrel: [*Laughing*] So do you see yourself as some odd kind of therapist for them? Or is this therapy for you?

Smith: It started out as therapy for me, but then I got into therapy, and it stopped being so therapeutic for me, because I could express this stuff in a real therapeutic setting.

Kasrel: Then it just became a way to make a living?

Smith: I guess it's remained therapeutic but in very different ways. I'd say I spent the first five years looking for a witness for it all. Then, through therapy and other means, I became my own witness, so I needed my audience less as a witness. But then my real work began, which is relaxing with people and relating to them. I became more comfortable in front of a crowd and more accepting of who I was. So I'd say I spent the next five years learning how to be at ease with people and comfortable in my own skin.

Kasrel: In the beginning, was the value of it for you the opportunity to talk about things that were pent up?

Smith: I was getting a lot of acceptance and validation. When I started, I had no self-esteem; when they laughed, it gave me a sense of value. As I gained value based on other, more real things, I required less acceptance from them. I just didn't require as much from them to be happy in my private life.

Kasrel: What led you to try stand-up comedy in the first place as a way to get that validation? It isn't a particularly easy path.

Smith: I've wanted to write since I was a teenager. My dad's real funny. Why am I doing this for a living? I guess I'm really narcissistic. And I really like to induce pleasure. I used to be a cook for a living. I never went to chef's school, but I worked in really nice restaurants and learned when I was young from people who were willing to train me. I cooked and I fed people, which doesn't seem much different from what I'm doing now. Feeding people savory dishes or feeding them funny lines—it's all about timing, you know. And appealing to their senses.

Kasrel: As you've grown more comfortable in your own skin and relaxed with the audience, how has your act changed?

Smith: I'm more accessible. There's less distance between the audience and myself. I talk more to them than *at* them. It's almost as though I'm talking *with* them, in a way. And instead of talking so much about myself, I talk about things outside myself. Of course, I have an attitude about whatever I'm saying, but it isn't so much "me, me, me" anymore.

Kasrel: What kind of things did you use to talk about that you no longer talk about so much anymore?

Smith: I used to talk about how I grew up in this obese family. Everyone was fat but me, and I used to have to hide in the bathroom to eat. That's the kind of stuff I don't feel the need to talk about anymore.

Kasrel: You focus more on your current experiences than on your background.

Smith: I'll talk a little bit about my family because that's what lets them know who I am. You have to tell them where you came from. Then maybe I'll talk about political stuff.

Kasrel: Do you always open your show by saying, "You guys sound like you're in a pretty good mood ... and that's what sets us apart"?

Smith: Yeah. I used to open with, "How 'bout that Kennedy assassination?" And they'd be like, What? Then I'd say, "Yeah, I've been *meaning* to write some new material." I look at that line now and think to myself, Well, it's an attention-grabber.

I guess I don't feel the need to be as aggressive as I used to be. I don't feel as angry, either. Bringing up your anger onstage is aggressive.

Kasrel: But you're still fairly cranky up there. You have this deadpan manner of delivery, and you make very sharp observations. How much of that is a persona that you've created for your act and how much is you?

Smith: Who I am onstage is part of who I am. I've become more integrated than I used to be, but I'm not where I'd like to be. You'd think that after thirteen years I'd have worked on everything I need to, but I really haven't.

Kasrel: Where do you still see room for improvement?

Smith: I'm still more physically inhibited than I'd like to be. In the last four years, I've begun to move around onstage, but before that I never even removed the mike from the stand. I'd get onstage with my thoughts and my ideas … and freeze. I just stood and hung onto the pole. I was afraid to move, which is weird, because offstage I've always been athletic.

Another change is what I wear onstage. One way of becoming my own person is to go onstage wearing what I want to wear, regardless of what anyone thinks.

Kasrel: And you didn't do that before?

Smith: I felt that if I wore something tight, they'd be looking at my breasts and not listening, so I'd wear real boxy stuff. Now I'm just beginning to think, Why am I so afraid to get up there and show that I have a beautiful figure?

In a lot of ways, the stage has been a place for me to grow up, to become my own person.

Kasrel: It can also be pretty tough, though, can't it? Audiences don't always make it easy for you. Or do they cut you a break?

Smith: Well, I used to think of them as the enemy. Then I realized one day, through therapy, that they want to like me. It's more fun for them to sit there for an hour if they do like me. Now I don't think everyone does like me, but I think that everyone wants to. And a lot of people do like me, you know. At least on stage.

Kasrel: I wanted to get back to the line you open your set with. It would seem to be a negative statement, yet people laugh. Why does that strike them as funny?

Smith: Because they believe it, and it isn't what they expect. And because the comic before me just got done acting like Mr. Comedy.

Kasrel: What's so funny about their believing that you're in a bad mood?

Smith: If I went onstage and just said, "Hi, I'm in a bad mood," they wouldn't laugh. But because I say, "Well, you guys sound like you're in a pretty good mood," I set up an expectation that what will follow will be my saying, "And I'm in a good mood, too." Instead, I say something they don't expect me to say.

People can relate to being in a bad mood. People are in bad moods a lot of the time. The question is, How seriously do you want to take your bad mood? Your problems aren't going to go away just because you take them a little less seriously. Laughing about them a little is just going to make you a little more comfortable in dealing with them.

Kasrel: When you deliver that line, they laugh because you're giving them something that they don't expect. In general, is telling people what they don't expect to hear an important part of your act?

Smith: That's part of it. A good friend of mine recently told me that she thinks I get laughs not because of what I say but because of how I say things. I think my act is funny because a lot of it is the truth, and when you tell the truth, people laugh.

Kasrel: Your friend must be right about your delivery, though, because people don't always laugh at the truth. Sometimes they get upset about it.

Smith: What makes me laugh at a particular comic is whether what he's doing, how he's doing it, and what he's talking about are organic to who he is. People used to try to get me to say Sam Kinison was wrong, that he was bad for women and evil. A lot of what Kinison said was offensive to me, but I couldn't criticize him, because what he said was all real and true to him.

Kasrel: Are you saying it's okay if somebody's act is racist or homophobic or misogynist if that's really who they are?

Smith: I'm talking about evaluating it artistically. You hear rap songs that appear to condone cop-killing, but that's this young kid's experience. When I watched the movie *Malcolm X* and saw his process of healing from his experience in this world, it made perfect sense to me. Had Sam Kinison lived, he may have gone on to say other things. I'm not saying I enjoyed what Kinison said, but I could appreciate the fact that he was telling the truth.

Kasrel: Do you think of your act as political?

Smith: That I'm onstage speaking to a room full of people is political. By *political* I mean that I think it moves women forward. Also, I don't say anything in my act that degrades women or makes women look bad in any way. People may not leave the club saying, "She didn't say anything racist or sexist or homophobic and she didn't put herself down," but it's a very conscious choice on my part not to include that kind of material.

Kasrel: Do you consider yourself a feminist?

Smith: Yeah.

Kasrel: Because you're being a woman who is commanding an audience?

Smith: I do think the fact that I have enough personal power to pull this off says something. I think the fact that I have so much self-respect warrants the respect of the observer. I never mention the word *feminist*, but I'm pro-woman, and I don't bash men, either. I think I come off as someone who is in favor of human rights and who doesn't judge the human condition.

Kasrel: Does your audience pick up on this nonjudgmental quality? Is that part of your appeal?

Smith: I think so. For instance, I'll be eating with another performer after the show, and someone will come up who's just seen the show and will start telling me things. One woman was telling me about how scared she was because she had to go in for surgery. After she walked away from the table, the other performer said, "I can't believe she just told you that." People confide in me: I've told her personal things and now she's going to tell me something personal. The other thing that makes them open up is that they see that I don't judge.

If you're in the audience and you're aware of the fact that people hide a lot of their reality, you might look at my act and say, "It gives me a lot of hope that she's saying it's okay to talk about these things instead of acting like none of us has problems." Whereas somebody else might be uncomfortable with it, because they don't believe in talking about private things in public.

From the time they are kids, people tuck pieces of themselves away, because it's not okay to be weak or to need. They do it with their sexuality. They do it with their thoughts. They do it with their hopes and dreams.

Kasrel: Are there any comics whose work you particularly like or who have influenced your comedy?

Smith: Woody Allen. I like the fact that he's silly one minute and the next minute he's telling you how hard it is to be with a woman and about his awkwardness and his experience with therapy. He gets beneath the surface. I like Steve Martin, because he's so multitalented. I also like George Carlin for his observations and his use of words and finding the tiniest little thing to observe and comment on.

My dad is a big influence on my comedy, as well. He's very funny and very charming.

Kasrel: If that's the case, I'm wondering why you choose in your act to portray him as a rather difficult alcoholic.

Smith: Because that was part of my experience, too. If you met my dad you'd love him, but you didn't have to be in the house with him every day.

Kasrel: How did you first discover you were funny?

Smith: I didn't hear too many kind words in the house I grew up in. Because I didn't get kind words at home, I had to go outside the house for kind words. Anything positive I got, I built on. In grade school, I heard that I was a good athlete. That's all I needed to hear. Then a high school teacher told me that I wrote well. Okay, I'm off and running with that. When I was fifteen, someone told me I was funny. Okay, I'm throwing that in the pot. Anything nice that anyone ever said to me I took and made something of it. Those were the things that people found about me to comment on, and that's exactly what I became.

Kasrel: You didn't see these things in yourself?

Smith: No, I had to be told. I'm sure that when you were young somebody told you that you were a good writer.

Kasrel: Yeah, but it didn't hit me right away.

Smith: Maybe you weren't as hungry as I was. Maybe you heard ten nice things. When you only hear one nice thing, you cling to it.

Kasrel: How did you get started in stand-up?

Smith: I went away to college, and I ran out of money and had to get a job. I got one at Second City because they said if I worked there I could get classes for half price. In Chicago I was in an improv group for a year, and I wrote sketch material with the friend who at fifteen had told me I was funny.

I worked at Second City for three and a half years and then moved to New York and started doing stand-up. Stand-up was a way of making friends and getting accepted and hiding that I was scared.

Kasrel: You mentioned before that performing itself was scary. I know you're saying that the audience wants to like you, but sometimes they don't.

Smith: At first, I couldn't even look at them, I was so scared. I operated entirely from fear. Even when they laughed, I was afraid. It would take me two months to get back onstage. I'd be devastated, and I'd cry on my way home.

Kasrel: I'm curious about why you'd put yourself through all that.

Smith: I don't know why. I just kept thinking, I know I can do this. I'd get laughs, and I wouldn't know why. One day the director videotaped us, and after watching myself I said, "I can't believe how slow I'm moving; I've got to pick up the pace." He said, "You don't understand—that's why they're laughing." I just had no idea.

Sometimes I still don't have any idea. Sometimes I'll go into therapy and say, "I don't know what they see in me."

Kasrel: What do you enjoy the most about being a stand-up?

Smith: I really like the hours, and the fact that I make money doing something I like doing. I'm in control when I'm out there onstage, and I like that.

Carrie Snow

by Deni Kasrel

Comedian Carrie Snow, self-proclaimed "America's girlfriend, gosh darn it," is every bitchin' babe's best bud. In her stand-up act, she shares her thoughts on a bunch of girl stuff: PMS and its primal link to housecleaning, the unique pleasure of binge shopping, and sex—the good, the bad, and the ugly of it. And like any faithful female friend, she disses men. They're good-for-nothings who are, on occasion, good for something.

Guys will never get the girl thing, insists Snow, who speaks in a slinky come-hither voice. They're too superficial. All the better. This way, ladies who attend a special one-woman show she's rigged up can laugh among themselves. Inspired by the same convivial spirit that's aroused at male strip-shows, they can whoop and holler and get rowdy in their own safe space.

Carrie calls her program an "interactive comedy escape," because it offers a give-and-take between the comic and her audience. The act started out as an alternative to "Monday Night Football." "I did it as a marketing technique," she explains. "The idea was to go into a club on what was normally a dark night and create our own reality." The gal-pal-getaway scheme has since evolved into a show Snow does on a regular basis.

As patrons arrive for this performance, they're handed a sheet of paper with two questions on it. One asks, "What is your idea of a real woman?" The other inquires if they have any questions for Carrie. The program opens with a half-hour of Snow doing a stand-up routine, much of it mauling the male gender. Then she gets to the questions posed by her fans. One woman asks, "How can you have great sex without an emotional attachment?" "Use an attachment," Carrie answers. Next, Snow pulls a few persons out of the audience to participate in a mock quiz show. The show concludes with wise-cracks on what is a real woman. The audience, made up primarily of females, howls throughout.

Snow believes ladies laugh more when they're in their own private space: "I think I could hook up electrodes to the audience and make a real scientific study … We [women] have more fun when we're together, and we can laugh easier when we're with each other, or at least in the majority."

Snow declares herself to be the "spokesmodel" for bitter angry women. "There's so many of us out there," she remarks. She's sure, for instance, that the movie *Shadowlands* is totally unrealistic. "In my act, I say I know it's a fantasy, because the guy was nice to her when she was sick—and women relate to that whether they've seen the film or not."

She touches on chords shared by women, especially those who continually go out on bad dates, as Carrie apparently does. While her act is sharply focused on topics of female interest, Snow objects to the suggestion that she's a feminist comic, preferring to consider what she does to be providing a forum for humor based on issues common to many. "It's like, 'Well, here's my head, what's inside your head?' Because I know a lot of 'em are thinking the same thing," she explains.

Collective levity provides a subversive source of empowerment, yet Snow frowns on the use of this word, finding it too strident. Besides, she emphasizes, her show isn't about empowerment; it's about having fun. Hence come lines like "A real woman can have her cake and jump out of it too."

The comedian claims a genetic predisposition toward being funny: a prankster mentality runs in the family. Snow's parents raised her to use humor as a coping mechanism for life. "It was considered a good thing to laugh and tease," she says of her upbringing. "They did stuff like, 'Stubbed your foot? Coulda been worse. Coulda been me'."

Comedy albums played frequently on the household turntable—Alan Sherman and Bill Cosby were favorites. Carrie's folks took her to see the top stand-ups of the day. However, her eagerness to enter the trade didn't tickle their fancy. For some reason, they weren't enamored of the notion of their daughter making a career of "talking dirty to strangers."

Regardless, young Carrie was drawn to jump up and jest in front of crowds. "I was so young, I'm not sure why I did it," she relates, conjecturing that it was in part a way of getting back at her mom and dad for all the ribbing they inflicted: "My parents were horrified, and that was a thrill, to find something to tweak them with. Heroin or tattoos weren't something I wanted to do."

Looking back, Carrie recognizes jobs she held prior to her becoming a professional stand-up as being good preparation for the role. An emcee spot she held at a male strip-joint, where she tagged herself the "Mattress of Ceremonies," afforded her handy practice at hosting a show. Another unusual employment—being a professional party guest—helped her hone skills for humorous interaction: "I'd go to parties and pretend to be somebody's cousin, and I'd put food in my pockets when people could see."

Even her college major, rhetoric, wound up being relevant to her comedic aspirations. Carrie took up this course of study at U.C. Berkeley, thinking she might go the pre-law route. Although she lost interest in the follow-through, acquiring a degree in the study of argumentative thinking and writing served as appropriate training for a career where quick-on-your-feet verbal response is a requisite skill.

The real clincher in her decision to become a bona fide comedian came when she saw "a good bad example" of someone trying their hand at the trade. It happened at a Martin Mull show, where the opening act was so bad Snow reckoned even she could do better. "I really felt it was inside of me," she recalls.

Snow took a comedy workshop and hit the clubs. Her first real stab at stand-up was well received. "It went great. It was intoxicating," she recollects. Another try fell flat: "The second time, I invited a bunch of friends, and I died. But you know what? I had already had the first drug, and the first drug was much more powerful. It's what I think beginner's luck is all about."

The jones of jokedom had seeped into her system. She dedicated her talents to developing as a stand-up. In those early days, Snow was heavy-set, and the topic of being overweight accounted for a regular portion of her material, as did grousing over men, family matters, current events, and just the general yin-yang of day-to-day living.

She's since slimmed down, so the fat jokes are out. Otherwise, Snow maintains the basic elements of the rest of her routine. She continues to use real-life experience as fodder for her funnies and has more recently gotten mileage out of her adventures at the plastic surgeon's.

Her material on personal remodeling is done with self-mockery, a device that Snow says serves to put her audience at ease: "It's a way for them to know that I'm human." When you're onstage, "you're different and you're special," thinks Carrie; a little good-natured self-deprecation helps establish a sense of common ground.

"It takes guts to do this, but I didn't realize it. I didn't know I was supposed to be afraid," says Snow.

Carol Steinel

by Anndee Hochman

She brandishes her acoustic guitar as if it might shoot sparks and growls a verse of the song that has become her trademark: "I'm dangerous, I'm a wild-eyed Amazon,/*I'm dangerous*, I don't use no Ban Roll-On."

West Coast comic Carol Steinel hardly exudes threat. She looks more like a puckish Guardian Angel in her usual performing uniform of faded jeans, white T-shirt, and three braids swinging from under a dark beret. What's dangerous about Steinel is the precision of her wit—a sharp, articulate take on politics, culture, and everyday life.

Steinel, who describes herself as a "small, flippant being" and as a "mad-cap songwright and troubadour," uses a blend of improvised patter, song, and anecdote to scissor away at topics ranging from fundamentalist politics to careers for the nineties. (Shoe-tying tutors will be needed, she says, for the generation of children who grew up with Velcro on their sneakers.)

Steinel grew up in the Midwest, where she claims she was born by mistake, because of a "metaphysical inner-ear problem." But she is surely not in Kansas anymore. In Portland, Oregon, where Steinel emcees a monthly women's coffeehouse, she also serves as the community's unofficial comic historian, a smart-mouthed chronicler of these peculiar times.

Her strongly feminist style of humor pokes a satiric finger at the recovery movement, visits from relatives, antigay activism, and lesbian break-ups. It's a blend with particular appeal to lesbian and gay listeners (Steinel routinely declares her entire audience "honorary lesbians" so they can feel free to laugh at her jokes) but with resonance for everyone.

"I'm not, in fact, a 'gold star' lesbian—that's a lesbian who's never slept with a man," she deadpans. "No, I know it's shocking but it's true—I did, once, accidentally, sleep with a man. For a year."

Steinel has opened for Tret Fure and Alix Dobkin. She has also performed in her original one-woman work, *Tacit Agreements: Graded Lessons in Sitting in a Chair*. She punctuates her comic performances with music, from the tongue-in-cheek "I'm Dangerous" to a country-western lament for the old hard-drinking crowd to a sing-along whose giddy chorus is "Nonmonogamy, nonmonogamy, nonmonogameeee … it don't work!"

In one signature piece, "The Laws of Relativity," Steinel uses an easel to graph the relationship between visits from relatives and one's irrational desire to clean house. The equation, she concludes, goes like this: the closer the relative, and the less you like that relative, the more frantically you will scrub.

Steinel is perhaps at her most dangerous when singing and talking about Oregon's fundamentalist right wing, which in recent years has sponsored numerous antigay ballot measures. In a trio of songs, she mourns for lesbians and gay men who are "Dying for Love," questions those who proclaim that "God is Love" but preach hate, and takes aim at "Biblical Schizophrenia." Why, she wonders, do people dwell on the Bible's injunctions against homosexuality while ignoring proscriptions against, say, wearing clothes of mixed fibers?

"I love what fundamentalists call us—things like 'unnatural'," she says. "And I love *who* calls us 'unnatural'—people like Tammy Faye Bakker! I mean, is she under there? Do you ever get the feeling that if you took a knife and started whittling away at the makeup, there'd be no one inside?"

What's subversive here is the way Steinel's wit nudges audiences to the edge of outrage, the way she exposes life's inequities by making people laugh at them. "I see humor as a way to work with people about issues that might otherwise be too intense," she says. "Good comedy invariably deals with truth, and if you bring truthful comedy to an issue, even an intense one, it often allows people to look at things in a new light. Besides, laughing keeps your Birkenstocks from cracking around the little cork part."

Judy Tenuta

by Kathi Maio, interview by Laura Post

Women comics seldom indulge in unabashed shtick. Some might argue that this is because few women were around back in the heyday of vaudeville, burlesque, or the borscht belt—when gimmickry and giddy foolishness were enthusiastically performed and enjoyed. Others might speculate that women show too much decorum (or native intelligence) to mess with violins or rubber chickens or goofy voices.

After all, these days, comedians and their audiences consider themselves more sophisticated. The question is, Is this a *good* thing?

You might just answer a resounding NO! after seeing Judy Tenuta perform for the first time.

Judy (Judy … Judy …) is the queen of shtick—or, as she prefers to be known, the Petite Flower, the Giver-Goddess, the Fashion Plate, the Saint. She enters (greeting her eager audience with, "Hi, Pigs!"), wearing a long gown or harem pant outfit of satin or chiffon. She wears a big posy in her long, curly hair. And, on her forehead and arms, she wears jewels that look like they were stolen from a road company of *Aida*.

She also wears that coolest of musical instruments, the accordion. This she plays to punctuate her stories and to accompany herself on ditties like "The Pope Song" ("I just want a cowboy in a long, white silky dress") and "My Dad" ("…makes lasagna with his feet").

As you can tell by even the briefest song snippets, Ms. Tenuta isn't exactly respectful of male authority. Comic contempt toward every fella from Santa Claus to a Southern police officer to her six interchangeable, dim-witted brothers (all named Bosco) is, in fact, her trademark. Although no one could call Judy a man-hater. She *loves* men. Especially when they're on all fours—the better to ride them around the stage cracking a bullwhip.

She is a goddess with a bad attitude, a Kali who sprang from a good Catholic family in America's heartland. Men, or "stud puppets" as she usually refers to them, must worship at her feet. But even the most adoring men in her audience—devout followers of the religion of "Judyism"—oft receive "abuse from the goddess of love." In the middle of a story about an encounter with yet another "squid in stretch pants," she might compare the man in her past with a member of her present audience: "Like you—but with a human head."

It is nearly impossible to describe the comedy of Judy Tenuta. Even in her own words, she doesn't translate easily to the page. (Her 1991 book, *The Power of Judyism*, simply can't capture the force of her comedy power like her recorded performances, including her Showtime special, *Worship Me, Pigs*, her HBO *One Night Stand* at the Fillmore, and her Elektra recording, *Buy This, Pigs!*) So much depends on Tenuta's costuming, her physical attitude, and her voice. Not to mention her squawking accordion, her pop-eyed, scrunched-up facial mugging, and the give-and-take of her interaction with her audience.

The appeal of Tenuta's humor is, however, quite easy to fathom. First and foremost, she is *not* just another stand-up comic. She is a one-of-a-kind stage presence from the mondo bizarro. Men—at least the ones who come to see her—seem to enjoy a woman who demands respect (nay, prostrate adoration!). And for women, her humor can hold special subversive magic.

Judy Tenuta has so completely rejected the self-hatred exhibited by so many other women comedians that she has arrived at its polar opposite. As Giver-Goddess, she has risen high above women's torturous self-esteem issues. The precious worth of Judyism's sole deity is undeniable, and she never masks it with modesty.

Ms. Tenuta's beauty and grace are, as she proclaims through every punch line and insult, more than any mere mortal man deserves. And this particular princess of power scoffs at all male domination. "You cannot possess me!" she hisses. And, by gum, you believe her.

It can be energizing as well as hilarious for a woman to see another woman who values herself so highly. But there *is*, it must be admitted, a downside to self-glorification. For *other* people, anyway. Tenuta's merciless ridicule of fat people (like a female friend who is "a landmass with a perm") is one example of the kind of comedic content that can leave sensitive audience members wincing.

But more often than not, the wacky performance art of Judy Tenuta leaves audiences rolling in the aisles, hoping for the chance to "come closer to the goddess," to listen once more to her extravagant effrontery and to the strains of her squeeze box.

Seldom has shtick been so funny. And it has certainly never been quite so divine.

Post: How did you come up with your Giver-Goddess persona? Did you just wake up one day and say, "I've got to do this?" or was it something you'd been working on for years?

Tenuta: A lot of it has to do with my upbringing. I was raised Catholic, in a big family. I was the oldest daughter. I was like Cinderella. I had six brothers and I had to wait on my brothers. That wasn't cool, so I guess you could say I rebelled. Everybody worshiped the blessed Virgin Mary. She had all these cool titles, like Queen of all Queens and Queen of Saints. I just said, "I deserve to have all these titles." I'm like a superhero; I represent all the positive aspects that a woman should be. I feel that woman really should be worshiped.

Post: Were you a rebel as a kid?

Tenuta: No. Listen, I want to thank my parents. I'm not one of these psychos like Roseanne who goes around saying, "Yeah, my parents took advantage of me and slept with me." I mean, come on. Look at her now. She should be kissing their feet! She really needs an ego enema. If it weren't for her parents, would she be doing what she's doing?

Post: Do you see yourself as a hero rather than a victim?

Tenuta: I think of myself as a champion, a Joan of Arc of comedy. That's why some men—idiotic men—don't like me. Most men like me. Certainly, gay men love me, because they all want to be a strong woman.

Post: What about your upbringing led you to develop your sense of humor?

Tenuta: I think what really motivated me was that we were always told to shut up. My mother was always saying, "Shut up and clean the house." When you're told to shut up all the time, your natural instinct is not to shut up, but to laugh and goof around.

I was the only girl for a while. Then my sister came along, but she was a tomboy and I was very feminine. I had to have all my dolls. I'd try to isolate myself, for privacy. I'd lock myself in my room and play the accordion in the closet.

Post: How did you learn to play the accordion?

Tenuta: There was a guy going door-to-door selling accordions. I was eight years old, and I thought, That looks cool; that's like a toy. I wanted one. My mom said, "Well, okay. If we get it you have to practice." I didn't know what that meant. Well, my mom didn't fool around. She was like Hitler. If you were going out, she'd say, "You're going in your room and you're playing that. I'm going to lock you in your closet until you can play "Lady of Spain" in the dark."

Post: And you did learn. The accordion is an important part of your act. Is it something you still like to play?

Tenuta: No, I don't like to play it. I just think it's a great way to abuse people.

Post: Did you have any idea when you were practicing the accordion in your closet as a kid that you were going to be a performer when you grew up?

Tenuta: No.

Post: So how did you get into this line of work?

Tenuta: Well, they didn't have enough openings for coal miners and rodeo riders. So I thought I'd do this, because it's not as glamorous, but there are still perks …

I needed to do it. I just said "I have to do this and nobody's going to stop me from doing it."

Post: How did you get started?

Tenuta: I'd just gotten out of college, and there was an article in the paper about a comedy club that was opening, and I went. It wasn't, "I just think I might try this." It was more like, "I have to do this or I might be seen on a rooftop with a rifle."

Post: When you first went on, did you love it?

Tenuta: Oh, of course. I was just crazy about it. I'd studied acting. I knew that I wanted to do some form of acting, but then I realized acting is such prostitution. It's almost locked in the layaway plan if you get a part. Like Kim Basinger hasn't been a mattress. You know what I mean?

The point is that I'm going to have my own gospel. I'm not going to mouth anybody else's words. I have a message: a lot of men are going to be furniture for women, and women are supposed to be worshiped.

Post: Did that first gig include elements of the gospel of Judyism?

Tenuta: I was very sassy. I was unconventional. All these comics—and it was basically all men comics—would say "Hey, you can't act like that." And I said, "Who's going to stop me?"

Post: Did you have any trouble breaking in, or did it come easily to you?

Tenuta: I don't think anything comes easy. It's hard, but I just said, "I'm going to do this. I'm dedicated to doing this." I didn't let anything stop me. A lot of people drop out when they don't make money. I wasn't making any money in the beginning, but I didn't let that stop me, because I just loved doing it.

Post: Did you have to work at other jobs to support yourself?

Tenuta: Are you kidding me? I used to dance on tables and be a waitress. I was a yogurt tester. I was a meat wrapper. I took inventory of nuns' and priests' habits. Poodle grooming … you name it.

Post: Did you get a big break at some point?

Tenuta: No. I worked very, very hard to get whatever I got. There are no breaks. Some people do get lucky, but I just worked very hard. I'm different, and you don't get rewarded easily for being different. You almost get punished. Except that the public loves you, because that's what the public wants. They can see run-of-the-mill all the time.

Post: You're now at a place in your career where you're playing very big venues and you've achieved a lot of success. You're saying that hard work and believing totally, unwaveringly in what you do has gotten you there?

Tenuta: Well, I love doing it, so nobody's going to stop me from doing it. Also, I really have fun doing it. With a lot of comics, it's like, "Okay, I'm going to do my forty minutes and then I'm out of here." That's not my attitude, boy. I go out there, and I have a riot.

Post: And people love you.

Tenuta: Because they know I'm totally dedicated. I've dedicated that hour and fifteen minutes to them totally. Not only that, but every moment up until then is dedicated to that moment.

Obviously, I've made life choices for my career. I haven't had any children. A lot of people say, "Well, why don't you have kids?" Yeah, well, excuse me, I don't really think that works for the lifestyle I have. Also, I really want a screaming mass of cells that one day shoots me for the Mazda, you know. *That's* a turn-on. This is a mission for me. It's not like, "Hey, this is cool, but if it doesn't work, I can always be an armpit sniffer for Ban Roll-on or something."

Post: Do you feel at this point that you've accomplished your mission?

Tenuta: No, I think I should be the biggest star in the world.

Post: You have an album and a book out. What about a video?

Tenuta: I'm working on it. As I said, it hasn't been easy for me because I'm different. For example, I'm not allowed on "The Tonight Show." I'm not allowed on Letterman. It's because I'm not just a woman who speaks out, but I'm an attractive woman. It would be okay if I were the side of a bus like Roseanne, you know—a big, fat, disgusting whale. All she's doing is rolling in mud and being obnoxious. I'm not. I'm sassy, but I'm also a sassy babe goddess.

Post: Yet you're a great guest. I saw you on Joan Rivers recently, and it was a terrific show.

Tenuta: She's totally cool. She knows what's happening. But with the other shows … I'm very rapid-fire and I've got a lot of energy. It's just sexist. Robin Williams is allowed to be all over the place, but with me it's, "She's not controllable." A woman has to be like in some kind of butt-harness with a bit on her teeth so you can control her. I mean, please.

Post: That's amazing.

Tenuta: Not, it's not amazing. It's typical.

Post: So you've run into obstacles for being an attractive and outspoken woman and for being "uncontrollable."

Tenuta: But I'm not complaining, because these are the same things that have made me very famous.

Post: How do you put your act together? Do your ideas just come to you? Do you sit down for a certain amount of time each day and write?

Tenuta: What can I tell you? I'm a comic genius.

Post: But what about the way you think allows you to come up with the stuff you do?

Tenuta: I enjoy words, and I enjoy playing around with them. My whole attitude is to have fun, so I play around with words.

Post: Some of your material is also very intellectual. For instance, your take on *Wuthering Heights*. You combine very contemporary language with what's really a feminist analysis of this classic piece of literature.

Tenuta: To me, *Wuthering Heights* just typifies how romantic love can only be achieved if the heroine dies. Why do you think Romeo and Juliet are so romantic? Because they both die. If they lived together, you know, they'd get like, "Uh, you big pig, I hate you." Because they'd get used to each other.

Post: Do you think romantic love is possible in this world?

Tenuta: Sure it is, but it can't be sustained forever. You have to work at it. You have to find a pig that's properly worshipful and willing to bring out the whipped cream, and, you know, be your sex donkey.

Post: With your being so down on men, it sounds like being with woman would be a good alternative.

Tenuta: I'm not down on men. I'm just telling them that they should elevate woman, because women have been oppressed. Hey, listen, if you want to switch to women, that's fine too. I'm telling all women, switch to whatever you want.

Post: Do you think women should elevate other women the same way that men should elevate women?

Tenuta: Basically, I feel that all women should worship me. And so should men.

Post: I read one review of your work by a critic who liked your act a lot but felt that perhaps the Judy Gospel was limiting.

Tenuta: It's not limiting at all. I'm a champion. I'm like a superhero for women. And for men who are women in training.

Post: You've appeared in a number of television commercials. Would you enjoy doing a television series or appearing in feature films?

Tenuta: I'm working on an animated live action series. And I'll be doing a movie with Kevin Costner: *Dances with Pigs.* What can I say? I've kept my clothes on. Hey, if you spread more easily, like Madonna, you can do it on the layaway plan.

Post: Have you ever met Madonna or Roseanne?

Tenuta: I know Roseanne. She's a big pig. I haven't met Madonna, but I like Madonna. I think she's talented. Roseanne is just an obnoxious pig-mouth. They needed some fat pig to champion all the fat women in America, what can I say? A lot of grazing cows can relate to that. I admire any farm animal that can make eight million a week.

Post: She's done very well.

Tenuta: There's a big market for grazing. That's what people do when they watch TV.

Post: You've reached the point where you're very successful, and you're really attuned to your audience. Do you ever have shows where it just doesn't work?

Tenuta: Oh sure. In Atlantic City, where everybody's a thug and all they want to figure out is how they can hide a body in their trunk and still win the jackpot.

Post: So what happened? Why didn't it work in Atlantic City?

Tenuta: Because they're all idiots. Well, no, I'll tell you why. Because the whole attitude of a casino is weird. Actually, it was only one show that was weird and then all my fans came in.

Let's face it, when you come to my show, you have to have an open mind. You also have to be somewhat hip and educated. Because I'm really sassy. I'm not just going to stand there like Buddy Hackass or Buddy Hackjob. I've got a whole three-dimensional universe that people can come into and have a lot of fun. I'm actually a healer. When people come to my show they say, "I've been transformed. I'm so happy. I was feeling horrible and now I feel great." It's very therapeutic for people.

Post: Do people come up afterward and give you that kind of positive feedback?

Tenuta: Yeah, they're totally worshipful. Not only that, but I'll be in the airport and total strangers will come up to me and say, "I love you." It's really cool.

Post: Do people ever come up and say negative things?

Tenuta: Once on an airplane a guy said, "You know, you're a lot thinner in person," and then he kept walking. I think he was just trying to get on my nerves, so I said, "Yeah, but you don't even look human in person!"

Post: Did you really say that?

Tenuta: Yeah! What am I going to do, let him get away with it? He's a pig! He obviously wanted to go out with me and he knew I'd totally reject him, so he had to say something negative to me.

Post: You said you think Madonna has talent. Who else out there do you think is really good?

Tenuta: Barbra Streisand. Oh, you know who was really sweet that I just met? Lily Tomlin. She's a sweetheart, a wonderful, warm person.

Post: That's nice to know. And speaking of wonderful and warm, you know Howard Stern, right?

Tenuta: Howard's a great entertainer, for what he does. I'd be a great guest for his show, if I wanted to be a bisexual masseuse. But I have a message and I have my own agenda, and on Howard's show, it's got to be *his* agenda. I'm a woman with a message, and instead it's like, "No, just show us your tits." I think he's very funny. I think he's hysterical. But he needs to submit to the Goddess.

Post: Getting back to the television talk shows—what is it about you that stops you from getting booked on these shows?

Tenuta: It's real simple; TV executives are stubborn, small-visioned idiots. They're just men who want to be in charge and have their big, fat male ego boss everything around. Like I was supposed to be on Arsenio and then he freaked out and said, "I don't think she can be controlled." Well, no, I can't be controlled, okay? But he's had wild people on his show. I saw Sally what's-her-name—that slut actress ...

Post: Sally Jesse Raphael?

Tenuta: No. That slut actress.

Post: Sally Field?

Tenuta: No. She's not a slut. That big blonde.

Post: Oh, I know who ...

Tenuta: Sally Kirkland. I mean, come on, she's, like, lying on him and everything. They're *scared* to have me on. They're threatened by the Love Goddess. What can I tell you?

Post: Is the Love Goddess continuing to evolve in terms of what she preaches? Is your show different than it was a few years ago?

Tenuta: There's a big difference. I'm wilder, and it's just more all-encompassing. And there's a lot more abuse. It's a lot more fun. I have more structure, and I do a lot more improv. That's because I've so much experience and freedom and I love the stage. Each time it's an opportunity to experiment.

Post: I assume you have no trouble responding to hecklers. Have you ever had a heckler you couldn't handle?

Tenuta: No, it's always a cool experience. I was in New York doing a big show recently, and I was saying, "The government said they didn't want any gays in the Navy—as if there would be a Navy without them." And a guy yells, "Hey, you lay off the Navy." So I ask him, "Sir, are you in the Navy?" and he says, "Yeah." So I say, "Well, come up here and submit." He kneels down on all fours, and he's trying to say, "There's no fags in the Navy" and I say, "Well, I'll tell you what, honey. You could use a fag to redo that hair of yours." Because he had this big queer haircut, you know? I said, "You need a gay man to get hold of your hair, shithead."

Post: What did he say?

Tenuta: He was laughing.

Post: Getting back to the network executives—what is it about you that scares them?

Tenuta: I'm wild. I'm not going to conform to standards and practices. "Oh, Judy, you can't say 'power tool'—it's too suggestive." I think it's important to be free, to speak whatever you want. I want people to break the mold.

Post: What would you do if a fat person came up to you and said they felt hurt by something you'd say about being fat?

Tenuta: I'd say, "Stop eating, okay? Pull away from the table!" You know, I'd like to sit around and inhale food like I'm going to the electric chair. I'd like to sit around like a fat house all day and inhale donuts, but come on! Have a little respect for yourself. Use a little self-control. Pull away from the table and say, "I'm done." How hard is that? Is it better for you to look like a school bus? I'd say, "I'm offended by the fact that you're a house when you should be a person, okay? So we're even!"

Post: Your act is pretty physical; you move around a lot. Do you work out to stay in shape?

Tenuta: No, I just jump from man to man. Keeps me active.

Post: What else do you like to do for fun?

Tenuta: Everything I do is fun. I don't isolate it: "Oh, you know what? I think I should have fun now." People have to learn that. Don't take a job that'll tie you down, like, "Yeah, but this will be secure." Sure, but you're going to be an unhappy jerk! Take a little risk. Maybe you'll be hungry for a while, but do something you really want to do. That's what I did, and that's why I'm happy.

You've got to make yourself happy, all the time. It's not like, "What do I do for fun?" Everything is fun for me. And that means driving in my car and blasting the music loud and then going to the mall and shopping and, you know, lying on top of my boyfriend. Everything is fun.

Post: Has your family seen your show? What do they think of it?

Tenuta: They don't care as long as they get some money. They think I'm the Bank of New York: "Yeah, Judy's great! Hey, Sis, how about a car?" They think I'm Elvis.

Post: Do your siblings have more standard kinds of jobs?

Tenuta: Yeah. My brothers are all electricians. My sister's a special education teacher.

Post: So none of them are gods or goddesses like you.

Tenuta: But you see, my whole message is that *everybody's* a god or goddess. You just have to figure out how to express that. That's the message of Judyism. I'm talking about men, too, not just women. Women have to be elevated to a more reasonable level, that's all. There's a lot of pressure put on men to perform. Becoming more equal with women would mean the burden to act like a macho pig wouldn't always be on them. Men should be more like women and women should be more like men. Everybody should be pigs who adore me. It could happen!

Robin Tyler

by Laura Post

Robin Tyler has had more impact on shaping the current women's comedy scene than most, because her role has never been limited to just performing. As the creator and producer of countless women's music and comedy festivals, Tyler has long taken responsibility for outreach as well. In 1970, as part of the ground-breaking feminist comedy duo Harrison and Tyler, she helped found the women's comedy scene. She and partner Patty Harrison cut two popular comedy albums (*Try It, You'll Like It* and *Wonder Women*) and enjoyed many television appearances, including making three pilots and starring on "The Kraft Comedy Hour."

Tyler went on to develop a successful solo act and continued to achieve many "firsts." An appearance on "The Phyllis Diller Show" in 1979 made her the first openly gay/lesbian performer to appear on national television; she was also the first openly gay comic to perform in the former Soviet Union. Tyler was also the first openly lesbian comedy recording artist, with the release of *Always a Bridesmaid, Never A Groom* in 1978 and *Just Kidding* in 1980.

For the past fifteen years, as producer of the West Coast Women's Music and Comedy Festival and the Southern Women's Music and Comedy Festival, Tyler has been responsible for launching and supporting the comedy careers of many other talented comics. She's led comedy tours worldwide and has been central to events like the 1990 Gay Games and all three of the lesbian/gay marches on Washington. In February 1994, she coproduced the First International Gay/Lesbian Comedy Festival in Sydney, Australia.

With Tyler's recent return to stand-up, it's clear that her wit is as sharply political as ever. Her current act combines classic bits like "The Birth of Baby Jesus" with cutting-edge social commentary, as in her characterization of Lorena Bobbitt as "the Rosa Parks of feminism."

Her activist role has been central to Tyler's life, and at age fifty-one her commitment to political change remains strong. Tyler's experience at the heart of several decades of lesbian/feminist comedy has given her plenty of insight into how comedy can work as a force for political change.

Post: You've been involved in feminist comedy from the beginning. How was your material influenced by feminism?

Tyler: Patty Harrison and I formed the comedy team of Harrison and Tyler in the early seventies, when the feminist movement was first coming alive. At first, our material wasn't feminist. Patty was a fashion model, and I'd joke, "She's so thin, she appeared in *Quo Vadis* and she was the third spear from the left." But in '71 we began to question why we were making fun of ourselves. It didn't feel comfortable. All of a sudden, we said, "Why aren't we talking about what bothers us, instead of what bothers them?" I'd read *The Feminine Mystique*, and it clicked. I realized that, as women, we'd been the object of humor and not the subject.

Post: How did that realization change your material?

Tyler: I did the same sexist jokes—I just turned them on men. "He's so fat …" "Take my husband, please." And you know what happened? Men have no sense of humor about themselves!

We joined Jane Fonda's FTA show, but she kicked us out because we kissed each other onstage and said, "Love means never having to say you're sorry." (She apologized years later for having been homophobic.) At that point, in the early seventies, we knew that war had something to do with guys, but we didn't know the word *patriarchy*. We knew that we had the right to love, but we didn't know the word *homophobia*. But we were already doing openly lesbian, feminist material. We were the first ones.

Post: Did you know when you first got into stand-up that you were going to be pioneering this kind of material?

Tyler: We didn't really know what we were doing. We did a sketch where I played a character named Brother Ripoff. I'd say, "This woman's come to me and she's a lesbian and she wants to be healed. I'm going to put my hand on her and I'm going to heal her. Hallelujah! You're now cured. You are now healed … And, you're still a lesbian!"

I didn't *know* I was "dealing with homophobia." I just did it, you know?

Post: You cut some albums at the time. Were they well received?

Tyler: The first album, in 1971, was *Try It, You'll Like It*. Unfortunately, we were blowing a man up on the album cover. Our second album, *Wonder Women*, was released by Twentieth Century Fox in 1974 and was actually hitting the charts. *Ms.* magazine reviewed it and said we were horrible. They called us the lunatic fringe. And we were. We carried that banner proudly.

At this time, Patty and I went on a radio show and took our clothes off to do a show about nudity. People called and threatened our lives. They didn't even want to hear people talking about nudity. They didn't even know if we were nude or not.

We didn't know that we were dealing with issues like the right to our own bodies, homophobia, and sexism, but nobody else had done it before, so we just did it. The field was wide open. We could talk about anything. We did a routine about the origin of the word *fuck* and material like that. This is in 1974.

Post: Were you able to perform material like that in the comedy clubs?

Tyler: I used to do openly lesbian material at the Comedy Store in the seventies. Mitzi Shore loved me. She was the only club owner who would allow it. I remember Bud Friedman throwing me out of his club for doing openly lesbian material.

There was a group of comics who hung out at the Comedy Store, including people like Cheech and Chong and Jay Leno. We struck the Comedy Store because we wanted to get paid. It was a very famous comedy strike. David Letterman was my strike partner.

Post: Returning to critical response to your first albums, were you surprised that *Ms.* gave you a bad review?

Tyler: It's not surprising that *Ms.* magazine really condemned us at first. You know, when Lenny Bruce started out, it was the Jewish reporters in *Variety* who said "This man is embarrassing." At that time, every Jew was trying to assimilate, and Lenny Bruce was doing a routine comparing Jewish and goyish—for instance: "Chocolate is Jewish; Fudge is goyish." He focused on the differences rather than trying to assimilate.

When Richard Pryor first started out, it was the white audiences who loved him. The black audiences were saying, "We have Bill Cosby to represent us! How can you say the word *nigger* and talk about being raised by whores?" Black audiences resisted him in the beginning. So it's only natural that our resistance in the beginning would come from feminist audiences.

Ms. magazine condemned us, but *Newsweek* said we were brilliant. They credited us with opening doors and changing women's comedy. After that, *Ms.* gave us a good review. You'd think your own people would appreciate you first, but humor is the razor-sharp edge of the truth, and the first people who don't want to hear the truth are your own community. But a comic, if she's truly terrific, has to have the perception to attack even what's around her.

Post: Is that what makes a comic great?

Tyler: The great comics and comedians have been the ones who dared to cross comedy with tragedy. That's what made Chaplin great. Carol Burnett, Lily Tomlin, and Richard Pryor all have the ability to cross humor with pathos. There's really only been one comic who's achieved this with stand-up—without using characters—and that's Lenny Bruce. That's why he's so admired.

Humor is the razor-sharp edge of the truth made funny. It's easier to hear the truth if it's funny.

Post: Humor is a way of communicating your truth?

Tyler: It's a tool. It's also a weapon. And because humor is about your perception of the truth, there's no such thing as "just kidding." Every time a man does a rape joke, every time someone does a faggot joke—they're telling their truth. There's always truth and seriousness behind humor. That's why people like Howard Stern are threatening. He uses humor to make that common bond with his audience.

Post: How did you start performing comedy?

Tyler: I was a singer, but I didn't want to travel with musicians, because they're always fighting. I wanted to be on my own. I started to do comedy just so I wouldn't have to work with a band. I never really wanted to be a comic. I always wanted to be a writer and producer. I'd rather be Barnum than the elephant. Mack Sennet is one of my heroes.

Post: What about Sennet's career inspires you?

Tyler: He was the movie producer who discovered Charlie Chaplin. He also discovered Mabel Norman, the forerunner of all the comedic "dumb blondes" in the movies. (And most of those blondes were brilliant. Judy Holliday had an l65 IQ. Gracie Allen was brilliant. You have to be brilliant to play it that stupid because you need timing.)

Mabel Norman became a heroin addict and died, and Sennet went broke. After that he said, "I'll never rely on one star again." He invented the Keystone Cops, which was the beginning of ensemble comedy.

It's important to understand the history of comedy, and especially the history of oppression in comedy. For instance, originally both women and men could be mimes. Then the Catholic church decided that comedy was a sin; they'd arrest the women as prostitutes. And now you think mime is a male thing, right?

You need a political analysis of how both religion and government have viewed comedy to see how powerful comedy is. I'm Jewish. If you're a Jew it's almost ... *not* to make humor is a sin. Question everything! With the Catholic church, it's: Question nothing!

A comic questions everything. You look at everything fourteen different ways, then through humor you try to somehow pierce the truth. And not only just pierce the truth, but influence other people.

Post: Changing people's minds is the purpose of good comedy?

Tyler: Trevor Griffith wrote a book called *The Comedians*. About teaching eight young male comics how to be comics. One comic does a sexist joke and says, "Aw, it's just a joke." The teacher says something like, "Any joke that gets a cheap laugh reinforces a stereotype, and that's nothing but cheap entertainment. But a true comic has to have the perception to change the way people think, to use humor to make a difference." He says, "You're better than that, damn you, and if you're not, you should damn well want to be!"

Post: How was your material influenced by the struggle for gay liberation and gay civil rights?

Tyler: Patty and I were doing gay material throughout the seventies. We were never in the closet. We told ABC that we were lesbians. We made them take the morals clause out of our contract. But I didn't yet know how to make the pain of growing up as a lesbian funny. How do you take the pain of coming out and make that funny? Nobody else had done it. I had nobody to emulate.

Then in 1977 Anita Bryant came along, and I just couldn't help but comment on Anita Bryant. I started to get up and talk about being a lesbian—all the stuff kids are doing now that's supposed to be unique. I did lines like, "Anita Bryant is to Christianity what paint by numbers is to art," and "Anita Bryant had to stop going to church because the choir insisted on singing 'Go Down, Moses'."

Even though we were starring on television, I couldn't go onstage and not talk about these things. Suddenly, I just began talking about coming out to my family, and it was like a torrent. I couldn't walk onstage and not do this material, because to be a great comic means to reveal yourself. So I became the first openly lesbian comic.

Post: You're saying that a great comic is somebody who isn't afraid to reveal herself. But what if the emotion you reveal is self-hatred? How do you feel about self-deprecating humor?

Tyler: Some feminists criticize Joan Rivers and Phyllis Diller, but they shouldn't. Joan is a brilliant comic. Nobody should knock either of these women, because when you work in show business, you're a factory worker. You do what you must to make a living.

Humor is the most aggressive medium there is. You always say, "I killed them," or "I died." By *aggressive*, I mean having power over others. You must have control over your audience. Some guy came up to me last night and said, "Oh, your audience was so together. It's so different with a lesbian audience." He's wrong. They're not together. I *brought* them together.

To be a comic, you must be aggressive. Until very recently, women weren't allowed to be assertive, let alone aggressive. The only way women were allowed to be aggressive was if they turned it on themselves, which is how self-deprecating jokes came about. So the men did, "She's so ugly ... and the women did, "I'm so ugly ..."

The victims of that consciousness were women comics. Don't blame the victim. These women had to turn this aggression on themselves in order to make it. Humor, remember, is the razor-sharp edge of the truth. Joan Rivers truly had to believe she was fat. Don't blame the victim. Don't even call them victims—they're survivors.

Anyway, so there I was doing lesbian humor. And who attacked me?

Post: Lesbians?

Tyler: Lesbians! I walk onstage in a tuxedo and they tell me I shouldn't wear a tuxedo. They're telling me I shouldn't say I'm a dyke. Well, what should I say? They're telling me I shouldn't talk about my Jewish mother. Well, who *was* my mother? My mother didn't say, "Do you want a cookie?" My mother said, "Eat or I'll kill you!"

Lesbians criticized me because I was beginning not only to pierce the homophobia around us but to pierce the hypocrisy of our community.

Post: You were the first comic to perform openly gay material?

Tyler: Yes. People like Kate Clinton and Lea Delaria came along years later. Everybody thinks we've just made this big breakthrough. Well, I did the "First Annual Phyllis Diller Funny Woman Show" on Showtime in 1979! I did all feminist and lesbian material. I was the first lesbian on national television. I'm not angry that people want to claim to be the first, but why would they claim somebody else's pioneering work, you know? It's kind of a rip-off.

Post: Don't you want to be recognized for having been first? Why aren't you angry about it?

Tyler: I don't feel competitive toward the comics that are coming up now. I gave birth to this comedy movement. They're my children. I don't mind being introduced as the mother of gay and lesbian comedy. I just don't want to be introduced as the grandmother.

There's nothing like being the pioneer, being the first. I had highs and lows that they can't possibly experience. It's exciting to be the first. It's like discovering another planet or being the first one to walk on the moon. It's a thrill, because nobody else has been there. You have to make your own path. I was first on the path. They didn't have the adventure of going first because there was already a path.

When I look at the young comics today on television or in *People*, I feel that I birthed them. I love them. It's like raising children. I've gotten a lot of attention for what I've accomplished. If the children are getting the attention now, it's fine.

Tracey Ullman

by Kathi Maio

For most women in comedy today, who they are is why they are funny. Their stand-up routines are slices of life. Their life. Their persona is what makes them believable. And their individual take on the world—be it dead-pan or whacked-out—is what makes us laugh.

Tracey Ullman is *not* that kind of comedic performer. She is not a stand-up comic. She is not a sitcomish "comedienne," à la Lucy. She is, simply, a character actor—one of the best of her generation.

When you watch her perform, you pick up few clues as to who the *real* Tracey Ullman might be, she is so possessed by her roles. And to intensify the mystery, she makes few public appearances and hardly ever hits the talk-show circuit. (Although one of her early American TV triumphs was her feisty response to David Letterman's standard guest harassment routine.)

Tracey is seldom seen, except in character. In the skit comedy for which she is best known, Ullman's characterizations bury the real woman beneath layers of pads, costumes, latex, makeup, and wigs, so that little more than her expressive eyes are left exposed.

One suspects that this is where Tracey Ullman is most comfortable: totally immersed in a role, with her self hidden safely away. Only when she is fully submerged in another human being can Tracey can come out to play.

A psychologist might be tempted to attribute this to childhood insecurities. A more generous soul might say that Ullman's deep-cover comedy indicates a healthy separation of her public life as an actor from her private life as a woman and mother. The known facts about Ullman's life could support either theory.

Tracey's early life as the daughter of a British mother and a Polish immigrant to Britain was comfortably middle class, until her lawyer father died of a heart attack when Tracey was six. Grief was quickly followed by financial insecurity, and later by the presence of a stepfather she didn't like.

At the age of twelve, Tracey won a scholarship to a stage school in London, where she studied dance and theater arts. She acted—and also acted out. When she was expelled from school at sixteen, Tracey joined a touring company of *Gigi* in Germany and later returned to London to find theatrical work.

Ullman's first major success was in an improvisational play at the Royal Court Theatre. Her role as a born-again club chanteuse named Beverly won her the London Theatre Critics Award as most promising new actress of 1981. It also gained the attention of British television producers. She then appeared in several English sitcoms, including an all-female (but hardly feminist) series called "Girls on Top," in which she played Candice, a gold-digging party girl, who constantly cheated and tricked her rather stupid flatmates.

In between the television jobs that made Ullman a household name in Britain (where the tabloids dubbed her "Our Trace"), Tracey continued to prove her considerable versatility. She appeared in the so-called legitimate theater (e.g., in Goldsmith's *She Stoops to Conquer*). She also won her first movie role in the film *Give My Regards to Broad Street* (1984).

The movie bombed. But the star of the film, none other than former Beatle Paul McCartney, was quite taken by her. So when Tracey became a pop singer, the fab Paul appeared in the video for "They Don't Know," which became a top-ten hit on both sides of the Atlantic. Her music is fun stuff (for a taste of her bouncy retro, girl-group sound, have a listen to the Rhino disc, *The Best of Tracey Ullman: You Broke My Heart in 17 Places*), but it hardly constitutes a great achievement in entertainment.

Cutesy rock and roll wasn't enough to occupy our versatile Trace, and she soon turned away from music and toward features films. She appeared as Meryl Streep's bohemian buddy in *Plenty* (1985) and then headed for Hollywood with her husband, television producer Allan McKeown.

Unfortunately, as is often the case with women actors who share few physical characteristics with Barbie, Tinseltown didn't exactly snatch Tracey up. (Blink and you'll miss her role in the 1986 Penny Marshall-directed Whoopi Goldberg comedy, *Jumpin' Jack Flash*.) But that doesn't mean that there weren't plenty of people in Hollywood aware of her many talents.

One of these people was filmmaker (*Terms of Endearment, Broadcast News*) and television producer ("Rhoda," "Taxi"), James L. Brooks. When plans for a CBS traditional sitcom fell through, Brooks and partners Heide Perlman, Jerry Belson, and Ken Estin came up with the idea of a half-hour variety show, or "skitcom," to showcase Ullman.

It was a simple but brilliant concept, backed up with a quality approach. Formulated as the flagship program of the new Fox network, "The Tracey Ullman Show" was launched in April of 1987 and featured some of the best writers on television, as well as the fine ensemble cast of Julie Kavner, Dan Castellaneta, Sam McMurray, Joe Malone, and for a time, Anna Levine.

Many of the skits were one-shots, but there were also several fascinating women characters who appeared frequently over the show's three-year run. A partial list of Tracey's recurring, fully-realized characters includes: Kay Clark, a shy spinster with (unnamed) physical challenges, whose quiet warmth and gutsy integrity constantly put her insensitive boss and harassing male coworkers to shame; Francesca, a bright pubescent girl learning life's lessons with the loving guidance of her two dads, David and William; Sarah, a high-end yuppie, who wants to have meaningful relationships with her husband and son, but who keeps getting caught up in the trappings and prestige games of her well-to-do lifestyle; Summer Storm, a burned-out, drug- and alcohol-abusing rock deejay who can't quite come to terms with the fact that the seventies are long gone; Tina, a postal worker whose love life stinks, but whose relationship with her best friend, Meg, is the real thing; Joanie, an ultrawholesome bride; Ginny, a seriously embittered, displaced homemaker; Lisa Morgan, a U.S.O. singer/dancer; and KiKi, an Australian pro golfer.

A typical show consisted of three comedy skits—as poignant as they were funny—the last of which segued into a song and dance number. The show concluded with a brief farewell in which the star, dressed in a chenille bathrobe, exhorted her audience to "Go Home!"

Guest stars as varied as Steven Spielberg and Isabella Rossellini happily appeared on a show they recognized as primo prime-time. Unfortunately, "The Tracey Ullman Show" was an expensive program for a fledgling network to maintain. In a typical Hollywood twist of fate, Tracey won an Emmy for Best Performance in a Variety Show (and co-won another for writing) two weeks after her show went off the air.

Since her program—which even now enjoys a repeat run on the Lifetime women's cable network—was cancelled, Tracey has done film and theatrical work. On stage, she did *The Taming of the Shrew* opposite Morgan Freeman for the New York Shakespeare Festival, and later performed a one-woman show as Florence Aadland, the mother of Errol Flynn's last underaged conquest.

Tracey Ullman's film career has continued to be, for her fans, as frustrating as ever. She has played lead characters in small films—e.g., Nancy Savoca's *Household Saints* (1993)—that nobody saw. More often, she has played small support roles in major movies—e.g., *Robin Hood: Men in Tights* (1993) and *I'll Do Anything* (1994)—that nobody saw.

The Hollywood movie machine is still clearly at a loss about how to utilize Tracey's talents. But all is not lost. HBO has recently given Ullman a few opportunities to do what she does best. In the fall of 1994, she starred in two one-hour skitcom specials featuring her full range of latex-covered and bewigged characters.

In the first, "Tracey Ullman Takes on New York," the star played both natives and out-of-towners with equal aplomb. The second special, even better than the first, allowed Tracey to take on something even bigger than the Big Apple, namely, the British class system. The intertwined, socially aware skits of *Tracey Ullman: A Class Act* represent her comic gifts in all their glory.

Tragicomedy with a satiric bite is far too rare in this culture. and no one does it better than Tracey Ullman in deep disguise. We can only hope that the entertainment industry continues to provide venues for this brilliant artist—whoever she *really* is.

Thea Vidale

by Trey Graham

In conversation, Thea Vidale sounds much more like her raucous, raunchy stand-up self than the hardworking widow and mother she played on her short-lived ABC sitcom. "I am so sick of straight white men makin' all the rules," she growls. Then she goes off on a riff about the American justice system, dishing Tonya Harding and moving on to trash the Menendez brothers.

"I tell a terrible joke about the Menendezes," she chuckles. "I say to the jury, 'You can't come up with a verdict. Try this: Close your damn eyes and pretend they're black. There's your fuckin' verdict!' 'Cause you know if these guys were black, they'd be in jail by now!"

Thea isn't what you'd call the word-mincing sort. Her stand-up comedy routine is positively notorious, full of blistering blue stories and jokes that would make Redd Foxx blush. She got her start, reportedly, as a wise-mouthed waitress at a Steak N Egg in Texas, where diners liked her cracks so much that she took a stab at stand-up, performing at the local improv club. Her husband disapproved—and he expressed it with his fists—but Thea was determined to succeed on her own terms. "I had the bug so bad that I couldn't stop doing stand-up," she told *First* magazine. "It was my savior. So every night, we'd duke it out."

Eventually, she left her husband, and though she allowed him custody of their children when she hit the comedy circuit, she never went back. And when he came after her, she was waiting with a gun. "I was tougher [then], and he was a little intimidated," she told *First*. "Of course, a .357 Magnum will do that to a person."

She's talked only a little in public about that time in her life, but she has offered advice to women who find themselves in similar situations: "If you're in a relationship that's bad, don't ever stay because you think no one else will want you," she told readers of *Big Beautiful Women*. "You deserve to be loved and nurtured and cared for. And you will be. You have to love yourself first, and the good things follow."

As for her views on men, they're fairly unequivocal. "Men do foolish things," she told a *USA Today* interviewer who asked her about the potshots her act takes at guys. "Men have ruined this country. Men want to tell women what to do with their bodies. Men are, overall, selfish people."

Thea's done all kinds of comedy, from stand-up sets in "redneck dives" to high-profile work on HBO's *Def Comedy Jam*. Most of it, as noted, has been risqué, to say the least. But the comic has no patience with conservative criticisms of her act. "Yes, I'm down and dirty," she says. "But don't tell me you're repulsed by it, 'cause you've already made Andrew Dice Clay a millionaire."

And another thing. Critics complain about her rough language, "but they don't tell you how I denounce Jesse Helms, they don't tell you how I knock on Rush Limbaugh. They don't tell you how I say it's wrong to not respect a woman's decision about what to do with her body. I'm gonna say what the fuck I wanna say. At least with me you're gonna hear about some issues."

Among those issues lately are AIDS, homophobia, and religion. "I'm not afraid to talk about the AIDS epidemic," she says. "I want my boys to be aware that while they're dippin' and dabbin', they need to be careful. And I want to make sure my girls know to protect themselves. I want them to know that if they get AIDS, that's something Mama can't help. Mama's gotta sit by and watch."

And about homophobia, Thea has definite ideas.

"To me, homophobia is racism. They're all together," she says. You want to hate somebody because they're not like you. And I'm not with that." She doesn't have time for religious right-wingers, either. "I'm sick of these people talking about God hates homosexuals," she says. "If Jesus was with us right now he'd be hanging with the homosexuals, the AIDS victims, with the gang bangers. He'd be with the downtrodden, not the people who've got everything."

That's not to say she doesn't have a kind of faith. "I believe in God immensely," Thea says. But I also know that I'm human. We all fall short in the eyes of God. I'm not a fanatic or a fundamentalist; I'm just a believer. And I believe God wants us to be kind to one another."

Fans who've seen Thea's act in gay bars say she's been known to talk about a girlfriend (a word that can, of course, be interpreted several ways). Would the comic care to clarify what she meant? "When you're in Rome, you do as the Romans do," she says coyly. "When I'm in a country and western bar, I can talk about country and western things. I adapt to many situations."

"Once again, please let me reiterate: I keep my options open, and my personal life is just that. But I do keep my options open. And please know that I have a love of all people, and love comes in many faces and all colors. I'm at that age when I don't have to be defending myself and my life to anybody."

Marsha Warfield

by Deni Kasrel

Marsha Warfield is a big, black, and proud kind of women. She stands up for herself, all right. And when she takes to the comedy stage she's more than just an all-right stand-up. Her jokes jostle your gut to elicit major belly laughs. No doubt about it, this woman dishes out a routine that goes for the gusto.

She uses her status of being a hefty African-American as part of her act, which in the appropriate setting can get rather raunchy. That's what some call it, anyway. Others might think Marsha merely sets things straight, both in and outside of the bedroom. Take older men: it's said they make better lovers because they have more sexual endurance. "Let's think about that," Warfield suggests. "Who wants to fuck an old man for a long time?"

She's got a wide feminist streak in her. "I like sex a lot," she reveals, "especially since I found out women are supposed to have orgasms." Her answer for safe sex and not having to hassle with loser guys is simple: "Don't date, masturbate."

There's no lack of self-confidence here. Warfield is delightedly brash and brawny. She loves every nook and cranny of her upfrontness. Heck, it comes with the territory of her proud heritage. "Black women, we have attitude," she assures. "We're the only people on earth born knowing how to roll our eyes with 'em closed."

Eyes may roll at Warfield's words. This is a highly independent woman who basks in being a freethinker. She's got a militant mouth, too. She blasts hypocrisy and real-life inequality. She wants to write a movie about black folks *not* scaring white people to be called *Black Men, Employed*. She slyly mocks how television presents grossly unreal programs built around black families. A show she would air about a poor black family that's got lots of troubles but who are nonetheless always upbeat would be called "We Be Happy." It's funny, and it makes a point, too: like, who are we all kidding?

The tell-it-like-it-is stance is her trademark. She is no doubt best known for her role as Roz, the take-no-prisoners bailiff of NBC's "Night Court." Roz is caustic, crusty, and always speaking her mind. On the other hand, in times of real distress, the aloofness melts away, and Roz bears a big, kind heart.

That's par for the course with TV characters. In a sitcom, there's usually goodness to everyone, deep down. It's also a reflection of the comedian herself. She's a tough cookie with inner sweetness.

Offstage she supports several socially conscious causes. She's even created her own award—the Jason Scott Inner City Incentive Scholarship—which is given to kids of her hometown, Chicago, in recognition of personal accomplishment.

Always a funny gal, Warfield says that in high school she was the class cut-up and a nonstop back-of-the-room commentator. Following the footsteps of her mom, she took a job as a telephone operator. Even then, she couldn't contain her desire to go for the laugh, "lousing up" on the phone lines when she felt the urge to imitate Flip Wilson's sassy Geraldine character.

She started doing stand-up on a dare. Marsha kept telling her friends she was going to try out at a local club's open-mike night, and they finally forced her to live up to the threat. She was pleased to find strangers laughing at her jokes, and soon enough she heard the beckoning call of the comedy scene. Her basic routine was bawdy and blue. In one early bit she conjectured what female members of the audience would say about their male companions when in the ladies' room.

This was in the mid-seventies, and at that time Chicago was severely lacking in comedy venues. To pursue her career aggressively, Warfield took off for where the action was, California. In 1979 she won a national stand-up contest, for which one of the prizes was touring as the opening act for Teddy Pendergrass. This gave her good exposure and also helped her land a spot on the "The Richard Pryor Show." While the program was short-lived, Warfield gained a strong sense of satisfaction working with someone to whom she felt a deep kinship.

A series of TV roles ensued. She was seen on "Riptide," "The Idi Amin Christmas Special," "The Marva Collins Story," and a few HBO specials. Her ready string of one-liners plus her ability to think fast on her feet caused her to fast become a favorite guest on the talk-show and game-show circuit.

The "Night Court" run lasted over a dozen years. As a follow-up, she took the role of Dr. Olivia on the NBC series "Empty Nest." She's done movies, too—*Gidget Goes to Harlem*, *Caddyshack II*, and *Mask*, among them. She landed these parts without a background in acting, though in a *TV Guide* interview Warfield noted that the rigors of doing comedy clubs provided good preparation for work in television and film. "To do stand-up success-fully, you've gotta be an instinctive actor, thinking quickly and reacting quickly," she said.

In 1990, she hosted "The Marsha Warfield Show," where celebrity guests came on and tackled topics in a less than serious manner. At the time of its air-ing, she made the comment, "We have to address women's issues. But we don't have to have a *Women's Wear Daily* attitude about it. Instead of saying, 'We're going to give you a brand-new you,' we say, 'Do you really need one?' "

There it is again, that potent ever-present irreverence. It's Marsha mixing up her funny stuff with a solid dose of attitude and social awareness. Most of her lines are doled out in deadpan fashion, which adds a subtle subversive flavor to it all. As part of her act she's observed: "Magic Johnson admits that he was sexually promiscuous, got the HIV virus, and possibly infected half the women he was with. And we call him a hero. Pee Wee Herman was in a theater, by himself, practicing safe sex ..." At this point the audience is howl-ing so hard that the comic doesn't even need to finish off the line. She's made her joke. And made a statement, too. That's signature Warfield wit.

Suzanne Westenhoeffer

by Victoria A. Brownworth, interview by Roz Warren

"I want to change the world. I want to be a spokesperson for the lesbian community," says Suzanne Westenhoefer. "Oh, and I want my own sitcom."

Such dichotomies are a way of life for this dyke, the rising star of lesbian comedy. As far as the thirty-four-year-old Westenhoefer is concerned, the personal is political, and the political is a punch line. She's been blitzing through the talk-show circuit on network and cable TV and also packing in sellout audiences at live performance venues from Peoria to New York. And now a joyous Westenhoefer is taping her first hour-long comedy special for HBO.

"It's the first-ever special like this for an out lesbian or gay comedian," she explains. "Ever. It's big. Very, very big."

After years of waiting tables and waiting for fame, Westenhoefer is a little surprised by her sudden popularity. "I believe," she quips, "this is what's called an overnight sensation."

The truly sensational part for Westenhoefer is that she's not only making it big but also making it as an openly lesbian stand-up comedian. Although naysayers around her predicted that doing queer comedy would be career suicide, Westenhoefer never had any intention of climbing into a closet to do her routines. She had a much bigger goal than that. She was determined to break the unwritten show-business rule: No one does queer comedy in straight clubs.

Explaining her dilemma to a straight instructor in a comedy class a few years back, Westenhoefer got just the push she needed. Her teacher told her candidly, "You're thirty years old. You aren't doing anything with your life anyway." He urged her to go for it, and he was right. "Now we're chic," she says. "Who knew?"

Today Westenhoefer has come to epitomize lesbian chic. Big, blond, and buff, she's every talk-show host's dream date. Uncompromisingly femme to look at, she talks endlessly about how great it is to be a dyke.

A small-town girl from Columbia, Pennsylvania, Westenhoefer went to a tiny Christian college, Clarion. It was there that she began her dual career as a big dyke on campus and lesbian cover girl. Like actress Sharon Stone, who hails from the same area, Westenhoefer is a former beauty queen. "It's not hype," she says, almost apologetically. "I'm not famous enough yet that we've begun to invent stories about me."

Westenhoefer admits that she's slightly annoyed by the media's focus on her looks. "It's this idea that there can only be one kind of lesbian, and she doesn't look good," she sighs. "But they're going a little overboard on the lipstick thing now. My first network TV appearance was on "Sally Jessy Raphael," on an episode called "Lesbians Who Don't Look Like Lesbians."

Still, to everyone from her manager, Olivia Productions cofounder Judy Dlugacz, to Geraldo to HBO, Westenhoefer may not look like a lesbian, but she sure looks like a rising star. "I first met Suzanne when she came into my office and made me laugh for about two hours nonstop," says Dlugacz. "She was fantastic." Singer Chris Williamson, with whom Suzanne often performs, is equally laudatory about the comic. "The girl is incredibly, wickedly funny," she says. "Standing up there onstage with Suzanne is great. And she's one of the kindest people I've ever met."

It isn't often that looks, talent, humor, and niceness come together in one package. But for those who are wondering how to get Westenhoefer's phone number, forget it—she's taken.

"Yes, I'm married, very, very married," she says. "Oh, and happily so. We have a house and two dogs—my stepchildren." Westenhoefer's girlfriend of two years is "about as deeply in the closet as you can get," she notes. "It used to really bother me. Now I just use it as material for my act. My girlfriend teaches in a small-town school."

Despite their marital bliss, family get-togethers can be "pretty weird. I'm totally out with my family," Westenhoefer says, "but at her house I'm just 'the friend.' I'm always talking nonstop there, because I'm afraid if things get quiet, I'll just lose it and yell, 'We're lesbians!' Her mother's seen me on TV, so it's very strange. She knows I'm a lesbian. It's like that T-shirt: 'I'm not a lesbian, but my girlfriend is.' We're living a T-shirt!"

Warren: Most comics are nervous before going on, but you've got not only the nervousness of just facing an audience but often the added component of being a lesbian comic about to face a straight audience. It's very courageous to get out in front of a straight audience and do lesbian comedy.

Westenhoefer: I don't think I'd use a word like *courageous* to describe myself. Although if I saw someone else do it I might say, "Wow, that's really brave." But it's just how I am. I have to do it this way.

Warren: Why do you think that is?

Westenhoefer: Ever since I can remember, from a very young age, I've felt I had to change the world. Whatever I was going to do with my life, that had to be part of it, you know? I had to fight for the underdog and fight for the rights of others.

Warren: What made you tune into that as a kid? Most young kids don't really focus on the fact that the world isn't fair or just.

Westenhoefer: My parents got divorced when I was two. We were very, very poor. This was the early sixties and there was a lot of prejudice about divorce. At school, I was the only kid with one parent, except for another kid whose mother had died. You stand out. You're different, so people make fun of you.

I had a teacher in fifth grade actually stand me up in front of the class and tell me I wouldn't be anything because I was from a broken home.

Warren: Do you think you developed your sense of humor as a way to cope with that kind of bullshit?

Westenhoefer: Not really. I don't stand out in my family in any way. We're all funny. We've been poor—we've had very little, but humor is something we've always had. We sit around and play cards and tell stories, and you laugh until your face hurts.

Warren: Your goal was always to perform out lesbian comedy for straight audiences. It's as if you've taken on the role of goodwill ambassador from the lesbian community to the straight world. It would be so much easier to perform for lesbian audiences—why try to win over the straights?

Westenhoefer: I came out to myself when I was twenty. I immediately came out to my mom, and to the world, and demanded acceptance. And got it. And when anyone gave me grief, I was able to overcome it. I'm a born arguer. I *want* to be an activist. Everything that made me who I am as I was growing up made me into an activist.

Some gays get thrust into the political limelight because they're successful entertainers, but they'll tell you, "I don't want to be a spokeperson for the gay community." Well, that's *all* I want to be.

Warren: You've said that what you try to do with your act is convince straight audiences that they're missing out on something. What are we missing out on?

Westenhoefer: Some people have misunderstood that. I'm *not* saying everyone should be gay. I'm saying that if you ignore gay culture you're missing out on a lot.

I'm a human being. Most of the time, I'm worried about paying my bills and will my car start and who's going to shovel out the snow and is the roof going to get fixed. You know, the same things everybody else cares about. But gays and lesbians are also a little different, and I don't mean about who we sleep with. There's an energy about us. There's a creative force. We shine a little in a different way. Gay people are like the gravy on the mashed potatoes of life. We're like icing on the cake. Like you've got your basic snow cone, and then you put the cherry flavoring on it.

It's *that* kind of thing you need. You don't need *us*. If all the gay people suddenly disappeared, the world would move forward. But that's all it would do. There wouldn't be the art. The culture would be different. We're like another force that creates a reason to live, to not just be plugging along.

Warren: When you were a little kid, did you want to grow up to be a famous movie star?

Westenhoefer: It's all I ever wanted. I never ever had another job thought for a second. I always wanted to be famous. I wanted an incredible amount of attention. I still need a lot of attention.

Warren: Who were your comic influences?

Westenhoefer: I always admired Carol Burnett. She could be almost buffoonish, but it never seemed self-deprecating. Sometimes female comics made fun of themselves to the degree that even though it was still funny you almost pitied them. Carol Burnett—and also Lily Tomlin—were the first women comics I saw who weren't just: "I'm so fat ..."

Joan Rivers was also an inspiration. She was one of the first women stand-ups who didn't just make fun of herself. She made fun of her circumstances. She seemed really in control of her life, in control of her destiny. She made fun of things that we weren't supposed to make fun of, and it was fun.

Warren: You don't look like the stereotype of what a lesbian looks like. Do your looks make it easier for an audience to accept you or trust you?

Westenhoefer: I don't look like what many people expect gay women to look like. When I get up onstage at the Improv or at Caroline's, I look like a guy's sister, or a woman he's dated. I don't see myself as pretty, but I do feel very confident. I always have.

Warren: Where do you think that confidence comes from, if not from your looks?

Westenhoefer: I think that I'm better than everyone else. When I was a kid, everyone told me I wouldn't be anything because we were poor and my parents had divorced and stuff like that. It just made me feel, I'm so much better than you. It's a defense mechanism. If somebody tells me I can't do something, that's what I want to do most.

Warren: And is that one of the reasons you started doing out comedy in front of straight audiences?

Westenhoefer: Everybody was saying you couldn't be an out lesbian comic. Not for straight audiences. But I knew they were wrong. When I started out auditioning—doing open mikes and stuff—in New York at the straight clubs nobody else was doing what I was doing.

Warren: When you first get up in front of a straight audience, you always tell them immediately that you're a lesbian.

Westenhoefer: I put it on the table immediately, because that's how I am in life: out, out, out. I cope with any negative reaction they might have by being very, very honest. I don't tell any jokes that aren't true. I'll adjust it to make it funnier. I'll say something happened yesterday when it really happened six years ago. But every single thing that I say is true and happened, so I'm being honest with them.

I think the audience gets off on my saying, "Look, I'm up here. I'm being honest. I'm not asking for your acceptance."

Warren: You're not?

Westenhoefer: No, I'm telling them to get with the program. I'm showing them that acceptance is the only way, if we're going to move forward.

Warren: Why is it important to tell a straight audience you're a lesbian up front, rather than easing into it?

Westenhoefer: I took a lot of speech classes in college. They teach you that when you give a speech the first thing you've got to do is establish your credibility. The audience is thinking, Who are you? Why should we listen to you? You have to anticipate any questions they might have and answer them. You can give a great speech, but if you beg the question on a couple of issues, your audience is going to go home thinking, Yeah, but what about this? So I try to answer all of the possible questions they could have and make them feel comfortable so they can lighten up, and we can let the comedy begin.

Warren: How do you develop your material?

Westenhoefer: It occurs to me as I say it. I try to tape every show, then I listen to them afterward. If I've said something new that's funny, I use it again. If you and I were to sit and watch videotapes of my show over the past three years, you could see the jokes and how they evolved. I keep adding, throwing out, and changing things until it becomes what it needs to be.

Warren: Do you ever get material from conversations with your friends?

Westenhoefer: Absolutely. All the time.

Warren: Do you ask permission, or do you just grab it and use it?

Westenhoefer: It depends. If I'm having a conversation with Kate Clinton and a joke comes up, she'll say, "Do you want to use it?" And I'll say, "No, no, you use that one." And we'll keep talking, and another joke will come up, and she'll say "Oh, can I have that one?" And I'll say, "No, I'm going to use that one."

Warren: Has Kate been a mentor? How did you become friends?

Westenhoefer: When I'd been doing comedy a little over a year, I did a weekend up in Provincetown. I was a big, big fan of Kate's, but we'd never met. After I got home, the phone rings, and it's Kate Clinton! I almost died. She said, "I heard that you were in Provincetown. I heard that you were openly gay. I'm so proud of you." She gave me advice about places to do my act and people to get in touch with. It was incredible. Kate is one of the most incredible beings who ever lived. I love her.

Warren: You make comedy from things that bother you. How do you go about transforming something that troubles you into something that will make people laugh?

Westenhoefer: You know, if I could tell you that ... There is no way to tell you that. Because that's exactly what comedy is—transforming something that is awful, sad, miserable, or that pisses you off into a joke.

You've done it. Something makes you angry. So you're home and you're talking about it with your boyfriend, girlfriend, whatever. And you're saying, "So, I'm coming down, and this guy sits right in front of me. I slip. I fall." You start to tell the story. They start to respond. You get into it a little more. Now you're adding a few little, tiny things to make it a little bigger, a little funnier. There's a whole bunch of details you don't need—get rid of those. You set it up. Give them the incident—the punch is right there.

That's how it works for me. Or else things just occur to me out of the blue. I was standing there waiting to go up onstage once, and I started thinking, If straight people are afraid of us, what are they afraid of? What do they think we're going to *do*? This was in Dallas, and there had just been a big car-jacking. I'm thinking, It's not like gays are the kind of people who would car-jack. What would gay people do? I'm standing there, waiting to go up onstage, watching the other comic and not listening. And suddenly I thought, "Well, maybe they're afraid a bunch of fags will *perm*-jack them, and make them get better hair." Boom! The joke is there.

Warren: One popular part of your act is the way you make fun of the questions straights are always asking gays.

Westenhoefer: That developed from years of being out to straight people and answering the same questions over and over. "Do you want to be a man?" Only if I can get paid like one. "How do people get to be homosexual?" Homosexuals are chosen first on talent, then interview, and then the swimsuit and evening gown competitions.

I was a bartender and I was out, so I answered the same questions over and over. You've seen gay people on talk shows—no matter what the subject matter of the show, they always get asked the same questions. "How did you get that way?" "Do your parents know?" "Do you want to be a guy?" It's the same six questions. So I just developed a little smart-shit answer for each of them.

Warren: My favorite is when a straight person asks what lesbians do in bed, and you answer, "We do everything you do, but one of us doesn't have to fake orgasm." What just kills me is to see the straight guys in your audience laughing at that. And they do! How do you pull that off?

Westenhoefer: It has to be the way I say it, because I've seen other comics say stuff like that and it doesn't work. I think most people get that I'm kidding. That I'm toying with them on purpose because they *do* say these things about us. So there's a grain of truth to it, although it's tongue-in-cheek. I'm laughing, but I'm saying, "It is sort of true, you guys, you know what I mean?"

Warren: You've done a lot of TV work. What do you like about being on TV?

Westenhoefer: Everything! I like the camera pointing at me. I like the attention. I like the exposure.

Warren: When they've got you on a show where you're supposed to represent something like "lesbians who don't look like lesbians," how do you break out of that narrow category?

Westenhoefer: I don't need to. I don't care. Label me. Feel free. Who cares? People only get bent out of shape by a label when it fits. If you're very confident about who and what you are, the label won't bother you.

Warren: There are several very successful women comics who are closeted lesbians. What's your take on that?

Westenhoefer: In all honesty, I think it's none of my fucking business. It's unfortunate if people feel that they can't be out, but nobody has the right to tell somebody else they have to be out. My job is to make it comfortable for everybody to come out and encourage everybody to come out.

Warren: You've said that you want to make the world better with your comedy.

Westenhoefer: I want the world to change and I want to do everything that I can, before I have to go, to change it.

Warren: For instance?

Westenhoefer: I want the gay issue to be a dead issue by the time I'm dead. I'd like racism and bigotry and prejudice to be dead.

Warren: That's a pretty big agenda.

Westenhoefer: I want people to be equal as possible before I go. Because I'm a Buddhist, so I know I'm coming back. And I don't want to have to come back and start over.

karen Williams

by Laura Post

The lesbian mother of two sons, Karen Williams describes herself as a "tall, thin, brown-skinned, bespectacled, African-American revolutionary warrior woman Buddhist." Williams is also the producer of the annual National Women's Comedy Conference, a gathering of like-minded funny women who share their knowledge through workshops on topics like ethnic humor and healing with comedy. Based in Ohio, Williams travels the country, playing gay clubs, Black clubs, universities and women's centers. She's also a popular MC at women's music festivals.

"I love the challenge," Williams says, "and the healing. There's something magical and magnificent about the sound of laughter, and I have the gift of giving it."

Calling her style "comic folklore," she specializes in spontaneous dialog with her audiences. Often wearing silver pumps and combat gear, Williams riffs about life in San Francisco: tofu, astrology, relationships, Birkenstocks and the rabbit coat she hides in her closet away from animal rights activists.

Williams was born in the Bronx ("What cities are so important that they're always called by the prefix 'the'? THE Bronx and THE Vatican.") She grew up in a public housing project, married early and moved to California in 1974. One evening Williams was at a nightclub with a friend who was cracking up at her description of riding the Oakland bus system. A local comic stopped by their table. Williams, on the spur of the moment, announced that she, too, did comedy. The comic offered her 5 minutes of his set and she was a hit.

Although she's never resorted to insults to get a laugh, Williams has built her rapport with audiences on a fault line that shifts between the tender and the tough. Her work is a smooth amalgam of correct political "issues" and her simple need to laugh at what she thinks is funny.

"If people's feathers get ruffled," says Williams, "let them process it."

Post: Tell me something about your background. Were your parents funny?

Williams: I found out recently that my dad was a frustrated comic. Both of my parents are hysterical; I get together with them and have laugh fests.

Growing up, my parents were both young—seventeen years older than me—and very creative. Their creativity came out in our home. We lived in the projects, but our apartment was very different from every other apartment. The living room had two blue walls and two white walls and my dad hung all kinds of art. My mother put mirrors on the walls with window flower boxes. There were six of us, a very tight-knit family. Along with all the creative energy in my family, there was verbal and emotional abuse. It was pretty crazy-making, but it was also freethinking, and I have drawn on all of it in my work.

Post: How have your experiences contributed to your comedy?

Williams: It's said that comedy is the flip side of tragedy, and I've had several tragedies. As a child, I felt like an ugly duckling; as an adult I realized that what had happened to me was really not much different than what happened to a lot of people. My response set me apart. I recognized that I had humor, that it was healing to me and to others and that it was a powerful way of connecting.

Post: What were some of your most significant life experiences?

Williams: As a child I was bussed to all-white elementary schools to be in the special progress classes. I skipped two grades and later graduated from the Bronx High School of Science at 16. One of the earlier tragedies of my life was that when I was in my early teens I had to testify against my father so that my mother could divorce him on the grounds of adultery. It was painful for me. Another early tragedy was that when I graduated from high school I was four months pregnant.

I went to California after graduation to be with my father. That November I had a baby boy, who was adopted at three days old. I was supposed to go to college and actually went back East to enroll at the University of Connecticut. I had a hard time living with myself after giving up the child, which I basically did to get a college degree that I still don't have. I spiraled down in a long, long cycle of drug use, which I later realized had to do with the adoption.

By the time I had the opportunity to have another child, Yusef (now 21), I went for it. I married a guy I met while at the University. Soon thereafter, he was sentenced to seven to ten years for armed robbery behind his heroin use. He got off with two years at a drug rehab. In the meantime I was pregnant and went ahead and had the baby.

My early life reads like a grade B movie, but it is definitely the salt and pepper of who I am.

Not only is my material drawn from what I see and what is real to me, but how I survive as a performer, how I work my whole life, has a lot to do with who I was and what I went through. Recently my dad said to me that there's a level of appreciation and gratitude that recovering dope fiends can have about their lives so they won't be caught up in the illusions about performing: thinking that one is more than they are, star-tripping, focusing on the material things, the privilege, the status. These days, when I wake up in a nice hotel I say "Great" and don't attach a lot to it. The trick is to remain right-sized, and my ability to do that is a gift, like my comedy.

Post: What are the circumstances of your coming out, and getting into performance comedy?

Williams: When my husband got out of the drug program, he didn't want to be married any more so we separated. Some time later I went to the National Black Feminist Organization Conference and I saw 2,000 Black women, feminists, mostly lesbians, and I was jazzed, really energized. I met my first lesbian lover there. I came out and we moved in together. Then Yusef's father started to harass me, trying to take the baby away. My lover wanted to stay and fight legally but this was 1974 in Connecticut. I was a theatre intern, without a "real job." She was a teacher and I didn't trust our circumstances. So I moved with my 2-year-old kid to Santa Monica. My lover was supposed to join us, but she never did. At the time, that was another tragedy.

I spent the next six years in the Los Angeles area, mostly doing temp work as a secretary. I moved to Oakland in 1980. It was in 1985 that, on a dare, I wrote a five-minute sketch which I performed at the Lucky Lion in Oakland. I was nervous but the audience liked me. For the next two years I did local venues, open mikes, and got some steady gigs.

I played mostly Black clubs and wasn't out as a lesbian. Interestingly, I had been out for 10 years during the seventies, then was involved with a man and had Keith (my son). In the 1980s I had my second coming out, as a lesbian comic. It was radical to appear as a Black woman comic—there weren't many of us. As a Black lesbian comic, I have experienced the homophobia of the Black community and the racism of the gay community.

Post: Do you address these issues in your act?

Williams: In my shows, I talk about African-American culture and lesbian culture. Even if I don't specifically come out in my shows, I don't include stuff that relates me to men sexually—and that sets me apart from "women comics" who talk about their boyfriends and husbands.

Post: You might be invisible as a lesbian, but you are visible as a Black woman. How do you address the issue of racism in your act?

Williams: I've done some stuff about the label "women of color" which I've made fun of as "woman o'color." I react to the nomenclature from the standpoint that it is not a name that we gave ourselves. I don't know any women of color who call themselves that. If I'm dealing with a Black women, we say we're Black women or we'll say African-American, or a Puerto Rican woman will say Puerto Rican or a Latina will say Latina. I prefer for people to self-identify, for us to name ourselves.

Post: Do you consider yourself a spokesperson or a leader? Describe your relationship with your audience.

Williams: As a public person, I try to be very clear that I am speaking only for me, from the life experience that I have and the small corner that I see. My politics came through out of sheer caring. I learn all the time, I write all the time. My work as a comic means for me, on a personal and artistic level, that I synthesize a lot of information. I have the ability to put it out there in a way that's not offensive. It can be shocking, but it will make people laugh. And, when we laugh, we can open up to the issues and begin to work on them.

I'm also playful with the audience. Part of my recovery is realizing that I grew up very quickly, that I didn't have a childhood. I'm probably about 14 now, rebelling and questioning and seeking. But still sincere. I am a Black woman up there who is playing with power. We don't see enough powerful Black people, we don't see enough powerful Black women, and we certainly don't see enough powerful Black lesbians. I know who I am, and I know that I tried to be who other people wanted me to be and that it didn't work. I grew up very repressed, unable to speak my piece, and I am enjoying my power.

Anita Wise

by Roz Warren, interview by Deni Kasrel

Anita Wise, an adorable blond with a sweet Shirley Temple voice and a sharp wit, has been doing stand-up for a decade, including TV appearances on "Tonight," "Seinfeld," and "Evening at the Improv." She also writes a column for *Kinesis* magazine. Her initial interest was in comedy writing, but after taking a comedy course requiring that students perform, Wise decided on a career in stand-up. Because her mother was a a ballet dancer: "from the time I was very little, I was always hanging around backstage." But taking the stage herself, at first, says Wise, was "the scariest experience I've ever voluntarily put myself through."

Onstage, Wise presents herself as a sweet, wispy-voiced blond with a tentative demeanor. But beneath that sweet surface, she's one sharp cookie. Sure, she pokes fun at herself (she wears a T-shirt saying, "Natural Blond—Speak Slowly"), but she's even better at making fun of guys: "A lot of guys think the larger a woman's breasts are, the less intelligent she is. I think it's the opposite—the larger a woman's breasts are, the less intelligent the men become." Men in the audience can laugh at jokes like that both because the comic herself looks so sweet but also because her comedy is basically kind. "I really like men," Wise claims, and her material bears this out. It's often critical, but it's never hostile. She doesn't "male bash," says Wise, but she delights in taking "loving pokes" at the differences between the sexes. For instance: "[Men] keep rushing through lovemaking. Which is the part I like, the beginning part. Most women are like that. We need time to warm up. Why is this hard for you guys to understand? You're the first people to tell us not to gun a cold engine. You want us to go from zero to sixty in a minute. We're not built like that. We stall."

Wise's act is by no means limited to joking about guys and gals. She's also very funny about topics ranging from kitty angst ("My cat's depressed—I had the exterminators in and they killed all his toys") to plastic surgery ("They can take the fat from your rear and use it to bang out the dents in your face. Now that's what I call recycling. It gives a whole new meaning to 'dancing cheek to cheek.'") Wise's wit also translates well; her act got rave reviews when she performed it entirely in French at the Just for Laughs festival in Montreal.

Kasrel: Your comic persona is that of a ditzy blond. You make keen observations, but almost as if you're unaware that you're making them.

Wise: I really didn't set out to create a "comic persona"; it wasn't a conscious choice. But I think being ditzy was my way of distancing myself from the fact that I was onstage, a way of not owning the things I was saying. Now I've come to realize that with the way I look and with my voice and demeanor, people don't take me seriously anyway! What I say will still take them by surprise: because of the way I look, they just aren't expecting me to say these things.

Kasrel: They don't expect you to be intelligent?

Wise: It's not that they expect me to be stupid, but they do think I'm going to be sweeter. I look delicate. I have a soft voice. I don't have the hard-hitting delivery you expect from a comic. People are always saying, "I want to take care of you when you're onstage." They feel protective of me, especially guys.

Kasrel: Because they feel protective and see you as sweet and gentle, the toughness of your remarks catches them off guard and gets a laugh. Is it always a positive thing that your audience feels protective of you?

Wise: It's good that they feel drawn to me, but you don't want them to worry that you're going to fall down on the job up there. The trick is to keep that feeling of vulnerability and yet reassure them that even though I look like this I really am in control. I know what I'm saying and what I'm doing, so just relax and enjoy it.

Kasrel: How do you communicate to an audience that you're in control?

Wise: When I started out, I'd actually practice getting up onstage and very confidently and smoothly pulling the mike out of the stand. It's a stupid little thing, but I thought this would convey that I'd done this before, you know? Like, "I'm here to do my work and this stuff is my equipment." Before that, I didn't take the mike out of the stand. Then I decided that working with the mike would telegraph to them that I was comfortable up there.

Kasrel: Has your style of delivery changed over the years?

Wise: I've gotten more physical and more animated.

One of my heroes is Richard Pryor. He's a genius on a lot of levels, but one of the things I really appreciate about him is that he's so eloquent physically. He's like a dancer up there.

An improv teacher who I learned a lot from, Martin Harvey Freeberg, once told me that comedy is a song and dance. The song is the words and how you say them, their rhythm and cadence. The dance part is what I'm working on now.

Kasrel: Are you more comfortable moving around on stage than you used to be?

Wise: When I started out I felt constrained. I was very low-key. You know Steven Wright? He paces back and forth, but you don't see an elaborate arm gesture from him very often. But I've gotten to the point where I feel very free onstage. I was so self-conscious growing up, and I'm still self-conscious in life. But onstage now I feel that somehow I have permission to just do whatever I want, and I really have fun.

Kasrel: Has this loosening-up changed the kind of jokes you're doing? Are you doing different material that might not have worked before?

Wise: I'm getting braver about trying certain things. I'm also looking at other acts and seeing what works. Wayne Kotter said to me recently that when you start out you're a real purist about just exactly what you want to do. Then later you just realize, hey, you're in show business, and you broaden your repertoire. He pointed out, for instance, that every comic has a bit in his act where he gets a laugh by talking very fast. You've memorized something that you can rattle off quickly, and it almost always gets an applause break. It's a real crowd-pleaser. And I realized that I've got a tirade like that in my own act, a bit I do about my aunt and uncle's poodle.

Kasrel: When you deliver a joke you often manage to get in several punch lines. I'm thinking of the joke where you start by saying that you just got to the city and that everybody seems to be really friendly. You say, "I was walking around a little bit and guys kept offering me rides. That was pretty nice … since there were already four or five of them in the car." You get a laugh there, then you add, "I didn't accept. I don't like candy," and that gets an extra laugh.

Wise: I do a lot of tags like that. They usually just evolve. I'll do a joke, and it'll get a laugh. And you want the laugh to continue, so all of a sudden something else pops out of your mouth. And if that gets a laugh, it stays in. I don't know how it happens. I don't write them. They just pop out of my mouth.

Kasrel: So your act isn't completely scripted? You leave room for being spontaneous?

Wise: The better the crowd is, the more spontaneous you can be. If the crowd is responsive, it's like a good conversation. They're with you and they're attentive, and even though they're not talking back to you they're *giving* back to you. So you open up and you share more with them.

Kasrel: Are you ever concerned that something might pop out of your mouth that doesn't work?

Wise: If the crowd is good and you say something that doesn't get a big laugh, they'll forgive you, because they like you. And you just move on. Unless you have really bad judgment, and you say something that really offends them all of a sudden. You might say something in the heat of the moment that turns out not to have been the best thing to say. Maybe because you've forgotten something critical—some current event might have made that particular comment hit a wrong note. That happens, but if it's a really good crowd, you move right on to the next thing, you know?

Kasrel: What does a good crowd look like from onstage?

Wise: Laughing and smiling. Open, receptive faces. Another comic recently described a tough audience to me as being "smooth." Like a flat ocean. It's a beautiful analogy. When you go bodysurfing and there are no waves, it's boring. It's like a bath. But when the waves are crashing, then it's really fun to be there, jumping around in the waves. That's what a good audience is like. You can see it. You don't even have to hear them. You don't even have to be onstage. You can look over the backs of an audience, or see them from the side, and tell if they're good or not, because when the audience is good, they're rocking. There's movement.

Kasrel: They're laughing so hard that they're moving?

Wise: I'll walk into a room before I do my set, and there'll be another comic onstage—and you can see the waves. They really do look like an ocean. You can see them rocking and moving, nudging each other, you know? But when they're not having a good time, they sit very still. Like that old vaudeville line about the audience sitting so still staring at you that they look like an oil painting.

Kasrel: What do you enjoy about performing, about being onstage?

Wise: It's very exciting. It's like a moment away from yourself, and yet you're never more connected with yourself. It's a strange state of being. It's like galloping on a horse. A moment where life is a little more intense.

It's a lot of fun. I love the whole thing. Getting ready for the show; getting dressed up and putting on my makeup and planning what I'm going to do; showing up at the club.

Kasrel: What do you do when for some reason it doesn't work? What if the audience just isn't responding?

Wise: You say to yourself, This will be over soon. The longest it can last is an hour, you know? I've realized that no one performance is going to end my career. It's not pleasant, it's not a happy experience, but at the same time—so what? It's a lot like going through root canal.

Kasrel: How do you develop material? What kind of subject matter appeals to you?

Wise: I like to get at the heart of things that bother people. Or talk about things that bug me. I do a joke about having moved from New York to L.A. I say, "Los Angeles is so much better. The crime is all spread out. Everything is so pretty here. Even the homeless have tans." It's a horrible joke really, but ...

Kasrel: Then why do you do it?

Wise: Because it's true. And there is something funny about it. And I'm making a point, which is that there are homeless people in L.A. L.A. has nothing over New York, except that there's sun. L.A. has no moral superiority over

New York, which everybody considers so crime-ridden. L.A. is just as bad. It's just New York with palm trees.

Kasrel: When you're doing material on a topic like the homeless, how do you make your point without mocking them? There's a delicate line between making fun of something and being funny about it.

Wise: There has to be compassion behind it. People could perceive my homeless joke as being a heartless comment, but given the context of my act and everything else I say, they recognize that what I'm saying is, "Isn't this tragic?" And people laugh, because it's true, and they agree with me.

Kasrel: You like to poke fun at guys a lot.

Wise: I poke fun at women, too. A lot of my material is about the differences between men and women. God's best sick joke is making men and women, and then making them have to live together. You know what I mean?

Kasrel: Only too well.

Wise: It's something we all deal with every day, and the stuff you deal with every day is what you end up joking about. You don't hear many jokes on the European economic communities coming together, you know? You make jokes about what you deal with immediately. Look at Jerry Seinfeld. He's made millions talking about the mundane.

Kasrel: Do you consider yourself a funny person offstage?

Wise: Yeah. What's funny for me is that unless people know I'm a comic I'll make a funny comment but they'll take it at face value. They don't understand that I'm joking. So I'm very amused during life.

Like if somebody is being condescending, I'll ask them a really stupid question. I know that I'm not stupid. I know exactly what I'm saying. But they'll answer me very seriously and continue to be condescending. It's very funny, because I'm actually poking fun at them and they don't know it.

Kasrel: Can you give me an example?

Wise: I was at an exhibit of miniature paintings done on these tiny, little wooden boxes. Tiny, little landscapes. It was very impressive and beautiful, with tiny, very intricate designs. I was admiring them, so the guy whipped one of these tiny, little boxes out of the case and started this whole big sales pitch. I wasn't going to buy one, I was just looking at it. He's telling me proudly how it's done with a single strand of camel hair and talking about how difficult it is to do. He even gave me a magnifying glass so I could study it. He's going on and on with this sales pitch. So finally I asked him, "Why don't they just get bigger boxes?"

The Onfuni Tribe

by Anita Wise

There it was, high up on the wall in the comedy club Green Room, which for once was actually green, printed in big, thick, black magic-marker letters, underlined four times. It popped out from the jumble of autographs, doodles, inside jokes, "thanks for the great time!"—the standard backwards writing spelling "Help! I'm trapped behind this wall!", the random and hideous red and orange spray-paint border, and the neat printing of comics so new you can sense their self-conscious pride as they predict, "I'll probably suck." I sat back on the sofa staring dully up at it in a fog of exhaustion, dread, and what I would soon learn was the first day of a major month-and-a-half flu. The writing on the wall said: "WOMEN AREN'T FUNNY."

Of course, it's been there all along, maybe not so graphic, but no less apparent. It lay couched beneath well-meaning remarks like "she's too pretty to be a comic," as if womanliness and humor are mutually exclusive concepts. It was implicit in the First Prize award for a comedy contest of a $100 gift certificate to a men's clothing store. It was tacit in nine club owners' instructions to never put two female comedians on back to back, as if too much estrogen would pollute the air.

When I first started doing comedy, after the sheer shock of finding myself on a stage with a microphone wore off, some nights I would get a distinct impression, like a giant thought-balloon hovering over the audience's heads. It said: "We're not going to like this," simply because I was a woman. Every female stand-up comic I've ever discussed this with has had a similar experience. You can never prove it; it's something you just know.

Several years ago, some comics came back from a comedy convention grumbling that they never realized the female comics resented so strongly being called "comediennes." It seems this point had been made rather *emphatically* by some women at one of the seminars. I didn't realize it either, but I was glad to hear the term was out of favor. It reminded me of the distinction made between the word *comic* and *comedian*. One says things funny, the other says funny things. I can never remember which is which. As for comediennes, it wasn't that I minded being lumped in with the likes of Lucille Ball or Carol Burnett so much as how some emcees would lean on that last syllable in the intro, "And now, coming to the stage, a comedi-*yanh* …" as if to tip off the audience, "Sorry, bear with us, this might suck."

Recently I had an emcee hop onstage and say, "You guys ready for a *female* comedian?" They weren't. Somehow I feel he would have had better luck getting the crowd revved if he'd said, "This next comedian's been on the "Tonight Show," "Seinfeld," and a recent NBC special with Bob Hope, please welcome …"

Not all, probably not most, but a lot of our comedy brothers share this anti-female comic bias. One night I overheard a colorful expression some use among themselves, "G.A.F." I pried its meaning from a very embarrassed and discomfited comic: "Gash Ain't Funny." Nice, huh?

So it wasn't with surprise that I contemplated the pronouncement on my gender on the Green Room wall, but with a numb sense of destiny. A feeling I had come to the end of a road. This would be the part where I left the paved surface and bounced over hard dirt ruts and rocks and bushes until I hit a tree or boulder.

As my club work experience and TV credits grew. there was a natural pressure to move up in the show from doing the middle spot to being the headliner. I'd been doing this by co-headlining, where the burden of carrying the show is shared, and by headlining smaller clubs. So far, so good.

Somehow I had landed this headlining spot at a good club in Atlanta for good money and now would have to come through as a full-fledged headliner, not just doing good shows, but getting publicity and being a draw. Well, not "somehow." I called the guy and asked for work and he gave it to me.

As the date neared, I began to feel very anxious. This gig wasn't that different from any other I'd done, except for the degree of responsibility I felt to do a good job. There was no co-headliner to share the time or trade off closing the rowdier late shows and no rationalization of not being paid that much if things didn't go well.

As for attracting an audience, I have anecdotal evidence from friends here and there that total strangers occasionally know who I am and sometimes even know my jokes. But whether this would translate into actual paying bodies in the seats, I hadn't a clue. I made no claims that they would, but I felt there might be that expectation.

My biggest concern was the late shows, when people tend to be drunk and tired and have less of a taste for the quieter, more thoughtful kind of humor that I do that they might have enjoyed earlier in the evening. As one friend says, "They like shiny objects." Since I was home for the holidays, it had been a few weeks since I'd done a really long set, which meant I was probably rusty. Among my colleagues there lately has been talk that the quality level of the audiences on the road has been dropping. The hipper people weren't coming out as much. Worst of all, the only comic I talked to who had actually done this room had a horrible time. It's not in Atlanta, she said, but outside, near the headquarters of the KKK. They're very conservative and redneck and they hate women. She told me they literally turned their backs when she got onstage—it was horrible!

Well, the first night's show went fine. Sometimes when your energy's slow you have just enough to focus on doing the show and none left to worry how it's going, which can be good. It was my first glimmer of hope that the week wouldn't be a total rout.

The next day as I got ready and the usual preshow preoccupation set in, I thought again of the statement on the wall. WOMEN AREN'T FUNNY. I found it so puzzling that anyone could come up with such a blanket indictment of 51 percent of the entire population. We're *all* not funny? Whom do you think is laughing at your jokes, butthead? Like the ancient theory of conception that the female is merely an incubator for the man's tiny, fully formed embryo, are we women merely empty comedy vessels, able only to receive humor, not make it?

The statement had inspired three responses on the wall, all in feminine handwriting. One suggested that "maybe women lose their sense of humor when they're around you!" Another claimed that "most men wouldn't know funny if it bit them on their male member!" I'd say that's one instance where they could be forgiven. The last one alleged that the offending remark was "probably written by a bitter, male, pencil-dick comic," and (my favorite part) "a Republican—*at best*!!" Sounds right to me. Well, it was high up on the wall.

Not bad. At least the ladies learned from their self-defense classes—when attacked go for the groin. I wanted to make the point that stereotypes are just stupid. If I could fill the wall with all the mindless things we say about each other, it might dilute the ugliness. The best I came up with that wouldn't have turned it into the Wall of Hate was "White Men Can't Jump." Not the knockout punch I wanted, barely a glancing blow, but I put it up there.

Again the show went all right, but I was far from reassured. This was only the second night. Still, the staff was friendly, I liked the other comics and their comedy, and so far, no pointy white hoods in the audience. I was having an okay time.

Thursday I spent in bed. I was beginning to think I was finally experiencing that mysterious ailment that seems to only afflict movie stars: exhaustion. At least they are the only people you ever hear of being "treated" for it.

I've known a lot of very tired people, including myself, but we never needed a hospital. I always suspected it was a euphemism for some exotic show-biz thing, like implant realignment. Well, I am in show business, sort of, and holidays were hectic … maybe this was it.

That night as I showered and dressed, I thought again about the person who wrote you-know-what on the wall. It probably was a guy and it's true that men and women don't always find the same things funny. How else to explain the Three Stooges? Men love them so much I'm surprised there aren't Stooges sightings. "Moe is alive! He came to me in my sleep and said, 'Why, you!! … Nyuck, nyuck, nyuck!!!' " Maybe this guy doesn't appreciate female sensibilities in humor. He just doesn't get it.

At the club later, I marched right over to the wall and wrote, "Small minds condemn what they don't comprehend.—Jesse Helms, NEA." The other comic came over to read what I had added, then he turned to me wide-eyed and said: "Wow! Did he really *say* that?" Ladies and gentlemen of the jury, can you spell I-R-O-N-Y?

By Friday I had realized two things. First, that I was really sick, not just tired with a cold. The other was that, in spite of this, things were going well. That night at the club, I was thrilled to find that I'd been favorably reviewed. The review was already on display as the owner greeted me, smiling and rubbing his hands, "Nothing like some press to get people to come out." Reservations were coming in and the shows were filling up. Whew! I'd been mentally avoiding this week so much I had put off sending my promo until the last minute. What a nice break.

That's when I started to get mad. I paid my dues and I'm doing my job. I've earned my right to be here, I belong in this Green Room and *that* there on the wall doesn't.

A non-comic friend wondered why I didn't just cross it out. The thought never occurred to me. As a group, comics are not particularly censorship-prone. We'd rather cut it to shreds with our rapierlike wit. As they say, the pen is mightier than the white-out. WOMEN AREN'T FUNNY. I drew my Bic and attacked again: "Das right, Massuh. We caint he'p it. We wimmins just ain't bilt right cuz we ain't gots no pickle. An' day say pickle is a funny word. You sho' nuff caint be funny widdout no pickle! We's jist tryin' to make you look even bettuh, Bossman.—luv, Kunta Kinki of the Onfuni Tribe" Then I drew the symbol of our tribe, the female Nabisco sign with a smiling face, only instead of a smile, just a straight line.

Unwinding after the shows, I came across a great interview with Roseanne Arnold on Charlie Rose's show. She was discussing a recent flap with a reviewer who insisted on including very personal attacks in his critiques of her work. She had responded in kind in a private fax to him to make the point of how hurtful it was to be reviled for something that's a part of your nature, in her case, her weight. It struck a chord with me, because I have a lot of difficulty with comics who do really mean fat jokes. It's hard to draw the line because any subject can be fair game if handled well. After all, part of the comedian's role in society is to be the court jester, the one who speaks what no one else dares. At its best, this serves a very healthy function; at its worst, it appears to validate extremely negative attitudes.

The biggest problem I have with those fat jokes is the unconcealed contempt for overweight people, especially overweight women. When I see a very heavy-set woman in the crowd in a very visible spot, I just die inside. I want to go warn her somehow that part of the show might make her feel very uncomfortable. But I haven't come up with any realistic scenario for how to do it. When I asked a comic if he didn't feel bad about that woman, how embarrassing and hurtful it must be for her to be the object of such cruel humor, he shrugged it off, "It's just jokes—it's a comedy club."

I think what bothers me about it is that for some people, being overweight is a buffer from pain they've already experienced, like abuse. Unfortunately, it's a very obvious buffer. I'd like to say to these people who think it's so funny, "What if your neuroses were visible? What if each of those cigarettes you chain smoke were a thousand calories, or each of those beers you have to have before you go onstage, or those joints you share with the bartender out back? How funny would all that crap be then?"

I'd never seen Roseanne so thoughtful and intelligent. I don't remember what she said exactly. All I know is that before the interview I would have said that making fun of fat people was not quite as bad as a racial slur and afterward I felt, no, it's just as bad. The words don't matter, they're just darts for the poison. And I felt a tremendous amount of respect and affection for this socially conscious, Emmy-winning, self-described "fat, smart, rich *funny* [emphasis mine] bitch." Go, girl!

By the next evening, I had worked myself up into a lather of self-righteousness (or was it the Sudafed?). Between sleeping I thought of little else than my answer to this affront on the wall. Maybe the author was only being provocative? I doubt it. Comedy club walls are not adorned with as many pearls of wit as you might think. It's mostly pretty sophomoric stuff. No, I think he meant it. So my reply wasn't a joke either, but I liked it a lot, having managed to make my point while combining a play on words, a nod to my favorite advertising maverick Jerry della Femina—who wrote a funny book called *From the Wonderful Folks Who Brought Us Pearl Harbor*—and a Nazi death-camp reference. Dennis Miller would be proud.

It read: "Another uplifting jingle from the wonderful folks who brought us 'Arbeit Macht Frei'." The other comic said, "But no one will get it!" That, I thought, would be the sweetest revenge.

Sunday night I was one of hundreds of comics across the country, getting paid, saying my good-byes; my mind already on the trip home. There'd been no records broken, no standing o's, but it was a good week and I felt a deep satisfaction. If I'd still been thinking about it, I might have gone back and added one last note, a phrase used by comics everywhere to end countless discussions on the elusive mysteries of comedy: "Hey, *funny* is funny."

Women in Hollywood:
No Laughing Matter

by Kathi Maio

It's a good-news–bad-news joke. Except this one isn't very funny. The good news is everywhere in the rest of this book: at long last, women are coming into their own in the field of comedy.

They are headliners in comedy clubs and are the stars of performance-art hit shows on the New York stage. It is no longer unusual to see a woman comic with her own HBO or Showtime special or to see a group show like Lifetime's "Girls' Night Out," designed specifically to showcase up-and-coming female comedic talent. And after the ground-breaking and brilliant success of "Roseanne," many funny women are also getting a shot at a network sitcom.

That's the good news.

The bad news is the Hollywood feature film. It is one of the last, great, still-to-be conquered bastions of sexism. The silver screen is, in fact, a realm where women have a harder time reaching the top today than we did fifty years ago. (Ain't progress grand?)

It is very rare for a woman to be allowed to "carry" a contemporary Hollywood film. In most movies of the eighties and nineties, female actors are relegated to secondary roles as the mom, wife/girlfriend, slut/temptress, or daughter of a male star. It's not just in film comedies that female performers come smack up against the proverbial glass ceiling. Be it tragedy, comedy, or something in between, the woman plays second banana—or, more likely, a matched set of casaba melons.

There are many theories about why this remains true—besides plain old misogyny, that is. The most obvious reason is that most movies are still written, directed, and financed by men. (Bless their self-involved hearts.)

Another popular justification has something to do with the notion that the film industry's target audience is males under the age of twenty-five. Indeed, young men *are*, statistically, the most *dangerous* demographic group. And we might all rest easier at night thinking that the adolescent males of America are down at the cineplex rather than out raping, pillaging, using one another for target practice, and driving dangerously through our towns. But beyond that comfort fantasy, there seems little reason to peg the laddies of the land as *the* primo audience.

Several studies, in fact, indicate that it is women over twenty-five who control most of the moviegoing dollars, as single viewers, and as the organizers of couple, family, and buddy outings to neighborhood flicks. Although this fact may bode ill for truly mindless and vile comedies, the surprise success of several sentimental comedy-dramas (e.g., *Ghost, Fried Green Tomatoes, A League of Their Own*) and New Age romantic comedies (e.g., *When Harry Met Sally, Sleepless in Seattle*) over the last five years shows that women are out there, eager to drag significant others to any relatively nondemeaning movie that says a little something about the messy realities of life and love *and* gives them an occasional chuckle in the bargain.

The problem is that every time a "women's" film of any description does well, Hollywood acts shocked—and lets the momentum pass. Conversely, a male performer like Eddie Murphy (who is believed to appeal to that young, male target group) can have lackluster showing after lackluster showing at the box office, yet still have his next project green-lighted.

When thinking about how hard it is for women in comedy to get a real shot at feature film success, Eddie Murphy brings us to an interesting comparison. Think about the various comedy-variety shows that have appeared in the last twenty-five years on the small screen. TV's sketch comedy shows have been a primary launching pad for big-screen comedy careers.

Mr. Murphy came out of the "Saturday Night Live" ensemble. So, too, did Bill Murray, the late John Belushi, Dan Ackroyd, Chevy Chase, Jim Belushi, and Billy Crystal. Each of these gentlemen has been afforded the opportunity to star in over half a dozen feature films. Whether their stars have remained high in the Hollywood firmament is almost besides the point. They were given a shot. Quite a few, actually.

Although not *all* of the male cast members of "SNL" made it to Hollywood, a good number of the late-night boys have taken that first-class flight from New York to L.A. More recent "SNL" cast members, including Robert Downey, Jr., Mike Myers, Dana Carvey, and Martin Short, have also been given the chance to carry movies through their comedic performances.

Now, consider the women of "SNL." If it's hard to name one who became a movie star, there's a reason for that.

In terms of a big-screen career, the most successful was undoubtedly the late, dearly lamented Gilda Radner. It is impossible to know what kind of Hollywood success Gilda might have achieved had she not been taken from us so soon. But I would wager that it wouldn't have been half the success she deserved.

Sadly, with the exception of her performance-art film, *Gilda Live*, Radner was sorely underutilized in all her few screen roles. She met her second husband, Gene Wilder, on the set of one of her biggest films, *Hanky Panky* (1982). Thereafter, she worked almost exclusively with him.

It should not reflect badly on Mr. Wilder—a marvelous comic talent and by all accounts a truly devoted husband—that *he* was the undisputed star of the movies he made with his wife. After all, he was an established lead actor and a known box-office quantity with a (then) excellent track record in screen comedy.

Still, when you see a film like the pathetically sexist *Woman in Red* (1984), with Gilda banished to bit-part status as a frustrated biddy who is the brunt of much slapstick humiliation, it breaks your heart to see her talents squandered so badly. She had so little time left! She should have been starring in movies written to showcase her own special comic gifts. But it never happened.

Of the other "SNL" women, Joan Cusack continues to make a name for herself as a support comedian. She's brilliant, but like male "SNL" equivalent Randy Quaid, she was already on her way as a character actor when she briefly sojourned at "SNL."

Jane Curtin became a major star, but on the small screen in the buddies sitcom "Kate and Allie." Julia Louis-Dreyfus shared a similar fate as the sole female in the "Seinfeld" cast. (More on that phenomenon later.) Mary Gross, Victoria Jackson, Julia Sweeney, Jan Hooks, Nora Dunn, and Danitra Vance have all appeared in films, but as either one-shot stars or as bit players.

Another comedy series, "Second City TV," also launched the careers of two male stars, the late John Candy and Rick Moranis, while two equally talented female cast members are still waiting for their big break. Catherine O'Hara is very funny and attractive enough to be a leading lady of comedy, but most moviegoers know her only as little Kevin's mom in the *Home Alone* movies. Andrea Martin's screen opportunities have also been less than stellar. Her feature highpoint was in a low-life project called *Too Much Sun*, a 1991 exercise in homophobic farce.

Recently, "In Living Color" has also offered break-out opportunities for men in the cast. Jim Carrey is one of the hottest comedy stars in Hollywood today. And Keenen Ivory Wayans and little brother Damon Wayans have both played the leading man. Little sister (and stand-up comic) Kim Wayans, on the other hand ...

Are you starting to see the pattern?

Now, you might observe that since women are given so few chances to strut their stuff in current variety programs it's no wonder that joining the cast of "SNL" or "In Living Color" does nothing for their careers. And you'd be right. Or at least many of the women who sign on with current comedy shows would agree with you.

The number of female-focused skits on "SNL" has dropped drastically since the days of Jane and Gilda. According to *TV Guide*, Julia Sweeney (the androgynous "Pat") cited sexism as a major reason for her recent departure from the show. Other female cast members before her have made similar claims when they walked away from the show.

Yet, crazy as it seems, even TV comedy-variety shows that headlined women performers could not launch their title stars into Hollywood fame. Carol Burnett, one of the comedy queens of television, has had a miserable time in feature films. Although most fans can name a favorite sketch from her classic show, few can name a movie she starred in. And except *Pete 'n' Tillie* (1972) and *The Four Seasons* (1981), it is probably better not to remember.

Tracey Ullman, who has, like Burnett, won Emmys for her television work, has had an even rougher time in Hollywood. The closest thing she's ever had to a lead in a feature comedy is her role as the wronged wife in the deadpan (nay, depressive) ensemble farce *I Love You to Death* (1990). The rest of her film work has either been serious roles in small-budget features (e.g., *Household Saints*) or cameos in comedies (e.g., *Robin Hood: Men in Tights*).

The only comedy-variety show I can think of where the women actually did better than the men was "Rowan and Martin's Laugh-In." The two breakout performers from that show were both female. You could put it down to the ambition and comic brilliance of Goldie Hawn and Lily Tomlin, but I suspect that the time period had something to do with it.

In the late sixties and early seventies, after a long dry spell for women performers, Hollywood was starting to reflect the influence of the various social change movements, including the second wave of feminism. Looking back on the decade of the seventies, some critics have termed it Hollywood's second golden age. Certainly, with fits and starts, women did get more screen time during the mid- to late seventies. After that, with backlash setting in and with most of the best comedy roles, even some "women's" comedy roles—like *Tootsie* and *Mr. Mom*—going to men, women's chances became more unpredictable.

Luckily for them, Goldie and Lily were two women at the right place (Burbank and environs) at the right time (the mid-seventies). They saw a window of opportunity (about the size of a porthole) and they dove for it. They have had two of the most successful comedy careers for Hollywood funnywomen in the last quarter century. But when you think about it, that's not saying much.

Throughout her extensive film career, haunted, no doubt, by her big break as the sock-it-to-me girl, Goldie Hawn has primarily been typecast as the sexy goof. (And you may well ask yourself whether her alluring bubble-blonde image is precisely the reason she has been so successful in Hollywood.) Goldie is capable of much more—as dramatic roles like 1992's *Crisscross* illustrate—but one gets the distinct impression that Ms. Hawn is a pragmatist and businesswoman first and foremost. She did what she needed to do to further her film career. With no regrets.

She does, however, understand that power behind the camera much improves the lot of the actor. (Proof that the wide-eyed waif routine was simply that.) She coproduced her best film, *Private Benjamin* (1980). Which is, not surprisingly, one of her few comedies to allow her character a little complexity (and acquired confidence and independence) along with the trademark fluff-head humor.

Goldie Hawn has had major roles in more than twenty Hollywood films. Some of them, including *Foul Play* (1978) and the more serious *Swing Shift* (1984), are well worth watching again. Many are not. As she ages, Goldie's ditzy babe act seems (as in 1992's *The Housesitter*) more and more incongruous and false.

Hollywood offers her few alternatives, however. (And she has yet to discover any for herself.) Certainly the rich shrew in *Overboard* (1987), who must be brutally mortified into a compliant wife/mother role, is no improvement. Nor is the piteous, body-obsessed woman-scorned she plays in the nasty "black comedy," *Death Becomes Her* (1992). That may be one reason she is doing more dramatic roles (like 1991's *Deceived*).

It may well be that Goldie Hawn has been the most successful feature comedian of the last twenty years specifically because she was such a throwback image of (seemingly) brainless beauty. And that may be one reason her sister in "Laugh-In"'s psychedelic silliness has had a much different career.

No one could ever mistake Lily Tomlin for a Malibu Barbie. And that, no doubt, has been her greatest challenge in Tinseltown, explaining why she has met with more success starring in one-woman stage shows and TV specials than in Hollywood films.

During that bright shining moment of the late seventies, it almost looked as though Lily would become a major screen star. Early outings like *The Late Show* (1977) and *9 to 5* (1980) demonstrated her potential. But then, with a little power, Lily made a couple of fateful missteps, in the form of films either written or written and directed by her partner, Jane Wagner.

Unfortunately, they weren't very good movies. And they most certainly didn't have the courage of their convictions. Perhaps Wagner and Tomlin compromised their craft, hoping to give Hollywood (and Hollywood's audiences) what they wanted. Perhaps their studio, Universal, interfered, as studios are wont to do. Whatever the reason, both *Moment by Moment* (1978) and *Incredible Shrinking Woman* (1981) were disappointments.

Moment by Moment, a romantic melodrama costarring John Travolta, is one of those legendary bombs that leave a crater the size of the San Fernando Valley. *Incredible Shrinking Woman* is a much more frustrating film, because it *almost* works.

Its major fault is that it went for agreeably cute and silly, rather than run with a tougher brand of humor suggested by its story of a housewife who shrinks after a new chemically derived perfume is spilled on her. A genuinely edgy comedy about a woman belittled by her suburban life and poisoned by the chemical potions of American consumer culture could have had substance and laughs. *Incredible Shrinking Woman* has too little of both. After her role as the shrinking woman, Lily's big-screen career seemed to diminish, as well.

Lily has made good films. *All of Me* (1984), in which she plays a dying heiress who possesses the body of Steve Martin, is very funny. But it's Steve Martin's film. Lily is just along for the ride. Lily Tomlin's greatest film accomplishment isn't really a film at all. The adaptation of her one-woman show, *The Search for Signs of Intelligent Life in the Universe* (1991), may well stand as her (and Ms. Wagner's) outstanding achievement. It is exquisite. But it doesn't so much work as a movie as stand as an important record of a theatrical event.

Whoopi Goldberg, that brilliant anomaly (a black performer with braided hair and a Jewish surname), is the only other woman of the last twenty years who has managed to create a substantive female presence in the comedy film. And her career has been, to put it kindly, uneven. Like Goldie, Whoopi supplements the questionable comedy scripts she is offered with frequent dramatic and serio-comic roles. And like Lily, she is also renowned for her one-woman stage shows.

Whoopi was discovered on the stage and called to Hollywood to make her screen debut as Celie in Steven Spielberg's less-than-faithful adaptation of Alice Walker's womanist classic, *The Color Purple* (1985). The movie was a mixed bag, to say the least. But Whoopi was an unmistakable treasure.

After they had her, however, Hollywood had no idea what to do with a dark-skinned African-American woman who sported something approaching a rasta-do. She clearly had star potential. But she didn't have that sultry, near-white beauty that could be easily exploited in those ebony temptress roles of which Hollywood is so fond.

Since Hollywood is not a land of originality, they had to plug Whoopi into an already existing image. And the studio's only reference point for African-American movie stars in the mid-eighties was Eddie Murphy. That's the ticket! Make Whoopi Goldberg a female Eddie Murphy! And that's what they set out to do.

Jumpin' Jack Flash (1986), which was Penny Marshall's directorial debut as well as Ms. Goldberg's first starring comedy, actually works, because it honors her femaleness as well as her funnyness. The same cannot be said for *Burglar* (1987) and *Fatal Beauty* (1987), which were wildly inappropriate vehicles for Whoopi's comic talents.

The downward slide continued with *The Telephone* (1988), an acrimonious project deemed so bad that it was dumped straight to video. And then came *Homer and Eddie* (1989), a film that audiences wisely declined to see.

The word was out. Whoopi Goldberg was history. But Whoopi herself wasn't listening. A supporting role in *Ghost* (1990) turned everything around. And with an Oscar in her hand, Whoopi was better able to pick and choose her scripts and directors. That has made all the difference.

Not all her films since *Ghost* have been great, but none of them have forced her to impersonate Eddie Murphy, either. Whoopi often seems content to forgo stardom for the joys of jazzing up an ensemble movie. Her tampon interrogation in Robert Altman's *The Player* (1992) is the most hilarious riff on the third degree that has ever been put to film. And the marvelous thing about *Sister Act* (1992)—which was sadly lacking in *Sister Act 2* (1993) —was that it gave many women a chance to shine.

One of those women was Kathy Najimy, who, like Goldberg, made her name on the stage, as one half of *The Kathy and Mo Show*. Although *Sister Act* wasn't Kathy's screen debut (take a closer look at *This is My Life*), it was the movie that made Hollywood sit up and take notice.

But, again like Whoopi, Hollywood has no idea what to do with Kathy Najimy. She's lovely, but she's large and ethnic looking—two things Tinseltown finds unacceptable in a woman. Kathy Najimy has tried to capitalize on all the positive buzz she received from *Sister Act*. But the choices were limited. She went for the chance to costar with one of her idols, Bette Midler, in a film called *Hocus Pocus* (1993). And who could blame her?

Actually, anyone who honors the history of women *could* blame her for that choice. The (male-written, male-directed) family comedy-adventure film has several wee problems. The first is that it's not much fun—especially for its target audience, kids. A movie in which the clownlike characters (Midler, Najimy, and Sarah Jessica Parker) run around trying to suck the life out of (and otherwise slaughter) children, isn't necessarily a good time for the kiddies. And that brings us to the other problem with the film. And it's a doozy.

The killer klowns of *Hocus Pocus* are witches. Not just any witches. They are *Salem* witches of the seventeenth century. Except these women aren't innocent victims of a small-scale holocaust, whose only sin was inheriting property and showing a little independent spirit. No! These witches really were sex slaves of the devil who lured innocent children to their destruction.

Talk about revisionist history! *Hocus Pocus* is a major outrage. All the more so because it went into production at the very time the town of Salem was solemnly marking the three-hundredth anniversary of the murder and false imprisonment of its citizens, dedicating a memorial to the innocent women (and men) who died in the witch hysteria.

Heck, that's just the kind of thing Hollywood would play for a few laughs.

It made me sad to see an acknowledged feminist like Kathy Najimy in a movie as treacherously woman-hating as *Hocus Pocus*. And it was even more dismaying to see her try to justify her involvement in this project. It would be easy to denounce her for making this choice. But how much choice did she really have?

She wants to work in film. She *deserves* to work in film. Even established stars like Goldie and Lily and Whoopi have trouble finding star comedy vehicles. (Whoopi recently agreed to do a film called T. Rex, realized how bad it was, and tried to get out of it. Threatened with a "Kim Basinger" multimillion dollar lawsuit, she ended up making it after all. So much for star power. If women who've made it have problems finding a decent movie to make, what must it be like for a newcomer like Kathy Najimy?

The thing is, women don't want to make stupid, offensive comedy films. (And most women don't want to see them, either.) Unfortunately, that's the only kind of comedy Hollywood seems to know how to make these days. And that's the sticking point.

What we need is a more humane and believable brand of screen humor for our female stars. It's out there. *Sister Act* is a modest example. And that's why it was a surprise, word-of-mouth hit.

But *Sister Act*, like its star, is a Hollywood anomaly—an irreproducible result. Nothing has changed for the better since the days when Gilda and Goldie and Lily tried to break into the movie business. It is still a hostile, uncomprehending (and incomprehensible) world for a funny woman to enter.

So what's a female comic wonder to do? Look around. They are all going into television, that woman-friendly medium. Ever since the days of Lucy, TV has given women the chances that the Hollywood film refused them. (Again, it has something to do with perceived demographics. The whiz-boys in the network boardrooms *know* that women are out there watching ... and making decisions about the consumer products they advertise.) Hence, female stars—both comic and dramatic—have a much better time in television movies and sitcoms than in the Tinseltown feature film.

Look at *TV Guide*. Joan Rivers or Bertice Berry might have a talk show. Carol Burnett might be doing a television "Movie of the Week." And following in the tradition of Lucille Ball, Jane Curtin, and Roseanne, any number of female comics—like Ellen Degeneres, Brett Butler, Margaret Cho, Stephanie Hodges—might have their own situation comedy on the air.

More power to 'em. It's nice to sit at home at night and do the couch potato thing, munching on a bowl of popcorn. It makes for a mellow end to the day, to watch some hilarious, bodacious broad take to the TV screen and make us laugh.

But we want to see more of them on the big screen, too. After all, sometimes you're in the mood to go out for some of that stale, killer popcorn they charge you five bucks for at the local movie palace. And all you want is a major motion picture featuring a bodacious and hilarious female star to go with it.

That's not too much to ask. Is it?

Writer's Bios

Toni Armstrong, Jr. has been publisher/managing editor of *HOTWIRE: The Journal of Women's Music & Culture* since 1984.

Victoria A. Brownworth is a nationally syndicated columnist for *The Philadelphia Daily News*. She has published eight books. Her collection of essays *Too Queer* will be published in 1996 by The Firebrand Press.

Susie Day is a freelance writer living in Brooklyn. She knows more than you think she does.

Trey Graham is an arts and entertainment writer for *The Washington Blade*. His profile of *Thea Vidale* is expanded from an interview which appeared there in February 1994.

Anndee Hochman is the author of *Everyday Acts & Small Subversions: Women Reinventing Family, Community and Home*.

Deni Kasrel is an all-purpose scribe, her favorite beat is covering arts and culture. Her articles appear in: *The Philadelphia Inquirer, Art Matters, Philadelphia Business Journal, Welcomat, The Press, Jewish Times* and *Ticket*.

Kathi Maio is the film editor of *Sojourner: The Women's Forum*, film columnist for *The Magazine of Fantasy and Science Fiction*, and contributing editor to *Visions Magazine*. Her film essays, *Feminist in the Dark* (1988) and *Popcorn and Sexual Politics* (1991) were published by The Crossing Press. She has every episode (but the elusive PMS show) of "Roseanne" on tape.

Patty Marx: "I've written *How to Regain Your Virginity* (with Charlotte Stuart), *You Can Never Go Wrong By Lying, Blockbuster* (with Douglas McGrath) and *Now Everyone Really Hates Me* (with Roz Chast). I've been a staff writer for "Saturday Night Live" and many other shows, including the Children's Television Workshop. My work's been in *The New York Times, The Atlantic* and *The New Yorker* (I write "Talk of the Towns") and *Spy*.

Ellen Orleans is the author of *Can't Keep A Straight Face* and *Who Cares If It's A Choice? Snappy Answers to 101 Nosy, Intrusive and Highly Personal Questions About Lesbians and Gay Men*. She lives in Boulder with two house plants and a non-cordless phone.

Andrea T. L. Peterson is a freelance writer/photographer. Her articles and reviews have appeared in *The Advocate, Deneuve*, and *Z* magazine.

Laura L. Post is a Jewish lesbian freelance writer, whose work has appeared in *Ms., Washington Blade, Sing Out!, Sojourner, Dirty Linen, off our backs, Victory*

Review, New Directions for Women, New Review of Records, Hot Wire, Visibilities, and *Deneuve.*

Samantha Rigg was an intern for *Sojourner* magazine at the time these pieces were written.

Janet Wollman Rusoff's articles have appeared in *The Washington Post, USA Today, Entertainment Weekly, TV Guide, The New York Times, Esquire,* etc. *How To Be Funny,* was coauthored with comedian Steve Allen.

Laurie Stone is a columnist and cultural critic for *The Village Voice* and for *Ms.* She is working on a book of autobiographical stories.

Essays about the following comics first appeared, in different form, in the following magazines and newspapers: *Abilities* (Geri Jewell); *The Washington Blade* (Lynn Lavner, Thea Vidale); *The Village Voice* (Betty, Louise DuArt, Sandra Bernhard); *Hotwire* (Kathy Najimy profile).

Photo Credits

Suzy Berger by Danielle Oviedo, Betty by Michael O'Brien, Brett Butler by AP/Wide World Photos, Kate Clinton by Paul Greco, Cathy Crimmons by Flash Rosenberg, Lea Delaria by Jim Flaherty, Dos Fallopia by Benham Studio/Gallery, Mo Gaffney by Cathy Blaivas, Lisa Geduldig by Leslie Katz, Sherry Glaser by Carol Rosegg/Martha Swope Assoc., Whoopie Goldberg by Marilyn Humphries, Marga Gomez by Irene Young, Lisa Kron by Dona Ann McAdams, Bette Midler by AP/Wide World Photos, Rosie O'Donnell by AP/Wide World Photos, Janice Perry by Erik Borg, Reno by Annie Liebovitz, Joan Rivers by AP/Wide World Photos, Roseanne by AP/Wide World Photos, Flash Rosenberg by Jim Graham, Rita Rudner by AP/Wide World Photos, Betsy Salkind by Lynn McCann, Judy Tenuta by Carol Bobolts, Tracey Ullman by AP/Wide World Photos, Karen Williams by Toni Armstrong Jr.